BEING DIRECT

Being Direct

Making Advertising Pay

Lester Wunderman

ADAMS MEDIA CORPORATION
HOLBROOK, MASSACHUSETTS

Published by Adams Media Corporation
260 Center Street, Holbrook, MA 02343
by arrangement with Random House, Inc.

Grateful acknowledgment is made to Harcourt Brace & Company and
Faber and Faber Limited for permission to reprint four lines from
"Little Gidding," in *Four Quartets*, by T.S. Eliot. Copyright © 1943 by
T.S. Eliot. Copyright renewed © 1971 by Esme Valerie Eliot.
Rights throughout the world, excluding the United States, are controlled
by Faber and Faber Limited. Reprinted by permission of Harcourt Brace
& Company and Faber and Faber Limited.

ISBN: 1-55850-834-1

Printed in the United States of America.

J I H G F E D C B A

Library of Congress Cataloging-in-Publication Data
Wunderman, Lester.
Being direct : making advertising pay / by Lester Wunderman.
p.   cm.
Originally published: Being direct : how I learned to make advertising pay. 1997.
Includes index.
ISBN 1-55850-834-1
1. Wunderman, Lester. 2. Advertisers—United States—Biography.
3. Direct marketing—United States. I. Title.
HG5810.W86A3   1998
659.1'092—dc21
[B]   97–39262
CIP

Book design by Carole Lowenstein

This book is available at quantity discounts for bulk purchases.
For information, call 1-800-872-5627 (in Massachusetts, 781-767-8100).

Visit our home page at http://www.adamsmedia.com

To my wife, Suzanne,
whose faith was stronger
than my fears

We shall not cease from exploration
And the end of all our exploring
Will be to arrive where we started
And know the place for the first time.

—T. S. ELIOT, "Little Gidding,"
  Four Quartets

Preface:
The Next Advertising

This is a book about direct marketing, about how to advertise profitably in a postindustrial, information-based society. It is a book about how manufacturers and consumers may engage in an interactive dialogue affecting the behavior of both. It is also a book about the changing paradigm of brands—which used to represent a cluster of product values but now increasingly identify clusters of consumers' individual needs.

I have written this book in the form of an autobiography to show, step by step, how I learned to make advertising pay. It is based not on theoretical hypotheses or secondhand case histories but on the recorded results of the many billions of dollars' worth of advertising I helped create and whose results I was able to measure.

I will describe the rules as I learned them and show how I discovered them—the facts, the hunches, the breakthroughs, and the frustrations—the experiences I used to create campaigns that succeeded and others that failed.

I am not sure whether I discovered direct marketing or it discovered me. I found its components one by one during a lifetime of trial and error. There was no single moment of revelation but a great many clues that led me in new and unexpected directions. Sometimes I would recognize the significance of an experience at once; other times it took years. And only recently did I realize that there was a pattern to successful direct marketing—nineteen things all successful direct marketing companies know. Those that fail or fall short of realizing their full potential neglect one or more of these fundamental rules.

It is as though I had put a jigsaw puzzle together with no picture on the box cover and no directions inside; each piece of the puzzle has a wonderful shape and color and its own peculiar meaning: Mrs. Schwartz, who bought her chickens from a kosher butcher in the Bronx and taught me how to measure the value of service; a box maker on Union Square in Manhattan who, by tapping on a radiator, taught me the first thing that clients expect to hear from an advertising agency; Ogobara Dolo, a chief of the Dogon tribe of Mali, who refused to be a "chief of straw"; a cantankerous chairman of American Express who ordered me to invent a credit card; two anonymous men in trench coats from CBS who started me on the road to success; the world's largest rose grower, who forced me to learn how to sell, satisfy, and loyalize his customers; and some sheep, geese, and a man named Jesús in Arizona who taught me about creativity and problem solving. There was also a chairman of a large American corporation who fainted on occasion to make his point; a Russian nobleman perched on the eighteenth-floor ledge of his office building from whom I learned a secret of getting new business; an African dancer in red shoes in Abidjan who taught me how ideas can transcend cultural differences; a 150-year-old legend in Gävle, Sweden, that helped me understand how the creation of ongoing relationships could revolutionize the future of packaged-goods marketing; the "Gold Box of Colorado," which revealed the secrets of media synergy; "Judy," the model housewife from Connecticut, who changed the history of television commercials; and, perhaps most important, the head of a division of the Ford Motor Company who agreed to sell cars and loyalize customers using techniques that B. F. Skinner had developed as a way of teaching pigeons to play the piano.

These are some of the pieces of my jigsaw puzzle, and it was from these and others that I discovered the grand design of direct marketing.

Hermann Hesse, in his novel *Siddhartha,* describes the long and difficult search of a young Indian for the ultimate truth. It took Siddhartha a lifetime to discover the secret. Along the way, he met the Buddha, Gautama, who asked Siddhartha whether he believed that he was the Buddha. Siddhartha said "Yes." The Buddha then asked Siddhartha to follow him on the path of truth. Siddhartha declined, and when the Buddha asked him to explain, Siddhartha replied, in effect,

"I want to know more than you know; I want to know how you felt when you found it out."

So, in that spirit, let me tell you what I found out, and I will try to put you onto the path to your own discovery—so that you too can learn how to make advertising pay.

Nineteen Things
All Successful
Direct Marketing
Companies Know

1. **Direct Marketing Is a Strategy, Not a Tactic**

   It's not an ad with a coupon; it's not a commercial with a toll-free number; it's not a mailing, a phone call, a promotion, a database, or a website. It's a commitment to getting and keeping valuable customers.

2. **The Consumer, Not the Product, Must Be the Hero**

   The product must create value for each of its consumers. It must satisfy consumers' unique differences, not their commonalities. The call of the Industrial Revolution was manufacturers saying, "This is what I make, don't you want it?" The call of the Information Age is consumers asking, "This is what I need, won't you make it?"

3. **Communicate with Each Customer or Prospect as an Audience of One**

   Advertising must be as relevant to each consumer as the product or service is. General advertising and more targeted direct marketing must both be part of a holistic communication strategy.

4. **Answer the Question "Why Should I?"**

   The most dangerous question a prospect or customer asks is "Why should I?" And he may ask it more than once—but never of you. The product and its communication stream must continue to provide him with both rational and emotional answers.

5. Advertising Must Change Behavior, Not Just Attitudes

Favorable consumer attitudes go only part of the way to creating sales. It's also the consumer's accountable actions such as inquiries, product trials, purchases, and repurchases that create profits.

6. The Next Step: Profitable Advertising

The results of advertising are increasingly measurable; they must now become accountable. Advertising can't be just a contribution to goodwill—it must become an investment in profits.

7. Build the "Brand Experience"

Customers have to know and feel the brand as an experience that serves their individual needs. It has to be a total and ongoing immersion in satisfaction that includes everything from packaging to point of purchase, repurchase, and after-sale service and communications.

8. Create Relationships

Relationships continue to grow—encounters do not. The better the buyer–seller relationship, the greater the profit.

9. Know and Invest in Each Customer's Lifetime Value

One automobile dealer calculated that a lifetime of cars sold to one customer would be worth $332,000. How much should a marketer spend to create such a loyal lifetime customer for a given product or service?

10. "Suspects" Are Not "Prospects"

"Prospects" are consumers who are able, ready, and willing to buy; "suspects" are merely eligible to do so. Communicating with prospects reduces the cost of sales; communicating with suspects raises the cost of advertising.

11. **Media Is a Contact Strategy**

    Measurable results from media, not the number of exposures, are what counts. Measurements such as "reach" and "frequency" are out of date. Only "contacts" can begin relationships.

12. **Be Accessible to Your Customers**

    Be there for your customers—be their database and source of information and service through as many channels of communication as possible. They can't tell you what they need unless they can reach you.

13. **Encourage Interactive Dialogues**

    Listen to consumers rather than talk at them. Let them "advertise" their individual needs. They'll be grateful for your responsiveness. Convert one-way advertising to two-way information sharing.

14. **Learn the Missing "When?"**

    The answer "Not now" is as dangerous to advertising as "Not this." Only consumers know when they are ready to buy, and they will tell you if you ask them in the right way.

15. **Create an Advertising Curriculum That Teaches as It Sells**

    A "curriculum" is a learning system that teaches one "bit" of information at a time. Each advertising message (bit) can build on the learning of the previous one. It can teach consumers why your product is superior and why they should buy it.

16. **Acquire Customers with the Intention to Loyalize Them**

    Promotions sell product trials—but not ongoing brand loyalty. They may also attract the wrong customers, who may never become loyal. The right customers must be acquired and persuaded to want what the product does and not what the promotion offers. The right customers may in fact be your competitors' best customers.

17. Loyalty Is a Continuity Program

"Totally satisfied" customers are least likely to fall away. Those who are merely "satisfied" may fall away without warning. To build ongoing relationships, rewards for good customers should be tenure-based (on previous purchases, usage behavior, and length of relationship). Rewarding "tenure" can prevent competitors from "conquesting" your best customers.

18. Your Share of Loyal Customers, Not Your Share of Market, Creates Profits

Spend more on the good customers you have. Ninety percent of most companies' profits come from repeat customers. It costs six to ten times as much to get a new customer as to keep an old one.

19. You Are What You Know

Data is an expense—knowledge is a bargain. Collect only data that can become information, which, in turn, can become knowledge. Only knowledge can build on success and minimize failure. A company is no better than what it knows.

Contents

Introduction:
Surfing on a
Tidal Wave

When I entered the conference room, a note was waiting at my place. It read, "The man in the gray suit is the target. We think he speaks English." I looked across the table and saw that my "target" was staring straight at me. Our eyes met, and neither of us blinked. Was he trying to stare me down? Or was he sizing me up, seeking to overcome the barriers of language and culture beyond the politically correct and generally sterile translations of our interpreters? Because he was my guest, I blinked first. His name was Duan Guichang, and he was the director, International Services, of the Ministry of Posts and Telecommunications of the People's Republic of China. He and an entourage of deputy ministers and deputy directors of his ministry had come from Beijing to find out how to increase the revenue of their postal service. We had been brought together by my company's client, the United States Postal Service, which wanted to do more business with China. Nonetheless I was wary because I had read so much about the belligerence of Chinese officials.

It was August 21, 1996. The meeting was taking place in Conference Room 4A of Wunderman Cato Johnson's headquarters in New York. It had started at 9:00 A.M., but, as planned, I didn't join the group until the USPS had almost finished its presentation. Our group had suggested that I present either the work our agency was doing or the list I had recently written of the "Nineteen Things All Successful Direct Marketing Companies Know." I told my colleagues that I would decide what to say when I sensed what our visitor from China really wanted to know.

I introduced myself as chairman of Wunderman Cato Johnson, a division of Young & Rubicam, Inc. WCJ, I told them, is the nineteenth largest agency in the world, with sixty-five offices in thirty-six countries. We are also the world's largest direct marketing agency, and—though I didn't mention it at the time—we are the agency that invented the term "direct marketing" and developed many of its techniques. I did tell them that we have offices in Hong Kong, Tokyo, Singapore, Taiwan, and Thailand but, as yet, no office in China. Expansion in Asia is a corporate priority. For modesty's sake, I added that our rate of growth had been not so much the result of extraordinary talent as of the dynamic global growth of direct marketing. What had begun as a ripple in a calm sea in the 1960s had become a tidal wave in the 1990s.

I then presented some statistics from the 1996 update of the report the Direct Marketing Association had commissioned WEFA (Wharton Economic Forecasting Associates) to make on the extent and impact of direct marketing in the United States. Direct marketers would spend $34.6 billion on direct mail advertising in the United States alone; $57.8 billion for telephone marketing; $15.5 billion on television; $13.9 billion in newspapers; $7.2 billion in magazines; and $4.7 billion on radio. The total expenditures for direct marketing in the United States alone would account for 58.3 percent of all U.S. advertising. Direct marketing expenditures were greater than those of general advertising. I paused to allow the interpreter to translate. I now knew that I had the group's attention. Duan Guichang's eyes had never left my face, and I was speaking directly to him. I sensed that he was reacting to what I said before the interpreter translated, but I couldn't be sure. Finally, I told him that 20 million workers are now employed in the United States as a result of direct marketing. I looked at my watch. It was time to move on.

I was relieved that the statistics were behind me; I prefer to discuss ideas. Duan Guichang smiled, too, as if he were reading my mind. If he spoke or understood English, it remained his secret. I then told the group that I would welcome questions. I could see that protocol was going to limit the dialogue to the director and the chairman. Duan Guichang spoke in Chinese. He opened his remarks by saying that in China telecommunications were growing much faster and more profitably than postal services. He wanted to find ways of building postal volume and revenue. He said this merely as a statement of fact that called for no immediate answer. I nodded, and he continued. The China Post had encouraged the formation of direct marketing enterprises in the various regions of China, but they were growing slowly and were not expertly managed. That didn't surprise me. Direct marketing was not a traditional Chinese way of selling manufactured goods. No infrastructure or training program existed to support it. Duan Guichang didn't ask any questions. He fired short bursts of information, waited for the translation, then continued immediately, saying that there was a great potential for China to use direct marketing for exports, employing the marketing infrastructure of other countries. The key concern in the United States was the reliability of American lists, since they were not created or sold by the government. I replied that while the U.S. government was not authorized to compile or sell lists, there were other reliable sources. He nodded and then said once again that he believed direct marketing could become an important marketing tool for China. I was beginning to understand that for him to ask a question would mean losing face. He was, after all, the director of the China Post. He understood that direct marketing could help build the China Post and the economy of China, but he didn't know how to start. He wanted help but refused to ask for it.

It was now time for me to answer the question that Duan Guichang would not ask. I told him that there were many ways of increasing the use of mail, but first I was going to give him a look at how one American consumer—me—was affected by direct marketing. Having anticipated that this was a tack I might take, I had brought some material with me. I showed him my copy of the August 23 issue of *The New Yorker* magazine, which had come in the mail that morning. I pointed out that because I was a subscriber, the magazine had been mailed to me—thereby requiring postage. I then opened the magazine, which contained one four-page ad on card stock; one twelve-page special advertising section; one single-page ad with a bound-in reply envelope; one two-page card-stock insert; one one-page ad with a postpaid card-stock business reply card bound in; one loose card; and two bound-in cards. I also showed him that week's issue of *TV Guide,* which contained two separate four-page card-stock inserts with business reply cards. I mentioned that my *New York Times* of the previous Sunday had contained seven special advertising sections, several of which had included cards or coupons to be mailed. I told him that my mail at home that very morning had contained eighteen catalogs, eleven from companies I had bought merchandise from and seven that were trying to make me a new customer. The catalogs had been mailed to me, and if I ordered, I would do so by phone. (The toll-free number is now responsible for more than 50 percent of all business calls in the United States.) But all the merchandise and additional catalogs would be sent by mail. Fifty-nine percent of American adults—113 million people—purchased from a catalog in 1995. I showed and commented on the four pieces of ad mail* I had received at home that morning. The best of them was a computerized letter from General Electric offering me a new three-year service contract for a dishwasher I had bought two years earlier. The original warranty had expired. General Electric was offering to extend it with a service contract that would retain me as a customer for an additional three years. It was direct mail at its best—databased, timely, clear, and relevant. I told him that last Sunday, while watching long infomercials on television, I had bought an electric toothbrush, which would be sent to me by mail. I told him that such advertising on television was creating more business for the USPS. I also showed him the five pieces of business-to-business mail I had received at the office that morning. Business-to-business is the fastest-growing segment of direct marketing. And I told him that it hadn't always been like that. Most of these new uses of mail and advertising were developed by our agency.

While describing direct marketing in the United States, an image suddenly appeared in my mind. I imagined a building holding a database of the more than one billion people who live in China, and there, standing at the entrance as the gatekeeper, was Duan Guichang. I left my seat and began to pace my side of the room. I then decided to share the vision with him. I said that what I had in mind required a number of assumptions and some leaps of faith, but if I were right, we could jump-start the development of direct marketing in China. Looking at Duan Guichang, I said that I assumed that the China Post had mastered the essentials of collecting, sorting, and delivering the mail. But could it add to its responsibilities the collection of data and the construction of a database? I thought I saw a nod even before the transla-

*The new name for commercial direct mail.

tion. Could the employees of the China Post who collect and deliver mail fill in a data form such as that used by the U.S. Census Bureau in the villages, towns, and cities they work in? Would the government cooperate by putting the data into order? I knew that this could be done more easily in cities than in farm communities. I also knew that 75 percent of the cities in Asia with more than one million people are in China. They could start with the cities and add the villages and farms later. A database of Chinese demographic segments could be the foundation of a direct marketing economy. The China Post would be the collector and gatekeeper of the database. It would rent the names to domestic and foreign companies that wanted access to specific segments of Chinese consumers and businesses. I said I believed that such a business would greatly increase the use of mail at a profit. I paused, expecting a discussion after the translation. There was much discussion among our guests, but none of it was translated for me. But judging by the animation of the group, I was sure I had hit home.

I could see that Duan Guichang was concerned with two problems: the first was how to increase the use of mail within China, the second, how to use mail to build international sales. Suddenly, I thought I had the answer. China is still ruled by a centralized authoritarian government, which can do pretty much as it pleases. Despite the rise of private ownership, the central government still owns part or all of many enterprises. I then turned once again to face my guest. I told him I had an idea for a radically new business that could provide China with a vast new market for its goods and a great opportunity for increasing the use of its postal facilities. His eyes narrowed. I suddenly realized that the director of International Services of the Ministry of Posts and Telecommunications of the People's Republic of China had probably never before seen anyone stand up and invent new businesses for his ministry, seemingly off the top of his head. I hoped I wasn't being impertinent, but this was how I had always done business. So I forged ahead and outlined the business I had in mind.

I told him that the Chinese factories that made goods for export were not building a secure or permanent economic base. They were manufacturing a variety of consumer goods for foreign companies, which sold them abroad under their own brand names. I believed that China could sell these goods at higher prices directly to consumers worldwide by entering the interactive world of direct marketing. The

China Post should begin, or encourage someone to begin, a catalog company to sell Chinese manufactured products globally with their own brand names that consumers would, in time, learn to recognize and value. These could be sold in every developed country with a direct marketing infrastructure, which is most of them. The China Post could create a site on the World Wide Web that would become a global electronic catalog. Printed catalogs, translated into each language, would be sent to lists of mail-order buyers in other countries. Space would be offered to those domestic enterprises that wished to participate. The catalogs, a showcase for Chinese enterprises, would contain pictures of the regions in China where the goods were made and would include photographs of Chinese workers, life, and customs. This would constitute a vast global promotion for China that could take place twice a year—a Chinese fair by mail that people could attend and shop at in their own homes. Such a catalog would have other benefits, as well: It would bring hard currency into China. It would help Chinese manufacturers sell goods at higher prices and more profitably. It would greatly expand China's use of its own postal services for international mail. It would put China into electronic marketing. And it would provide profitable global advertising for Chinese brands. It would be direct marketing at its best.

Then, as our guests were on a tight schedule, the meeting ended. As he left, Duan Guichang handed me a gift collection of Chinese stamps and said to me in perfect English, "Thank you, Father of Direct Marketing." It was the end of the meeting but not the end of the story. My new friend Duan Guichang and I would meet again and, I hope, often.

Direct marketing makes things happen. It now attracts the attention of nations, the press, universities, and large and small businesses everywhere. In the past twelve months, I have addressed groups in Cupertino (California), New York, Barcelona, Byfleet (U.K.), São Paulo, Buenos Aires, Frankfurt, Paris, Toronto, Lisbon, Copenhagen, Mexico City, Manzanillo (Mexico), Monterey (California), Sirmione (Italy), Brussels, and Mougins (France).

But it wasn't always like that. Direct marketing and I had humbler beginnings. To explain how and why this came about, I will have to take you back to the times and places where it all began.

BEING DIRECT

1
How It All Began

I was born in New York City in a tenement in the east Bronx. My father had just opened a small business, manufacturing fur coats. We were very poor. The business improved, and five years later we moved to a brand-new apartment house with a roof garden in the west Bronx. My father drove a Packard limousine. My older brother, Irving, and I had expensive clothes and a German nanny. It was the American dream. But when I was nine, my father became terminally ill. His business suffered, and a year after he died, we were poor again.

I grew up during the Great Depression. I knew that banks failed not because I read about them in the newspapers but because my mother and her friends had lined up in panic at the United States Bank at 170th Street off the Grand Concourse in the Bronx to find their savings gone.

I saw my friends' fathers—heads of households who drove taxis or sewed or sold cloth or fur—drift home and weep from fear and shame as they lost their jobs, their savings, and their dreams. In those days, there was no unemployment insurance, no Social Security, and no welfare—when you lost everything, you had nothing left.

Thus, I soon developed a different way of looking at the world. As a "gifted" student in the New York City school system, I was enrolled in a fast academic track and graduated from De Witt Clinton High School before my sixteenth birthday. But my formal education came to an end after a year at Brooklyn College. It was free to those who qualified, but even a free college was beyond my means when my childhood ran out and I had to go to work for survival, ready or not.

When I was still in high school, my first job was delivering chickens after school on Fridays for Izzy, the local kosher butcher. Izzy didn't pay me; I had to make do with tips. Since our neighborhood was predominantly Jewish, Izzy sold a lot of chickens on Friday, traditionally the day for making chicken soup.

There were two kinds of buildings in our neighborhood—five-story walk-ups and taller ones with elevators. The higher the floor in a walk-up, the lower the rent, but the opposite was true of the elevator buildings. Though I hadn't yet learned the word "demographics," I thought I could figure out where the big tippers were most likely to live. I quickly learned I was wrong.

The job was simple. By sundown on Friday night, Izzy had to deliver his last chicken and close his shop. Izzy would hand me as many bags of chickens as I could carry—about fifty pounds. He had no cart and I had no bicycle, so I carried the chickens in my arms to their owners. On a typical Friday, tips from customers in the elevator buildings were scant. But my last delivery one afternoon was to Mrs. Schwartz, who lived on the top floor of a walk-up. Mrs. Schwartz gave me a lavish tip of seven cents, and I couldn't help asking, "Mrs. Schwartz, how is it that you never tip me less than a nickel for bringing your chickens, but none of the ladies in the elevator buildings give me more than two cents, if that?" She smiled at me and said, "Lester, I need you more."

I have never forgotten this lesson. To this day, I teach our employees the "Mrs. Schwartz Rule of Service." Charges for services should not be based on what the services cost or on the customer's ability to pay. The price of a service should be based on the value that service provides to the person or company that uses it. The "Mrs. Schwartz Rule" led me to recommend in 1958 that American Express launch its credit card at a $15 annual fee, even though Diners Club was charging only $5, because potential cardmembers had a greater need for the new and expanded services that I proposed American Express offer. The "Mrs. Schwartz Rule" will become even more important in the years ahead as our society continues to change its focus from manufacturing commodities to creating and selling services.

In June 1937, my formal college education ended, and I knew I would have to join the grown-ups and make a living. What would I do? What could I do? My one and only role model was my mother's youngest brother, a dashing figure who carried a walking stick.

Uncle Isac was one of a group of Jewish intellectuals who gathered at the Café Royale on Second Avenue in Manhattan, and I loved to accompany him there. I would sit and listen to passionate writers and actors discussing books and plays and places they had traveled to. Their world seemed large and bright compared to mine.

My world consisted mainly of the employment agencies I visited that posted handwritten cardboard signs announcing the jobs to be filled: dishwasher, delivery boy, short order cook—all my depressing prospects.

I finally found a job with a collection agency on Madison Avenue and Forty-third Street. The ad in *The New York Times* had called for "some college education"—and so I became an office boy at $10 for a five-and-a-half-day week. Herman Steinberg's collection agency had "clients," not customers. I was in the service business now—and on Madison Avenue! The firm had two kinds of clients: industrial companies such as Owens Illinois Glass and expensive shops such as Saks Fifth Avenue and Cartier. The Depression was still on, and there was plenty of work for collection agencies.

I opened the mail, filed, ran errands, and put stamps on the outgoing mail. Steinberg, a genial, gentle man, always summoned me by shouting "Boy!" It took him months to learn my name. Since there were no staplers in those days, I kept Steinberg's desk supplied with pins for attaching papers. I also deposited his paycheck, which was $165 a week, more money than I could believe, since $100 a week was then big money. Steinberg lived in the East Sixties in Manhattan and drove a Cadillac.

Bill Shea, one of my colleagues at the agency, could dictate letters to a machine faster than I could speak. Each night in the mail room I saw how good they were. They requested, explained, demanded, and threatened with great economy. The letters were original, dictated on the instant—and they worked. It was the first time I saw letters that produced responses with money enclosed. It was my first view of the power of direct mail.

Frank DeBoers specialized in collecting from movie stars, playboys, and phonies who owed money to the fine shops. The reports Frank would dictate on his phone calls and visits read like a Sunday tabloid. For example, there was the playboy who refused to pay Cartier for a piece of diamond jewelry he had bought for a celebrated movie star. She said it wasn't good enough, crushed it with her foot, and flushed it down the toilet. The playboy never paid the bill—and the matter never went to court. Then there was the wealthy man who bought a mink coat for his girlfriend at Revillon Frères; it was accidentally delivered to his wife with his girlfriend's name embroidered in the lining. That bill didn't get collected either. I learned from Frank DeBoers that when mail didn't work, a personal visit or phone call might. I didn't realize it then, of course, but I was beginning to learn the elements of direct marketing. Bill and Frank encouraged me to help them with their work. They gave me letters to write and calls to make, and I was soon good at it. Bill said I had a feel for the business, though I didn't feel good about doing it.

Then came the day Congress voted the first minimum wage act, $12 a week, which was how I got my first raise.

However, even with this great sum, our family couldn't make ends meet. My brother, Irving, who was two and a half years older, was making $15 a week as a production assistant at a foreign-language advertising agency, a job that Uncle Isac had found for him. Isac wrote copy for the same agency, which placed ads in the Yiddish press. Since Irving couldn't read Yiddish, his prospects were no better than mine.

We met for lunch several times a week in Bryant Park behind the public library at Forty-second Street and Fifth Avenue. We didn't talk about what our lives were really like. Life was too awful. Instead, we would imagine other and better lives. Looking back at those years now, I can see a pattern. I was propelled into fantasy by fear, trying to calm the horrors of the moment by dreaming of tomorrow.

We had to move frequently from one block to another in our neighborhood. Times were hard and apartments difficult to rent, so landlords offered "concessions" of one or more months' free rent at the beginning of a lease. It was the "apartment-of-the-month club." If you agreed to pay so much rent for a given period, you got so many months' free rent for moving in. As an extra bonus, you could get a free paint job for a room or for the whole apartment if you acted "now." My mother was a good negotiator, so we moved every time our lease expired. That was how I first learned about giving premiums in exchange for a long-term commitment to purchase, knowledge that would eventually create billions of dollars of profitable advertising.

My mother finally negotiated us into a ground-floor apartment at 1475 Wythe Place, one block west of the Grand Concourse. My good friend Gil Tschomsky lived nearby. Gil's mother owned a small millinery shop that featured "Paris models" in the window. The Tschomskys lived in back of the store, and to visit Gil I had to walk through the store. When there were no customers, Mrs. Tschomsky would greet me in her heavy accent, "Hallo, Lester." One day, she proposed that Gil and I open a millinery store. She would buy the hats in the millinery center on Thirty-eighth Street. Gil, she was convinced, would be a good businessman, and with my "mouth" we were sure to be a big success. I wanted nothing to do with hats or stores.

I said, "Mrs. Tschomsky, a lot of women don't wear hats anymore. What if they all stop?" But she was stubborn. "What does every girl want?" she demanded.

"I don't know, Mrs. Tschomsky."

"Every girl wants a husband, Lester. To find a husband, she first has to find a hat. A hat that makes her feel beautiful. You think girls will ever give up wanting husbands?" she asked triumphantly.

Mrs. Tschomsky was right, of course. Women are never just looking for hats, they are looking for love. I tucked that away too for future use, though not in the millinery trade.

Mr. and Mrs. Harry Klein and their daughter, Gladys, were our downstairs neighbors on Wythe Place. He said he was in the "promotion" business, but he really owned a box factory. Since Irving was already working in advertising and Mr. Klein thought I showed some creative ability, he encouraged us to start an advertising agency in the small penthouse on the top floor of the building where he had his business.

What should we call it? How should we start? Where would we find the money to begin? Our mother had one piece of jewelry left from the good years, a diamond-and-emerald bracelet my father had given her on their tenth anniversary. She sold it without hesitation. Soon we had a bank account of $3,000, a name, "Coronet Advertising Service," a business card, and a lease. The word "service" in the name rather than "agency" was deliberate. We didn't know what advertising agencies did. We believed a service would cover anything a client needed. We would do anything and everything until we learned the right path to success. I was president and Irving was executive vice president, and our first location was in a penthouse at 874 Broadway, just a block above Union Square. My career in advertising literally began at the top.

2

How Not to Start an Advertising Agency

I was nineteen years old and knew nothing about starting or running a business and less about advertising. Irving didn't know much more, and what little he knew was how to do it in Yiddish.

To cover our costs—mainly rent and phone—and our living expenses, we had to take in $50 a week more than we spent, almost double what we had made in our previous jobs. We had to make a profit of $217 a month.

We needed a plan. Our lives depended on it. The plan we came up with had these objectives:

First: Get going—get into business as fast as we can.

Second: Learn advertising—read, study, listen, try.

Third: Get business—any kind of business.

Harry Klein, who on Wythe Place seemed weak and timid, seemed tall and strong at work. He told us where to buy cheap used furniture. We needed stationery and visited our first paper dealer. I still remember him holding the paper up to the light so we could read the watermark: Hammermill. We bought reams of light blue paper for letters, envelopes, and bills, and card stock for business cards. Then we found a printer, George Thermopoulous, a Greek who had come to America as a teenager.

I looked around George's shop. Next to the entrance was a wall covered with dollar bills. I asked, in jest, if he had printed them? He went over to the wall, put his finger on the portrait on one dollar bill, and told me that George Washington was his hero, which was why he had named his print shop "George's Washington Press." We were looking at the American dream come true. Maybe it could happen to us.

Our office was one floor above Mr. Klein's factory. To get to it, you had to get off the elevator at Mr. Klein's floor and walk up a curving flight of stairs to the "penthouse." Our door was made of heavy dark wood with a frosted-glass panel set in the top half. We had CORONET ADVERTISING SERVICE lettered on the glass. I remember looking at it a lot from inside, where you had to read it backward. It looked important.

We had not thought about who would answer the telephone while we were out looking for business. There were no answering machines in those days, so Mr. Klein suggested that we run an extension from his telephone up to our office. Someone was always in his office to answer the phone. If a call was for us, he would let us know.

I asked him how he would signal when the call was for us. No problem, he said. He would tap on the radiator with a hammer, and when we heard the tap through our radiator, we would then pick up the phone. For outgoing calls, we kept a record and reimbursed Mr. Klein. The incoming calls were more interesting. Mr. Klein or one of his workers would answer the phone—and respond by giving the phone number. If a call was for Coronet Advertising Service, Irving or Lester Wunderman, Phillip Irving, Jim Lester, or any of several other "department heads" whose names we invented, Mr. Klein would bang on the radiator and one of us would pick up the phone.

Our first assignment was from George Thermopoulous.

One afternoon, we were in the print shop watching George print our letterheads on a small circular press, one sheet at a time. George chanted and talked to the press and us as he worked. "Isn't that a beautiful press? Look at the wonderful sheet. So you have an advertising service. What do you know how to make?" The song went on, and each time the press opened, a letterhead that read "Coronet Advertising Service" came out. George continued his chant, but suddenly the words changed.

I couldn't believe it. All at once, I was listening to the preamble to the Constitution sung in a broad Greek accent to the rhythm of a printing press:

...provide for the common defense, promote the general welfare,
and secure the blessings of liberty to ourselves and our posterity,
do ordain and establish this Constitution for the United States of
America.

I told him he was singing the Constitution of the United States. "Of course," he acknowledged. "They are the most beautiful words in the world." Then he asked if we could sell them. Could we sell copies of the Constitution to banks as premiums? We said we'd try. George would print them; our job was to write a letter to sell them.

And so we had our first job. It took us a week to finish the copy to both George's satisfaction and our own. But we didn't know what to charge because only the results of the mailing would determine its true value. Finally, I suggested to Irving that we ask George to pay what he thought it was worth. George thought about it for a few minutes, reached into his wallet and said, "The letter is wonderful—it's worth two pictures of George Washington."

Thus we earned our first two dollars. Our first job was a business-to-business letter that actually sold thousands of booklets to banks. We discovered we knew how to write. Next, we had to learn how to get paid. We did—but much later.

There is no way to get new business except to go after it relentlessly, day after day, in every way possible. It was true then, and it is true today. I began by going door to door in the buildings near our offices, where it was easy to get in. I would start selling on my way in. "I'm from the Coronet Advertising Service," I would say, "and I'm here to help you sell what you make. We do ads, counter cards, letters, brochures, anything you need. We do it well, and it costs less than you think."

People were nice to me—but I got no orders. "We'll call you if we need you, sonny," was the usual response. But I looked, listened, and papered the area with my business cards, and I learned something from every visit. I made a list of the people I called on and what their reactions were. When I visited the second or third time, I could address the prospect by name and knew something about his business and his needs for advertising or printing. I felt that if I could keep that up, we would begin to get business. You can't get new business without understanding the prospect and what he needs. And it works only when you build a relationship of mutual respect.

So I went up and down, from building to building, for weeks. We were asked to quote prices for a few jobs, and we began to understand printing, engraving, and typesetting. We also found suppliers who would work with us. In those days, they were as desperate for business as we were. The country was just emerging from the Depression, and everyone needed sales.

I would tell the following story to any prospective customer who would listen. It was about a peanut vendor who sold hot peanuts from a wheeled cart equipped with a firebox, a steam whistle, and bags of peanuts. "There was this peanut vendor," I would say, "and he was finding it hard to sell his peanuts. So he had to reduce his costs. Since his only expenses were charcoal and peanuts, he decided to give up the charcoal fire. He would light it only when he needed to heat peanuts for a customer. What he forgot was that when his fire went out, his whistle stopped blowing, and the whistle was his advertising. Without it, nobody noticed his peanuts. He finally went out of business. In hard times," I declared, "you had better blow your whistle." The story gave me a chance to talk to people. Talk was my whistle, and I was afraid to stop blowing it.

Then I got our first client. I was in a building on Broadway between Twenty-first and Twenty-second streets, and as usual I took the elevator to the top floor. As I got off, I saw that a man had opened the window at the end of the hall and seemed about to jump. "Stop!" I yelled and dashed for him. In an instant we were struggling. He was screaming in a language I didn't understand, and I was screaming too, terrified that we would both fall out. But I was younger, stronger, and more determined to live than he was to die. I dragged him down the hallway from the window, pushed him to the floor, and sat on him, wondering what to do next. The building was industrial, and the doors were all made of heavy, soundproof steel. Nobody heard us, and no one came out to help. The man I was sitting on was weeping hysterically and moaning unintelligibly. I kept saying soothing things to him, not knowing whether I was getting through. Suddenly, he began to speak English with a French accent. He said he was all right and I could let him up.

I asked whether I could trust him to sit still until I closed the window. He nodded yes. He then invited me into his office. As we entered it, I smelled an extraordinary scent.

He took a bottle of cognac out of a desk drawer and asked me if I wanted a drink. We both needed one. We sat and drank and talked.

His name was on the office door, but I won't use it. Let's call him Michel Camelot. He was in the cosmetics business, which explained the wonderful fragrance I had smelled.

Standing in a line were bottles of a white, creamy liquid that read MICHEL CAMELOT, APRÈS BAIN, some printed display stands, and other advertising matter. I didn't pay much attention to them at first, as I was more interested in the man. He could see I was curious and began to tell me about himself.

"It's a long story," he said, "but if you have the time, I'll tell you." He said that he was not French but Russian; that he had spoken French since childhood because he had come from a wealthy, titled family in Russia and had been brought up in the tsar's court. He had lived the life of a nobleman until 1917, when Russia had gone to war with Germany and he had been sent to America by the tsar as a purchasing agent. Russia had needed everything: guns, bullets, food, clothing. But soon after Michel had arrived in America, the tsar was overthrown.

Suddenly, he found himself in a new country with no job and no money. Though he had been trained as a lawyer in Russia, his real skills were those of a connoisseur of women, wine, and food, qualities not needed in World War I America.

So he went back to Paris, which had been his second home. But even in Paris he was misplaced; he couldn't get a job. Then he was saved by a gift he had received in Russia from one of the ladies of the tsar's court. It was a perfumed after-bath lotion, and its formula had been a gift of love. He began to make the lotion and sold it successfully in Paris. Then he returned to New York, where the lotion was also selling well. So what, I wondered, was his problem?

He paused to refill our glasses and continued. Five years ago, he said, he had developed psoriasis and had become increasingly depressed. That day, on impulse, he decided to kill himself. He thanked me profusely for saving his life and asked what he could do to repay my kindness.

I said, "You could give me your advertising account."

And so he became our first client.

I never learned whether his story was true, but the business he gave us was real. It paid part of our rent and expenses. Within the year, however, Mr. Camelot sold his business to a large cosmetics company that had its own advertising agency, and that was the end of that. I had saved Michel Camelot's life, and he helped save ours, for a while.

It was our next client who got us into direct marketing—but I didn't know it at first.

One day, while I was canvassing the buildings in our neighborhood, I came upon the New York office of *Specialty Salesman Magazine,* "The National Institutional Monthly for Men and Women Who Sell." The magazine was for door-to-door salespeople. It was 1939, and the economy was barely recovering. People who couldn't find regular jobs or whose jobs paid too little turned to door-to-door selling for additional income. Companies that wanted to recruit them took out ads in *Specialty Salesman Magazine.*

The industry was called "direct selling," and it was growing rapidly. I heard about it for the first time the day I wandered into the office of *Specialty Salesman Magazine.* Jim Peckworth, the manager, spent most of his time calling on potential advertisers, but I was lucky and found him in. I handed him my business card, and he assumed I was there to buy advertising for a client. He couldn't have been nicer—or more wrong—but the scenario was so pleasant that I let it play out for a while. Being a buyer was clearly better than being a seller. Jim gave me coffee, a comfortable chair, and a complete sales pitch. I was embarrassed and suddenly wished I had a client who could advertise in *Specialty Salesman.* Jim Peckworth told me that direct selling was a far larger business than I had imagined. Big companies used it to demonstrate their goods in people's homes, farms, or other businesses. Successful companies sold vacuum cleaners, sewing machines, typewriters, garden equipment, cosmetics, foods, encyclopedias, housewares, clothing, office equipment, retail window displays, real estate, and so on through independent door-to-door salesmen. Peckworth told me he could prove that his magazine worked by counting the inquiries and orders his advertisers received. If these ads didn't work, why did advertisers keep coming back again and again?

Jim told me his advertisers needed to create and place ads and follow up their prospects by mail with booklets and other materials. Salesmen needed promotional pieces for their prospects. Suddenly I had a vision of thousands of salespeople distributing thousands of circulars created and printed by us.

I could tell that Jim was about to come to his closing argument. I didn't know how to slow him down. I asked if this was the presentation he made to all his prospects. Annoyed by the interruption, he gave me a peremptory "Yes." Before he could resume, I told him that it was one of the most persuasive presentations I had heard and asked if he had created it himself. Again, an impatient "Yes." He was trying to get me to listen to his closing argument so he could ask for an order. But I couldn't let him get that far because that would end the conversation, and out I would go.

So I pressed on with my interruptions, moving the conversation sideways until we could go forward together in another direction. I asked him why his magazine wasn't filled with ads.

He explained that many advertisers were interested when he could get their attention but that their advertising agencies wouldn't listen because his space rates were too low. It didn't pay an agency to create an ad for one small magazine. It wasn't only the creation of the ad that discouraged agencies; follow-up letters and promotion pieces also had to be written and designed to explain the product and the deal. They had to persuade salesmen to sell and motivate them to keep selling. Agencies would rather create effective ads for mass-circulation magazines. And they were hardly eager to create ads whose results could be measured precisely. Many of his smaller potential advertisers didn't have agencies of their own, and he wasn't equipped to do ads for them.

Jim didn't know that he had just outlined the opportunity that was going to put us into the advertising agency business. I asked him how he would feel about an agency whose main business was meeting the special needs of direct selling clients.

He said it would be an answer to his prayers. I suggested that I come back the following morning with my brother to discuss whether we could be that agency. As I left he called out, "Hey, what was the deal you came in to discuss?"

"Tell you tomorrow," I answered.

I ran back to our office and told Irving what had happened. I said that if we went on the way we were going, we would fail. We had no facilities and little experience. The general printing services we offered were of no special value. If we tried to do general advertising, it would take too long to become as good at it as other agencies were. We needed to be the best at something of our own, no matter how small. We would have to specialize. Direct selling was a big industry, and large agencies wanted no part of it. But they were wrong: it was advertising and selling in its purest form. We would be measured by results—and nothing else.

Irving agreed, and so began my life in direct marketing.

The next day, we saw Jim and discussed what his advertisers needed. We talked about how an agency could help his advertisers. By the end of the day, we had a deal. With his help, we would learn the direct selling industry. Jim would recommend us to advertisers who came to him without an agency or whose agencies didn't want to get involved in direct selling. And we would get a steady flow of new clients—however small they might be.

We would get the usual 15 percent commission his magazine paid to agencies for the ads they placed. That wouldn't be much. But we were gambling that we would produce results. If we did, the advertisers would place our ads repeatedly. In those days, a successful response ad could run for years. The commissions from subsequent placements would be like royalties on a hit song.

So we had a business idea, and now we had to make it work.

We assembled a file of successful direct selling ads, follow-up materials, brochures, and so on. That was easy. We answered ads in *Specialty Salesman* and *Opportunity* magazines and gave our home address. Mail came pouring in, usually followed by salesmen. In a few weeks, we had examples of sales letters, circulars, sales manuals, and price lists from all kinds of companies. We then took part-time jobs selling brushes and books door to door, on commission. Selling the stuff was more difficult than writing about it, but we began to understand the problems salespeople faced. Jim also arranged for us to take training courses from sales managers of local direct selling companies.

We had to be ready to produce good ads and letters fast and, we hoped, in quantity. We knew we could write copy, buy space, and do the correspondence and billing, but we needed artists and designers to create layouts and finished artwork just as quickly. It was then that the always helpful Mr. Klein introduced us to Bela Proper.

Bela was a Hungarian, pink-skinned and round with many chins. His face was divided horizontally by an enormous waxed moustache. With his striped green shirt and bright pink velvet bow tie, Bela looked like a newly packed, gaudy snowman who should have been holding a candy cane rather than an artist's brush. But that was how Bela announced that he was an artist—not just any artist, but a Hungarian artist.

We would also discover that Bela's tastes and values were absolute. There was only good art and bad art—good goulash and bad goulash—good people and bad people. No middle ground. Bela's first question after saying hello was whether we did good work. If it was bad, we shouldn't waste his time. He already had enough lousy work to do. He didn't need any more.

I told him we were terrific. We had great ideas and wrote wonderful copy. What we needed was good design and finished art to bring it to life. Could he help us?

Bela didn't answer until he decided whether to believe us. Instead, he took an enormous engraved gold watch from his vest and said it was lunchtime. Let's have a goulash, he said, and then we would talk about business. Thus I discovered how much of the advertising business is done over lunch.

We had learned at home to appreciate good goulash, and that day we passed the goulash test. After lunch, we went to Bela's studio, located on a lower floor of the same building in which we had our office. The Bela Proper Art Studio consisted of Bela and two freelance artists, each of whom, we eventually learned, was charged half the rent. The three of them worked for shared and individual clients doing everything from layouts to finished art and mechanicals. Bela was the landlord, the salesman, and the organizer—and he seemed good at it.

We told him of our plan to become a specialized advertising service that could create ads, booklets, circulars, sales manuals, package designs—everything direct selling clients would need. Bela said that if we were serious and good and we wanted to be better and we paid our bills on time, he would be our art studio.

Thus the pieces of a business began to fit together. Our hopes were high, our needs small, yet the potential for disaster was great. We were short of time and money, and every minute counted. In addition to paying our business overhead, we had to withdraw money from our capital each week for food and rent. That week I had torn a hole in the seat of the trousers of my only suit. I couldn't afford a new one, so my mother patched the pants. I was the only advertising agency president in New York who could never turn his back on a client.

Days, weeks, and months passed at a frenzied pace. Jim Peckworth came through as promised. The clients we got through him were mainly large companies with small direct selling advertising budgets.

And we came closer and closer to breaking even. Our monthly expenses remained $350: $200 to live on and $150 for the business. By April 1940, we were selling an average of $1,500 worth of advertising a month. The 15 percent commission we earned on $1,500 was $225, and we had begun to make some additional money on printing and copy. And we were recognized by media associations.

Most important, we were learning our trade. We did retail promotions and printing for a cosmetic maker and for a housewares manufacturer. We also represented a large company that made flamethrowers for clearing farm fields of weeds. Another sold toy battery-driven dogs that barked. Another made paper draperies for people who couldn't afford cloth—a good business in a depressed economy.

I phoned, wrote, and visited companies asking for just a little of their time to explain "direct selling," a wonderful new marketing idea that could help their businesses grow. Some companies replied that they didn't want to sell direct but wanted new and original marketing ideas. Soon I found that many businessmen were willing to talk about their companies and their problems—if they thought you could provide a unique solution—and in this way I learned that the most important service an advertising agency can provide is a new and better marketing idea.

Our first success at selling an idea was for the Economy Ribbon Mills on lower Broadway. I had been recommended to the owner by a mutual friend, and when I called him, he said he had heard I was giving away good ideas. Did I have one for him?

I said I'd be right over and would bring a good idea with me. When I arrived, he was ready to listen, but I didn't have an idea to give him. I asked him to tell me about the ribbon business and what he thought was his most difficult problem.

He told me that business was terrible. He was not selling enough ribbon to make a living. I asked him why not. Were other people's ribbons better or cheaper?

That was not the problem. His ribbons were as good as anyone's, probably better than most, and his prices were fair. He just couldn't seem to get the attention of department-store buyers. They believed all ribbons were the same, and they wouldn't take the time to learn the difference.

He wanted to know if we could help him, since he had tried everything. He sent free samples of his ribbons to buyers every season. His salesman followed up the samples with personal visits, letters, and phone calls. What more could he do? Sending out whole lines of free samples was expensive—and he had to do it twice a year.

That might be his problem, I told him. Buyers probably received samples from many companies at the same time. How could they tell the difference?

He shrugged, and then I recommended that he let us create a quarter-page magazine ad that would offer to enroll his prospects and customers in a "ribbon-of-the-month club." Membership would be free. Each month, the Economy Ribbon Mills would send a sample of the month's hottest-selling ribbon plus a full description of the fabric, the colors, and how best to use and sell it. It would tell whether it was a classic design or a new one. We would give each ribbon a name. Economy would no longer be just another company sending samples to people who hadn't asked for them; he would become a unique source of information and service. The ribbons he sent out each month would get attention, and they would differentiate his company from his competitors'. I had never talked faster or thought more quickly—and I can still remember how much I enjoyed it. It was the first time I had had a chance to convert a commodity into a brand and a service.

The Ribbon-of-the-Month Club was a success, and so we had another client who advertised regularly and who needed monthly mailings. The account was small but steady.

But something more important had happened. I had discovered that I could create ideas and solve problems—and that I could do so on demand. For the first time, I began to believe that I really belonged in the advertising business and that I had something original to contribute.

Our ideas weren't always good—they weren't always bought—they didn't always work—but they were always exciting. Each problem suggested a possibility, and a life of possibilities began to replace the fears I had lived with for so long.

Meanwhile, Irving developed another way of getting business. He was too shy for face-to-face presentations. But he was a fierce letter writer. He looked through magazines for ads he thought we could improve. As Phillip Irving, creative director, he shook up many an advertiser with his keenly written analysis of what was wrong with its current advertising and how it could be improved—and soon his letters began to bring responses. Most of them said, "Thank you, but no thank you." Others suggested that we mind our own business and leave theirs alone. However, while my gentle, shy brother Irving might have taken "No" for an answer, Phillip Irving was indomitable and persistent.

Irving found a legitimate prospect for us in the *Saturday Evening Post*, at the time America's largest-circulation and most expensive magazine for advertisers. In a current issue was a full-page, full-color ad selling men's ties by mail order. The ad had a coupon, and respondents were asked to choose the tie or ties they wanted right off the page. The advertiser was the Haband Tie Company of Teaneck, New Jersey. Irving's letter to them was devastating. "Your ad is too large," he wrote. "Its very cost makes it impossible for you to get a sufficient return to cover your expenses. I am sure we can get a lower cost per sale from a one-inch, black-and-white ad run regularly than you are getting from the full-page, full-color ad you run occasionally." Our suggestion of a low-priced solution was seductive to a company that had built its tie business mainly by direct mail rather than space advertising. One day, a bang on the radiator sounded the telephone alert. It was Mr. Habernickel, the owner of the Haband Tie Company, wanting to talk to Mr. Phillip Irving. He said that many agencies had written to him, but we were the first to promise more orders for less money. He wanted to test our idea. We created and placed a series of one-inch humorous ads for Haband in the *Saturday Evening Post*. Imagine our excitement: a one-inch ad in the *Saturday Evening Post* cost more than a full-page ad in *Specialty Salesman*! Unfortunately, our small ads didn't work. We learned a lot from the Haband experience, but we lost the account. We learned that while small ads with cute copy might not sell, they could create inquiries. I still believe a subsequent mailing of a full brochure to prospects would have worked if we hadn't sacrificed information for humor in those first ads.

Our next important response was from the Mapleine Company of Seattle, Washington, which marketed an imitation maple syrup through grocery stores. It was a large national advertising account—and the company was a client of one of the large general agencies. Phillip Irving's unsolicited analysis caught Mapleine's attention, and several executives wanted to come to New York to see us about their account. That created a problem. We were two kids in a dinky office above a box factory. Our "creative department" on another floor in the building consisted of a goulash expert and his two tenants. Our client list wasn't distinguished—and I still wore my patched trousers. Irving suggested we rent a hotel suite for the meeting, but that would be expensive. And then what if we were offered the account? We couldn't afford the fare to Seattle. We needed the business, but we weren't ready for it, even if we could fake our way into a sale. We gave up. Phillip Irving wrote to Mapleine, explaining that we had to withdraw since our plans for expansion to the West Coast were not yet firm. They sent us a nice letter and a case of Mapleine. It was welcome.

We found out that it was a waste of time to sell what we couldn't deliver. It was a hard lesson, but even the largest agencies learn in time that it's better to help a client by selling his product—not your agency.

By specializing in the business of direct selling, we got new business we could handle and our income slowly grew. By September 1940, we had begun to break even. After a little more than a year, we were ready for our next move.

The Mapleine experience troubled us. We couldn't continue to say "No" to clients or prospects who wanted to visit our offices to see our work. We needed a real office, we needed our own telephone, and we had to show our clients people at work. We were now "playing on the house's money." The losses from our original capital had been recovered; our monthly income equaled our expenses, both business and personal; and I had a new suit. In our optimism, we even bought an old car to visit our growing list of clients in Brooklyn, New Jersey, Pennsylvania, and Westchester County. The car, a black 1932 Chevrolet coupe, cost $35. It had a rumble seat, but the floorboards under the front seats were missing. There was a working radio; you could hear it only when the car was standing still. When it was in motion, the worn-out muffler drowned out the radio and all conversation. But it was a car. We were still living on Wythe Place in the Bronx, so we drove to work every day down the then-new West Side Drive.

Bela helped us solve our office problem. Thanks to our clients, his art business had expanded. He now had four freelance artists, each paying half the rent, so he was feeling good. I suggested we move to larger quarters together so that we could look like a real advertising agency. "Let's have a goulash," he said. "We'll talk after lunch."

We found a perfect suite of offices just a block south, at 41 Union Square. There was a large room facing north, up Broadway, for Bela's group, and on the right another large room for Irving, myself, and some better secondhand furniture. The rent was higher, but so were our expectations. Bela could now have five artists in addition to himself, with room enough in the studio for a copywriter when we could afford one. The little reception room could one day house a typist and a bookkeeper. I insisted that the only name on the door be "Coronet Advertising Service" and told Bela that his clients wouldn't object as long as his name and the names of his artists were listed in the building directory downstairs. We signed the lease, sublet part of the office to him, and divided the rent equally—but Bela, as usual, subdivided his among the artists in his studio. We were a major source of Bela's business. He shared in our success, and we began to feel like a real team. The greater volume of work attracted better freelancers, and soon we had a reasonably talented group.

We were on the brink of war but didn't know it. The Depression was ending, and businessmen were more willing to try new ideas. The direct selling business began to grow, and so did we. We were now specialists at creating ads, letters, and sales presentations that paid. We could actually count the number of responses to each ad. Our job then was to convert those inquiries into sales of our clients' products. We also had to maintain the enthusiasm of the sales force by mail. We created newsletters, contests, and house organs and celebrated the success of the door-to-door salespeople who did well.

Door-to-door selling is a cruel and difficult business. As one salesman put it, "To succeed you need a face with a smile that never fades, an ego strong enough to believe that any prospect who doesn't buy has made a mistake, a spit-proof eye, legs that won't move backwards, shoe leather that never wears out—and a family to support and bills to pay."

Much of the American economy had been built by such men. The Yankee Pedlars had opened the vast spaces of America to commerce. Marshall Field and other merchant princes had begun by selling door to door. Direct selling remains an effective business. Avon products, Tupperware, Amway, and Mary Kay cosmetics are large companies that still sell door to door.

Direct selling—and creating advertising that paid—was the business we were learning at Coronet—and we were learning it from the ground up. By trial and error, I was discovering how to conceive ideas, how to write copy that worked, and how to make layouts that presented those ideas clearly and dramatically. At first, I failed more often than I succeeded. I was also learning how to specify and order type, make paste-ups, use a ruling pen, place media orders, estimate and buy paper and printing, address sales meetings, do bookkeeping, calculate taxes, type letters, control overhead, bill clients, pay media, and collect bills. Some of these skills we mastered easily; others we had to learn the hard way.

Because our company was small and we were young and new at the business, we were forced to prove that the ads we recommended not only worked—but worked *better* than those offered by our competitors. We learned to test ads and letters and also had our clients record the results they were getting. We were discovering some surprising truths about response advertising. For example, despite what we had told Haband, large ads, though more expensive, were more cost-effective and more profitable than small ads. We learned that the most powerful word in advertising was "FREE" and the second most powerful was "NEW." And most important, we could prove that some of the ads we created paid. We also began to understand the reasons why some didn't.

A good way we found to test ads was the "split run," in which two different ads for the same product were printed alternately in a magazine or newspaper. We tested even our best ads and mailings this way to see which ad got better results. Clients and prospects alike began to respect the fact that we sold results, not opinions—objective proof, not subjective judgments.

These techniques began to win us new accounts. One was the Pocono Hosiery Mills, makers of thermal socks. The mill had built a profitable mail-order business with an ad headlined COLD FEET. The copy promised that the thermal socks would keep the cold out. The president of the company asked how we would test it against our new ad. He didn't want to do expensive research. I explained the split-run technique and said that the research would cost him nothing. Our headline promised "Warm Feet." It outpulled "Cold Feet" two to one. And we won another regular client.

Soon afterward, we discovered a powerful advertising offer that won every split-run test in which it was used. It was "Buy one and get one FREE." With this simple idea, we converted failures to successes and successes to big winners. Even then, we realized that to be successful a response advertisement in any medium had to get attention, break the barrier of inertia, and stimulate immediate action. When that happened, response advertising could achieve better results than most people thought possible.

By the beginning of 1941, we were creating advertising for more than a dozen clients and were beginning to get some attention in the direct selling and mail-order industry.

We were still writing all the copy ourselves, buying media and printing, overseeing production, and keeping Bela's expanded art staff busy. Bela now had six artists. We hired a secretary–bookkeeper–phone-answerer–receptionist. Our business was growing, and as we learned more about advertising and selling, we were ready for a large account—and we got one. I will call it the Formost Merchandising Corp., and its headquarters were just a block away, on the north side of Union Square.

Formost's advertising recruited salesmen to sell electric turntables for retail window displays. Formost spent $10,000 a month for advertising and direct mail. For us, that was a large account. Our income from it would be $1,500 a month. The extra income seemed like a fortune. I remember thinking, the day we were awarded the account, "Here I am not yet twenty-one, and I am going to be making as much money as the people I used to work for."

When I told Irving the good news, we hugged each other. Bela announced, "Everybody out for goulash." That day the goulash was accompanied by champagne.

In retrospect, I realized I had never asked Formost why it had hired us. Its account was large enough to attract larger agencies, but we seemed to win the business without competition. We had presented our work and offered some ideas, and we were hired at once. The company was well staffed, its offices luxurious, and the executives we met seemed highly competent. The product was a good one that worked as advertised. It seemed that nothing could go wrong. With hindsight, one might have wondered if it was too good to be true. I still find it painful to admit that we were being set up.

After a hectic first month's work, everything seemed in order. The budget of $10,000 was spent as promised, and we billed the client on the usual advertising agency terms: it was to pay us in thirty days, but it could earn a 2 percent discount if it paid us in ten. We had to pay the media, printers, and so on, within ten days to earn our commission. We paid; the client didn't. I went to see the people at Formost and was reassured by the company's president that it were changing its accounting system and we shouldn't worry. We then placed the second month's advertising, another $10,000, based on the assurances we had received. Formost now owed us $20,000. I called Formost to demand payment. No one answered the phone. Suddenly frightened, I ran across the square to the Formost office. The doors were locked, and there was a marshal's notice of bankruptcy on the door. We owed the better part of $20,000, and we didn't have it.

Formost Merchandising was a corporation, and therefore its owners were not liable for its debts, but by digging I found out that the principal owner was a countess. Frantically, I called and asked to see her. She refused. She said that the corporation was bankrupt and we would be treated like all the other creditors. Then she hung up. I called her again and told her that I desperately needed to see her, if only for a few minutes. Grudgingly, she offered to see me in her apartment that afternoon. A uniformed servant opened the door, and I was taken through a foyer with mirrored and damasked walls into a living room larger than our entire apartment on Wythe Place.

After what seemed to me a painfully long wait, a slim, elegant woman entered the room, introduced herself as the Countess de Valmont (not her real name), and asked what was so urgent.

I told her that I was not like the other creditors. If she did not pay her bill, my brother, my mother, and I would not have enough money for food and rent. I didn't want to hear about bankruptcy laws. I only wanted her to tell me how she was going to pay us so that we could continue to live. I hadn't come for a discussion. All I wanted was a check.

She sat quietly and then told me that while she was indeed the Countess de Valmont, she was not French. She had been born poor on a farm in Montana, but she had lived a life of elegance and splendor in France as the wife of the wealthy Count de Valmont. When France had succumbed to Hitler, he had stayed there to fight in the underground. His properties and money had been seized by the Nazis and the Vichy government, so she had fled to America with enough money to invest in Formost as a way of supporting herself until the war ended. Unhappily, the business had failed. Her lawyers had advised her that a bankrupt company could not favor any single creditor. But after hearing my story, she decided to give me a personal check. I was so astonished, I could hardly breathe. She left the room and returned with a check made out to the Coronet Advertising Service. I thanked her and hurried out.

The next day, I went to her bank to cash the check. The bank manager asked if I had seen the countess. I told him that I had, just the day before, at her apartment. He said that he was sorry but there was not enough money in her account to cover the check.

So it really was over. We closed the Coronet Advertising Service that week. We didn't declare bankruptcy or explain anything to anyone. I had learned a bitter lesson. I was just a kid, and I had been had. We hoped we could pay our debts in time—but we didn't know how or when. We just packed up and left the office. Bela took over the lease. We still needed $50 a week, and somehow we would have to find a way to earn it.

We applied for unemployment compensation. Irving got a part-time job at the post office. Tempted by the security of civil service, he decided to take the next civil service test for postal clerk. I didn't know what I wanted to do.

Our mother set us straight. She told Irving the idea of working for the post office was foolish. Our cousin Morris was a postman, but he hadn't even finished high school. Irving could do better. She told me to stop dreaming. She said that I reminded her of her brother Isac when he was my age. She had asked him what he thought we should do, and he had told her we should go on. He had said we had talent and would find some way to succeed.

She had a point. We should look for jobs in advertising. We hadn't failed. On the contrary, we had begun to learn how to make advertising pay. And we had learned some things about advertising that no one else knew.

3

Buy One, Get One Free

So we wrote our résumés. Irving looked for work as a copywriter, I as an account executive. To support ourselves, we would each have to earn $25 a week. The few agencies I saw asked first about my education, what degrees I had earned, and how I had ranked in my class. When I responded "Brooklyn College" and "No degree," the interviews ended just as I was adding that I had been forced to stop school because I had had to go to work. I told them I had worked in advertising for two years. They wanted to know where. "The Coronet Advertising Service"—they had never heard of it. When they asked why I had left, I had to admit that I had been one of its owners—and that it had gone out of business.

My credentials were not impressive. I tried to explain how much I wanted to work in advertising. I tried to tell them what I had learned about advertising that paid, but they were more interested in hiring graduates from Ivy League schools. They wouldn't break the rules for people who didn't fit the mold.

Irving's interviews were much the same. We suffered from the same disadvantages that had forced us to open our own business two years earlier: wrong education; wrong experience; wrong side of the tracks.

The large agencies' clients shared the same values. Small agencies and their clients were equally unpromising. They wanted beginners who would work as office boys or errand boys for a meager wage. When they needed to hire professionals, they recruited from the larger agencies to build their own prestige.

When Japan attacked Pearl Harbor, we were still unemployed. One evening, I went to register at our neighborhood draft board in P.S. 64, my old elementary school. I learned I would have to wait to see if I would be drafted. Meanwhile, I had to find a job.

Walking home from the draft board, I had an idea—an idea that seemed crazy but one that I knew would work. That night, I explained it to Irving. Since we didn't seem likely to get jobs in the usual way at the wages we needed, we would have to try something different. We would have to go job hunting together, a two-man team seeking one job. We could write ads, make layouts, get clients, handle accounts, and make a profit for an employer. We had proved that by doing it for ourselves. Each of us was worth $50 a week. An agency could hire either one of us, paying him $50 a week, and the other would work for free. We would make prospective employers the same offer we had used so successfully for clients: "Buy one, get one free!"

So we made another round of the advertising agencies, offering our unique proposition. The executives we met were not as interested in the deal as they were in the imagination that had created it.

As we made our rounds, one agency head asked if we had tried Casper Pinsker. Pinsker had his own mail-order advertising agency. He specialized in ads that sold products by mail in magazines and newspapers. I called and asked if we could arrange to see him. I said we had something to offer him free. His "Yes" was instantaneous.

We saw Casper Pinsker for the first time on the morning of February 9, 1942. His offices were downtown at 150 Nassau Street, a strange location for an advertising agency. We took some comfort from the fact that in those days, most of the New York newspapers were published on Park Row, just off Nassau Street; maybe it wasn't so illogical a location after all; certainly no worse than Union Square.

We passed the Bowery, then New York's center for men who had failed. We parked near city hall and walked to Nassau Street trying not to notice the beggars and bums. I saw threateningly little distance between us and them.

Forty-one Union Square had been shabby but genteel; 150 Nassau Street was just shabby. At Pinsker's office, we entered a large reception room filled with filing cabinets and were greeted by his secretary. She knocked on his door and announced us. The same gruff voice I had spoken to on the telephone invited us in.

Casper Pinsker sat at a large desk placed in the center of the room.

A small desk to the right was for his assistant, Mathilda Reimers. The furniture was worn and yellow with old varnish. Like Pinsker himself, his desk was oversized. He wore metal-rimmed glasses over ruddy cheeks and heavy jowls. He was smoking an enormous cigar. As we entered, he greeted us with a warm "Howareya?"

I noticed at once the curious way Casper Pinsker used his hands. As he sat in his swivel chair, he used his left hand for a cigar, the phone, or a pencil—but the other hand seemed never to leave the side of his neck. He held on as if his head would fall sideways if he let go. "Tellmeaboutyourself," he said. "Wouldyoulikeadrink?" "No—thank—you," I said, hoping I could get his words separated. If I couldn't, we were not going to have much of a conversation that day.

I plunged in, thinking that if I got to the point quickly we'd be in or out in a hurry. I wasn't certain I wanted to stay there any longer than necessary. So I said, "Mr. Pinsker, we're here to—" He interrupted to say, "CallmeCap." "Cap," I went on, "we're here with a proposition that could change your life and ours. We've been told you're in the business of writing mail-order ads, ads that have to pay out. Is that true?"

"Yes," he answered, "that'sallIdo." I went on to explain that we also created ads that paid. We had been doing it for two years and thought we could help him build his agency. "I thought you had come here to offer me something free," he said. "I never buy anything unless I get something free." Either his speech had suddenly cleared up or I was getting to understand him better.

I said we did have something free to offer. He could have either one of us absolutely free—all he had to do was make a choice. "What's the catch?" he asked. "I know nothing is free—you always have to buy something." His speech was getting clearer, and I noticed he had removed his hand from his neck. That was true, I admitted. If he hired one of us for $50 a week, the other would work for nothing. The choice was his.

"That's the damnedest offer I've ever heard," he said, laughing. "I've been offered many things free in this office, but this is the first time I've been offered a person. Are you guys any good? Are you for real? Tell me what you've been doing."

He not only asked to see our sample ads, he wanted to see the results. It didn't take long for us to realize that Cap Pinsker knew more about response advertising than we did. He questioned us about head-lines, offers, and the media we had used. Why had we done this? Why hadn't we done that? We had talked for two hours when he told his sec-retary to cancel his luncheon appointment and make reservations for three at Whyte's, a well-known downtown seafood restaurant. He said we could continue to talk at lunch, and we did.

After lunch, Cap invited us back to his office. We sensed that we would get a decision before the day was over. Back at the office, he showed us a series of large scrapbooks that contained his work. He went through it, describing each client, the problem to be solved, and the success or failure of each ad. The products were all second-rate; the ads plain, the style crude. The artwork looked like an afterthought. As Cap turned the pages of his advertising scrapbook, we could trace the course of his professional life—that of a nice man who had achieved mediocrity.

Cap's largest account was Harvest House, a publishing company. Its best-selling book had first been published as an article in *National Ge-ographic* magazine. It was about the life of an African tribe. Harvest House had bought the rights to the article and published it as a book entitled *The Secret Museum of Mankind*. The ad showed a drawing of a bare-breasted African woman and promised many real-life photos of the subject of the drawing. Harvest House was the bread-and-butter account of Cap's agency. It paid for his Havana cigars, flamboyant clothes, and good food. Advertising agencies developed reputations and personalities based on key clients. The Marlboro Man and Green Giant stood for Leo Burnett; Jell-O, Sanka, Dr Pepper, and Lincoln-Mercury were Young & Rubicam; and so on. These identities lingered even after the clients had left an agency. Cap Pinsker's professional standing was expressed by *The Secret Museum of Mankind,* and I knew it would always be so, no matter what Irving or I might contribute.

But fortunately, that was not the whole story. Pinsker had other clients and a philosophy about advertising. As he explained it, he cre-ated the best ads he could for a client. He tested and retested them. When he was sure he had the most effective one, he "went shopping" for media. I asked him what he meant by "went shopping." Didn't he just look up the advertising rates as published? He said that was how the large general agencies did it. He had to determine how much he could pay per reader to make an ad pay out. He gave us an example. If a book sold for $3.95, the client could usually afford an advertising cost of $1 for each mail order. The balance of $2.95 was used for the cost of manufacture, overhead, postage, profit, and so on. Cap's advertising had to produce sales for $1 per order. He couldn't pay more. After testing, he determined how many orders he could expect an ad to produce from the circulation of any newspaper or magazine. He didn't care what the publisher's rates were; Cap's rate was $1 an order, take it or leave it.

He showed us all the ads of his current clients. Each ad had a dollar figure written on it that represented what each of them could pay for orders received. Cap said that when publishers' representatives visited him, he spread the ads out. They could have all the business they wanted as long as they gave him low enough advertising rates to meet his targets. Most often, space salesmen came to him after they had sold all the advertising they could to the large agencies. Pinsker insisted that his ads run and rerun until his client received the needed number of orders. He did most of his business that way. The publishers' representatives might come to him last, but they were certain they could sell space if they guaranteed Cap Pinsker a profit for his clients.

Cap closed his scrapbooks, turned to us, and said he guessed we had come to him as a last resort, just as the publishers did. He knew we needed to make a deal. I answered that we had already given him our best offer. He could hire either one of us at $50 a week, because that's the least we could live on, and the other would work for free.

He stared at us for what seemed an eternity. Then he put out his hand to Irving and told him that he was hired as a copywriter at $50 a week. He turned to me and said that I had better make myself useful, because I was the "vigorish" in the deal.

So we had jobs again. Irving was earning $50 a week, the usual wage at the time for a copywriter. I was the "vigorish," but I had no idea what that meant in Cap's mind. I would work that out for myself.

The Casper Pinsker Agency was really a discount house. From his point of view, there was no such thing as an ad that received too few responses, only publications that charged too much. Other agencies differentiated themselves by claiming that their creative work or their strategic thinking added value. Cap thought he also created good ads, but because he bought media for less, he gave his clients more exposure and more profit for every dollar they spent. He lived in a world of "incremental" sales. Publishers could sell to him for less because he didn't care when an ad ran or how often, as long as it paid. His clients were the bargain hunters of the advertising business, and as long as there was unsold space to be bought at cut prices, they would make a profit.

As I studied the ads and results, I began to notice variables. For example, an ad that ran in a January issue of a magazine, distributed in late December, produced almost twice as many orders as the same ad placed in a May issue, on sale in late April. A back cover of a magazine produced more than double the number of orders as an inside page. The first three right-hand pages of a magazine pulled at least one third more orders than left-hand pages further back. The exception was the left-hand page facing the inside back cover of a magazine, which was worth as much as the first right-hand page, because many people opened a magazine from back to front. News and weather, good or bad, affected results. In those days, most magazines and newspapers were sold on newsstands. Bad news would bring people to the newsstand; bad weather would keep them away. Our media knowledge was a dramatic talking point that differentiated us from other agencies. Before the advent of sophisticated research, neither we nor anyone else knew much about why consumers acted or didn't—but we could measure with extraordinary accuracy what they did or didn't do.

I tried to create a presentation that highlighted the agency's skills. It was difficult because it really wasn't an agency but a one-man office. Cap understood that headlines, copy, and layouts had to get the reader's attention. But his copy was heavy-handed. I discovered that he didn't actually write ads, he dictated them to his secretary. He was an old-fashioned salesman. His ads were selling arguments nailed together. I was determined to use Cap's skill at buying media to get accounts. Irving and I would then try to enhance results by creating better copy and illustrations. I searched for new business, as I always had. My role as the "vigorish" would be justified only if I contributed to Cap's profits.

So I didn't sell the agency's skills, I sold its results. I sold ways of helping a client expand its business. At Coronet I had, in the main, presented to clients who had no agencies. For Pinsker, I fought for clients who were already advertising. We weren't trying to create new advertising budgets. We had to transfer existing ones to our agency and expand them by making them more profitable.

My first victory came from Ballco Products, a company owned by an elegant Swedish man-about-town named Eric Eweson. He had patented a small handheld device called the Vacutex that removed facial blackheads. The ads for Vacutex ran in the large women's service magazines of the time. I told Eweson that the Casper Pinsker Agency could increase his profits and his sales. I argued that while he successfully advertised in a number of magazines, there were many more he hadn't yet used. If that were not true, I would have seen his ad everywhere. His answer taught me one of the fundamental principles of mail-order advertising. He said he didn't have an advertising budget, what he had was an allowable cost per sale; he would spend as much as he could on advertising that earned a profit. If I could expand that, he would be interested. To do that, I needed to know where he had advertised and what results he had achieved from every ad. He said he didn't know me well enough to reveal that. He didn't share that information even with his current agency, with which he had been doing business for years. I told him he was doing his agency's work. Our agency had scientific ways of creating and testing copy, and Cap Pinsker was a genius at negotiating low media rates. Eweson was slow to respond, but he finally said he would need a letter from me promising that no one but Pinsker and I would see his advertising costs and results. We would then be required to make a written proposal indicating how our prices compared with the rates he was paying. He wouldn't change agencies on promises; he wanted proof.

I agreed to provide the proposal if he would give me the data I needed. However, I, too, needed a promise. He would have to keep the information we provided confidential. He couldn't show it to his agency or to magazine publishers. He couldn't use our prices as a bargaining chip. I also wanted his assurance that he would give us his account if we could prove that we could help make his business more profitable.

I hurried back to the office to tell Cap what I had done. He complimented me on my effort but said I might have promised too much. I asked why. He told me he would explain when I brought him Eweson's schedules, rates, and results.

That worried me. I had promised bargains, but Cap was not so sure. I had also told Irving that we needed to create a better ad. Then, if Cap couldn't deliver lower rates, we could still deliver better results. We studied the Vacutex ad. It was a seventy-line ad, one column by five inches. The headline read REMOVE BLACKHEADS. It made a direct promise in the prosaic tradition of patent medicine advertising. The illustration showing the Vacutex made it look like an unwieldy instrument. Our copy would have to be more compelling and our graphics more attractive. We rewrote the headline. It read UGLY BLACKHEADS OUT IN SECONDS. We changed our illustration to make the Vacutex look like a small cosmetic appliance.

When I took the Vacutex media costs and results to Cap, he told me he couldn't get reduced rates on small ads in major women's magazines, particularly those that Eweson was already using. I said that if we couldn't reduce the costs of Eweson's current media, perhaps we could place ads in others. I had already done some research on blackheads at the public library. They were more prevalent in young people, who were prone to be embarrassed by them. I was certain that there were magazines for young people that Eweson had not tried.

Cap agreed that I was onto something. There were many new picture magazines and comic books being published for young people, and he could buy most of them inexpensively and have a look.

I went back to see Eweson. I told him that we could deliver what I had promised but somewhat differently. We couldn't promise to reduce the rates he had been paying in the large-circulation women's magazines. Publishers wouldn't sell us the same space he had been buying for less money. We could, however, assure him that his ads in those magazines would appear in better positions, which I knew would improve his results. We could also place his ad in a great many more magazines at very low rates. In addition, we had created a new ad that we believed would pull better than his old one.

He asked who would be in charge of his account at our agency. I told him I would, hoping it was the right answer. He said it was a deal if I agreed to spend not less than a half day with him each week. Together, we would try to understand why some insertions failed and others succeeded.

He then said that he had not believed we could buy major media at lower rates. And he didn't know if our new ad was any better than his old one. He was certain, however, that I wanted his account more than his present agency did.

Eric Eweson remained my client for seven years. Our new ad turned out to be 20 percent more effective than his old one. I also found out that his former agency had been rebating to him half the commissions it received from media because Eweson had been making all the advertising and media decisions himself. I learned many lessons from the experience.

I had sold bargains and delivered personal service. Price was only one aspect of service, and, while there is an irreducible minimum, there is no limit to the added value of service and talent. Because the ad Irving and I had created improved results by 20 percent, it alone was worth more than the entire 15 percent commission we earned and more than double the rebate Eweson had been receiving from his prior agency. The new media we used to reach young people were also much more successful than the mass-circulation women's magazines.

Creating better ads and researching the potential of new audiences were creative solutions Cap Pinsker had never considered. We were going to show him that a better idea could be more profitable than a better deal.

Irving was Pinsker's first full-time copywriter. Before hiring us, Cap had written all the copy himself. Irving and I hoped our success with Ballco Products would protect our jobs. The commissions on the Ballco account were greater than the $50 a week Cap Pinsker was paying Irving. As I was still the free "vigorish," Cap had a real bargain. When we heard that he had boasted to his cronies that he had found a first-class mail-order copywriter who was worth more than the $50 a week he paid him and that he had acquired another able person free, we began to feel more secure.

Then an unexpected problem arose. When we had closed Coronet in the fall of 1941, we had not declared bankruptcy. We had completed the work we had been doing for clients, and we had given every cent we had to our creditors. We owed relatively little. Our major creditor was *Specialty Salesman Magazine*. Jim Peckworth felt responsible for our failure because he had introduced us to the Formost Merchandising Corporation. None of our creditors pressed to collect their outstanding bills. But after we went to work for Cap Pinsker, one photoengraver sued for the money we owed him, and suddenly Irving's $50-a-week salary was garnished for the maximum legal amount, 10 percent. The $5 a week was more than we could afford to pay.

All this took place after we had gotten the Ballco account. We explained the problem to Cap, and he raised Irving's wage to $55 a week.

That solved our problem until Irving was drafted in September 1942. He got married the night before he left. That left me as my mother's sole support, but I was still working as the free "vigorish." The deal with Cap had to be changed. In less than a year, we had made a real difference to his business. I had brought in several new accounts, and more people had been added to his staff. The agency was beginning to be taken more seriously.

When Irving was drafted, I told Cap I couldn't continue to work without pay. Cap was not surprised. He said he appreciated the work that I had done and offered to pay me the same $55 a week. I had to be careful because Cap was an experienced, tough negotiator. I didn't want him to feel that this was an argument he had to win. I thanked him, but said I felt that it would be a short-term solution and that before long we would be talking about money again. I wanted him to think longer term.

He asked what was on my mind. I told him that I, too, might be drafted, and then none of this conversation would be meaningful. But if I were not, a number of new possibilities could arise. I had already been receiving job offers from other agencies. As their employees were drafted, they needed replacements. I knew I could get a job with a number of larger agencies, and I was tempted.

Cap understood. But I told him I didn't really like the idea of being a replacement for someone who was going off to war. I didn't want to be chosen as a leftover. I preferred to talk to him about an agreement to remain for the duration of the war if I were not drafted.

Cap sensed I was being honest. If I wanted to make a deal for the duration, he was ready. He asked what I wanted. I told him that Irving and I were a team. I wanted to be certain that when he came back from the army, he would have his job back. Cap agreed. Then I told him I would accept the $55 a week for now because that had been the deal. But I wanted it not as a wage but as a guarantee against commissions. I knew I could help build the business, but I wanted one third of the commissions on all the new business I brought in or worked on. I also expected that he would continue to improve the services his agency offered.

He asked if I wanted a written contract. I said a handshake would do. He held out his hand, and it was done. I had finally begun to learn how to make advertising pay—for me. The first year of our new deal, my income was $9,000. It soon rose to $15,000. The agreement I had made with Cap was fair. He never stopped calling me his "vigorish"—and perhaps he was right.

Shortly after I made my deal with Cap, I was called for military service. The medical examination disclosed that I had a physical problem that, while not severe, made me ineligible for service in the army. So the deal I had made with Cap Pinsker really would be for the duration of the war.

Now, for the first time, I began to feel economically secure. I needed time to fill in some of the blanks that had been left in my life by the death of my father and the worldwide economic disaster that had followed. My education had been aborted when I had been forced to leave college, so I began to explore night courses at local universities. I enrolled in courses ranging from psychology and anthropology to English literature and the art of Egypt's XVIII Dynasty. I have pursued this quest for knowledge informally ever since. I could never have discovered the secrets of successful advertising without the perspectives that grew from this ongoing education.

Casper Pinsker was a good teacher of the things he knew, but his skills were limited. His ability to buy media inexpensively was a way of passing on the inefficiency of many of his ads to publishers. Any ad will succeed if you pay little enough for the media. However, the lessons I learned about media from him were clues to creating advertising that paid. While low rates were a crutch to support mediocre execution, unreasonably high rates were insupportable even for great advertising. Perhaps the best lesson Cap Pinsker taught me was that there are more media available than I had imagined, and they were not all listed in *Standard Rate & Data*. Later, I was to discover that a medium is any conduit or combination of conduits that reaches consumers. To be profitable, advertising would have to create its own tools. It was Cap Pinsker who first taught me how varied those tools could be.

When I joined Pinsker, none of the products or services he sold were found in stores. He was a mail-order man. He didn't think of himself as being in the advertising business, nor did the general agencies accept him as a peer. The separation of general and mail-order advertising at that time was even greater than it had been in earlier years. In the days of Albert Lasker and the copy geniuses who had worked for him, advertisers had used mail-order techniques to supplement their general advertising. Lasker's agency, Lord & Thomas, for example, was proud of its "results department," which could show that a request for samples or information from an ad for a store-distributed product was a measure of an ad's readership and of readers' interest in a product. Lasker was convinced that there was a direct correlation between the number of responses to offers in ads and the effect of advertising on the sales of products in stores.

The form and function of general advertising were changing. World War II and the shortages it created, as well as changes in distribution from "mom-and-pop" grocery and drugstores to supermarkets and drug chains and the development of new media such as radio and later television, would have a major impact. So would the psychological theories of Sigmund Freud and others, which provided new research tools for understanding human motivations and attitudes.

It seemed to me that I was building a career in what looked like an advertising dead end: no esoteric research, no radio commercials, no brand images, no attitudinal modification, no large budgets—and no large clients.

Why did I stay? Because I had made a promise I meant to keep. But also because every day I was discovering that mail-order advertising could be the most exciting business in the world, and although it seemed old-fashioned, it was as yet almost totally unexplored. It was a potential gold mine in which no one else seemed to be staking a claim.

4
How to Discover a New Medium

A mong the things I discovered during my years with Pinsker was an unlikely new advertising medium: comic books. Large advertisers and their agencies believed these magazines were read only by children, teenagers, or illiterates, none of them appropriate targets for brand-image advertising. I thought they were wrong. Despite the wartime paper shortages and restrictions on printing, comic books, using inexpensive paper, were printed by the tens of millions. And they sold out. The salesmen who represented them became my friends, and we talked regularly. They were convinced that comic books were right for the times. They had an enormous circulation among teenagers, in the armed forces, in the lunch pails of American industrial workers, and even in some businessmen's briefcases. Comic books were the precursors of television, probably the first truly "mass" medium; they had easy-to-understand graphics and text, lots of action, simple dialogue. But national advertisers wouldn't try them even though their advertising rates were ridiculously low.

I tested comic books for a few clients, and the results were astonishing. Comic book readers really read the magazines and the advertising. I told Cap that we could get ongoing options on the preferred positions in the best comic books at very low rates. Cap knew a media bonanza when he saw one. We contracted for back covers on all the major comic magazines, and the publishers were grateful. We were going to "break the ice" for them. The advertising we attracted for comic books more than doubled Cap Pinsker's business. Within months, new clients came knocking at our door. If they wanted access to comic books, they had to buy it from us.

The first time my name was ever mentioned in a serious publication was in a scholarly book of research entitled *Magazines of the Twentieth Century,* in which Cap and I were credited with the discovery of comic books as the most successful wartime advertising medium. The commission arrangement I had with Cap gave me a share of the profits. No such windfall would ever come Cap's way again. But years later, I would be able to build an advertising agency of my own by discovering other innovative media.

5

How to Invent a Best-Seller

At Cap Pinsker's I learned how mail-order advertising could transform failure into success. I found a book few were buying and drove it onto the best-seller list.

A publisher came to me with a strange story. He said that Adolf Hitler's personal physician, a Dr. Kurt Krueger, had escaped from Germany and was hiding in Brooklyn. Dr. Krueger feared he might be killed because he had written about aspects of Adolf Hitler's personal life that had never before been revealed. He was in touch with the publisher through a mysterious intermediary, but he himself never appeared. He wanted the book published on the condition that he would hold no interviews, nor would he surface in any way to support the sale of the book.

When I heard the story, an edition of the book had already been published and distributed to the trade under the title *Inside Hitler*. It hadn't sold. But the publisher believed in the book and asked if I could sell it by mail. I read the book and said "Yes." The book portrayed Adolf Hitler as a man suffering from strange psychological, sexual, and physical disorders. The author claimed to have been Hitler's psychiatrist as well as his physician and to have treated Hitler for his unusual mental and physical problems during his rise to power. For him, Hitler had been just another patient. The Hippocratic oath was his justification for having tried to heal him.

I realize now that there were many questions I should have asked before I agreed to work on the project: How had Hitler's doctor escaped? How had he gotten into America? Why did the FBI not know of him—

and why had he chosen to sell his rights to a small publisher? *The New York Times* had asked similar questions and had decided not to review the book or accept advertising for it. If those questions crossed my mind then, I don't recall them now. My job was to sell the book, and I was excited by the prospect of doing so.

I proposed that the title be changed from *Inside Hitler*, which promised nothing, to *I Was Hitler's Doctor*, which promised everything. Then I wrote an ad whose headline suggested the book would reveal secrets of Adolf Hitler's personal life that only his physician and psychiatrist could know. The ad explained that the author was in hiding and Hitler would surely have him killed if he could find him. The ad was designed to look like editorial matter, and it was spectacularly productive. In those days, as now, an ad that imitated an editorial format had to carry the warning "advertisement" in small type. However, if the material is sensational and dramatic enough, the word "advertisement" is the last place the reader's eye will fall. While the front page is usually where the news is, it has been my experience that an ad containing sensational new information becomes its own front page.

The ads sold copies of *I Was Hitler's Doctor* by mail as fast as the publisher could print them. We expanded the schedule from newspapers to newsmagazines and from newsmagazines to picture magazines and then to scandal tabloids. And they all worked. We adapted the editorial style of the ad for each type of publication, and it always outpulled the more conventional-looking ads we continued to test. We didn't have a picture of Hitler's doctor to use as an illustration, but pictures of Hitler himself were easy to find.

The ads were profitable and effective. Every $1,000 we spent on advertising produced 2,000 direct sales and hundreds more through bookstores, thereby earning a direct and immediate profit.

Hitler was news. His speeches were broadcast frequently from Berlin. Everyone followed his actions daily. I felt that Hitler's doctor should be news as well. The success of our editorial format in print had proved it. I believed we could do the same thing on radio. I created a radio commercial and decided to place it in general programming, not on news shows. It opened with an announcer saying, "Ladies and Gentlemen, we interrupt this program for an important transcribed announcement by Adolf Hitler from Berlin." We would then play portions of a recorded speech by Adolf Hitler—a hysterical diatribe.

Since few people understood German, it didn't matter what he was actually saying. What mattered was how he said it. Two "news analysts" followed the speech with a discussion of why this madman wanted to destroy the world. Next came an actor who played the role of Hitler's doctor and who told about the book. He said that the doctor wanted to tell the whole story himself personally but the actor would have to speak for him because he didn't dare to come out of hiding. To understand Hitler, all the audience had to do was send for the book.

Radio turned out to be even more successful than print, and it also provided support for retailers. Radio rates were flexible. Unsold "remnant" time could be bought for very little, and "remnant" didn't necessarily mean bad time, but any time that had remained unsold too long. We rolled the commercial out nationally. Its format was predictive of today's talk shows, which build the sale of books through radio and TV interviews. The commercial was, in fact, an early "infomercial."

With no salesmen and no retail distribution, *I Was Hitler's Doctor* began to appear in bookstore windows as customers began to ask for it and booksellers ordered it. We watched it climb up the best-seller lists. A mail-order book—with mail-order advertising—had become a best-seller at retail. It sold 250,000 copies. We might have sold a million, but wartime paper quotas limited the paper available to print them.

When I went to work for Cap Pinsker, I wasn't sure I approved of the advertising business. But I quickly became so taken with the game that I did whatever seemed necessary to win. I did feel twinges of conscience, and in retrospect I should have felt more, but at the time I never questioned a client's product, even one as far-fetched as *I Was Hitler's Doctor.*

After that success, we accomplished the same result for another timely book. Our client was its publisher, the Arco Publishing Company, whose books helped people prepare for civil service examinations. Arco published many specialized manuals, but its best-selling book was entitled *Practice for the Army Tests.* It helped draftees succeed at the classification tests given by the armed forces for the officers training corps or technical jobs.

Again, we did only mail-order advertising for the book, and it, too, became a runaway best-seller, by mail and in stores. Comic books were the perfect medium. The results were astonishing. *Practice for the Army Tests* also made the retail best-seller lists as the result of mail-order advertising. I learned that mail-order ads could stimulate retail sales as well as or even better than general advertising. I was continuing to discover new ways to make advertising pay.

But I was becoming discouraged and depressed because being paid a commission by a small-time advertising agency wasn't likely to lead anywhere. One of the clients I had acquired for Pinsker was a small news service called Facts on File. The business was owned by a refugee from Holland named Edward Van Westerborg, and we became close friends. One day when I was complaining to him about my career, Van Westerborg offered me some personal advice I have never forgotten. He told me to forget about money—to put it out of my mind. The important thing was to try as hard as I could every day to learn how to make advertising pay. If I continued to discover what others didn't yet know, the money and the career would come.

I had gone to work for Casper Pinsker because I was literally penniless. The money and promotions that followed were gratifying, of course, but I knew Edward was right. Every job I have had since that day—and every business I have run—has reflected that principle. I never quarreled about my income. No one has ever paid me enough to keep me in a dead-end job or too little to make me leave a place where I could follow my own star. Edward Van Westerborg was a big man who happened to be running a small business. I remember him with a special gratitude because so often it is the other way around.

The war was just ending, and my deal with Cap Pinsker would soon end as well. Irving would return to the agency, whose client list had diversified and expanded. We had come a long way from *The Secret Museum of Mankind*, but I was getting restless.

At the time, I lived in the downtown Manhattan neighborhood called Chelsea. Most of my friends were painters, writers, and professors trying to make sense of the postwar world. The times seemed full of promise. I wanted to speak out for ideas I believed in, and while mail-order products still had to be sold, so too, I felt, did a better way of life.

The depression that had ended with World War II had scarred the American psyche. Many people felt helpless before the seemingly uncontrollable cycles of the economy, and they were looking for political solutions. The School of Living, founded by Ralph Borsodi, offered one answer. Borsodi was an economist who, along with architect Frank Lloyd Wright, author Louis Adamic, and some others, had a vision of America as a nation of small towns governed by local town meetings.

Ralph Borsodi was the economic theorist of the group. He had written a number of books, including *Flight from the City,* which described how he and his family had left urban life to escape their dependency on wage employment, cash, and landlords. Borsodi and his wife, Myrtle, had bought a tract of land in Suffern, New York, a rural area about fifty miles from New York City. There, they had built a house with their own hands. They had taught themselves to mix cement, do carpentry, farm the land, and prepare and preserve food. They milled flour, baked bread, wove cloth, and made their own clothes. They needed only a little cash, which they earned by occasional writing, teaching, and lecturing. They were educating their two sons at home. The boys literally went from home to Harvard.

Borsodi believed that America would soon suffer a devastating postwar inflation. He wrote and published a book entitled *Inflation Is Coming* and sold it for $1 a copy. He began with a small edition, distributed on newsstands through a wholesaler. The initial sales were good, so he reprinted 80,000 additional copies. Sixty-four thousand of them were unsold.

Because of my success at selling books by mail, the Borsodis came to me. Once again, I represented a publisher with no sales force, no distribution, no reviews, and no advertising budget. I studied the book and created a new ad for it. We tested it in *The Hartford Courant* in a full-page ad that cost $125. The ad sold 250 books by mail, and bookstore sales in Hartford more than matched the direct coupon sales from the advertising. We expanded the campaign. A $1,000 ad in Philadelphia sold 2,000 books through the mail and 2,500 through bookstores. A $500 ad in Cleveland sold 1,000 books by mail and an additional 1,200 books at retail. We expanded the campaign, and *Inflation Is Coming* became the third best-seller I helped create through mail order. This time it was not just a book but an introduction to a way of thinking and living. When I visited the Borsodis in Suffern, I marveled at the simplicity and beauty of their life. They were the gentlest, hardest-working people I had ever known. In a single afternoon I would find them baking bread, conducting Socratic dialogues, playing music, and mixing cement.

To visit the Borsodis was to enter a totally different world. They had created a small utopia for themselves, and people flocked to the School of Living to learn to do the same. While *Inflation Is Coming* became a huge success, the advertising account was secondary to the relationship I developed with the Borsodis. I had inadvertently become their spokesman. I began to write materials for the school and take part in their seminars and sessions. The Borsodis wanted me to join their school as a teacher. It was a tempting alternative to the life I was living. I didn't accept, but I did take some of their teachings into my world.

Years later, Mary Lasker, Albert Lasker's widow, called on me frequently to write political ads (as a volunteer) for her many good causes. I still treasure the letter she sent me describing how many senators and even the vice president had been influenced by the sacks of mail they had received as a result of ads I had written for her. Our agency also named and launched Common Cause for John Gardner. Good advertising, we found, could sell not only products but ideas.

The war was over, and clearly it was time to leave Casper Pinsker. I had kept my promise to stay for the duration, and Irving had his job back. I had begun writing some fiction for radio and became involved in politics as a ghostwriter for several congressmen and senators. At the same time, I was studying photography at the Photo League, in a basement just north of Washington Square. I discovered that I was good at photography—good enough to be given an exhibition at the Photo League and be invited to work with Dan Wiener, a well-known photographer for whom I had great respect.

So I had some options. I could write, take pictures, work in politics, and more. I was twenty-six years old and free—free to make a choice for the first time in my life. The one choice I couldn't make was to continue working for Casper Pinsker. I was encountering ideas, art, forms of expressions, and means of communication that were beyond him, his agency, and its clients. My friends insisted that all advertising was vulgar and without social value. The book *The Hucksters* had just come out, confirming that view. I still remember the cocktail parties where to admit that I was in advertising invited contempt. When I said I was in mail-order advertising, people would ask, "What's that?" and in response to the name "Casper Pinsker," they would ask, "Who's that?" Nobody asked me if I was good at it or why I was doing it. In those days, it was better to be a failed poet, a poor painter, or a philosopher-fool than to succeed in advertising—and perhaps it still is.

I resented the scorn, though I knew it was ignorant and pretentious.

I knew better than anyone else the deficiencies of mail-order advertising as it was then practiced. But when I looked beyond the bad craftsmanship, I saw something revolutionary and wonderful: a world of measurable causes and effects. An absurd event triggered my next discovery.

While we were still at Pinsker's, Irving and I had a client named Willy Novak, an immigrant from Poland who spoke unintelligible English. But Willy, a book publisher, had discovered the mail-order business and had been successful. Despite his difficulties with English, his taste in books was astute and informed. He had just published a book entitled *What Men Don't Like About Women,* a timeless subject. Fortunately, it was still long before the woman's movement, because "what men don't like about women" was almost everything.

Willy's first attempt to describe the book to me was so garbled that I had to ask him to try again. Instead, he wrote the title on a piece of paper. I asked what made him think anyone would buy a book on such a subject. He replied with five words I did understand: "Ask Sigmund Freud," he said. "He knows." We never did that, but after reading the manuscript, we were able to produce a lively, humorous ad. I am embarrassed now by its chauvinism, but at the time it seemed like harmless fun. As it turned out, the ad was successful, and Willy had once again made the right choice. What he—and we—didn't know was that this book was going to change our lives.

Maxwell Sackheim, a legendary mail-order copywriter, had recently opened Maxwell Sackheim & Company in an office over the Doubleday Book Shop, then on the southwest corner of Fifty-third Street and Fifth Avenue. He had been awarded the account of the Literary Guild, Doubleday's major book club. Doubleday provided Max Sackheim with office space above its shop, and the agency, as it was on the second floor, had lettering on its Fifth Avenue windows: MAXWELL SACKHEIM & COMPANY, ADVERTISING.

Max wrote great copy, knew about books, book clubs, and mail-order advertising, and was determined to build a successful mail-order advertising agency. Just after Willy Novak published *What Men Don't Like About Women,* Max called him. Sackheim, who had written one of the great ads of all time—"Do You Make These Mistakes in English?"—was soliciting an account from a man for whom the headline might have been written. Sackheim probably didn't understand much of what Willy said to him, but Willy certainly understood that Sackheim had offered to write a free ad for *What Men Don't Like About Women*. He would test it against our ad at his own expense, and if he succeeded, he would get Willy Novak's substantial advertising account. More than that, he was going to help put Willy into the book club business. For Willy Novak, that was big-time talk.

Willy explained to us what was happening, and we were worried. This was a real threat to our security. Sackheim was a great mail-order man—the best—and he was after our client.

Sackheim soon finished his ad for *What Men Don't Like About Women,* and the competition was on. Willy asked us if we wanted to do another ad, but we said we'd stay with the one we had. After all, it was selling books. Sackheim created a split-run competition: his ad against ours, winner take all. If we won, we would keep the account we already had. If we lost—it was gone. Irving and I cringed when we received the first copies of the split run of the New York *Daily News* that carried the two ads. We expected lightning bolts, but when we saw it, we knew at once that Sackheim had committed a fatal blunder. He had taken *What Men Don't Like About Women* seriously. His ad was a solemn argument against women, and our ad beat his two to one. Willy Novak may have made mistakes in English, but he didn't make them about money. We kept his account.

Sackheim didn't make many mistakes, either. He decided to hire Irving and me. Walter Lowen, the best (and only) headhunter in the advertising business in those days, arranged a meeting.

Irving and I went to see Sackheim at his offices at 670 Fifth Avenue. The entrance to the building was on Fifty-third Street, a few doors away from the Museum of Modern Art. The space the agency occupied was long and narrow with a carpeted corridor down the center and glass-partitioned offices on each side. I still remember the nameplates on each partition: LEAH ROTH, MEDIA DIRECTOR; EDWIN C. RICOTTA, ART DIRECTOR; DON BROWN, COPY CHIEF; AL BERKE, PRODUCTION MANAGER. We entered a large office at the end of the hallway, and a man about five feet tall stood up and glared at us through rimless glasses. It was Max himself. He greeted us cordially, but he still seemed forbidding. Later, I would learn that he had a demanding mind and a hot and ready temper.

Max began with a brief summary of his career. He had been born in the Midwest; had become advertising manager of Sears, Roebuck and Company at an early age; had left when he thought it couldn't grow any larger; had come to New York; had become copy chief of Ruthrauff & Ryan; had left to join Harry Scherman and open Sackheim & Scherman. There, they had invented the Book-of-the-Month Club and the negative-option selling system. He had owned a large share of the business but had sold it to Scherman because he thought the club couldn't continue to grow. This was the story of his career: promising business ventures abandoned for what he thought was a lack of growth potential. He had just opened Maxwell Sackheim & Company because he finally realized he had always been too impatient. This time he was going to stay with it until his agency was larger than any mail-order agency had ever been. But he needed good young men to help him build it, and in particular men who could write great mail-order copy. He offered Irving a job at once. Irving had been earning $55 a week at Casper Pinsker's; Sackheim offered him $150. As for me, he wanted another meeting at which only he and I would be present. He understood that Irving would not give him an answer until this meeting had taken place. I made an appointment to see him the next day.

When I arrived, he was all business. What did I really do, he wanted to know? I told him that I got clients and helped them with their marketing. What did that mean? he asked. A strange question, I thought, from such an experienced advertising executive. I answered, as calmly as I could, that I helped companies build their businesses. I gave them ideas and advice. I helped the agency help clients solve their problems. Finally, he said I might be the person he had been seeking for a long time—the person to help him do his job. He couldn't build his agency alone. He was not young enough to do it by himself anymore, and if I could do what I said, I would have a good chance of eventually becoming a partner and owner of his company. I almost fell out of my chair. He asked how much I earned. I replied, about $15,000 a year in commissions. He didn't want my accounts and told me to leave them with Pinsker. He offered to hire me at a wage of $10,000 a year plus bonuses to be determined if I succeeded. That came as a shock. He wanted to reduce my income by a third.

I told him that he was asking me to give up one job and take another for less money. He was asking me to give up $5,000 a year—which I really needed as I was planning to get married the next month. Why should I accept that? I asked. Because, he told me, he would teach me about the mail-order advertising. business as nobody else could. He went on to say that he could be a son of a bitch to work for, but if I had any talent, he would get it out of me one way or another. He promised that I would learn how to make advertising pay. I would learn to tell good copy from bad and how to sell mail-order advertising to companies that had never dreamed of being in the mail-order business. He would challenge me to succeed, and if I did, his agency would one day be mine. I was less than half his age, and I could wait my turn. I didn't hesitate. I told him I would do it. What he didn't know was that I would have worked for him for nothing just for the chance to learn. What I didn't know was that soon I would.

And so Irving and I gave notice to Cap Pinsker, and he accepted graciously. He knew it was time for us to move on.

6

"Great Copy Is Great Advertising"

—Maxwell Sackheim

Irving and I began work at Maxwell Sackheim & Company in April 1947, and after a short period of indoctrination Irving was promoted to copy chief. Things didn't go as smoothly for me. In May I got married, in June I got worried, and in July I got fired.

Max Sackheim was a genius with a temper that equaled his talent. Everyone employed at the agency was highly skilled and ambitious, having been hand-picked by Max—but no one could satisfy him. When he summoned people, they walked down the long hall to his office wondering what they had done wrong. When they got to Max's office, the door would close, and you would only hear the sounds of Max's rage.

I couldn't say I hadn't been warned. Max had told me he was a son of a bitch when he hired me. I'd thought at the time that it was hyperbole; only later did I discover that whatever Max said was—like his copy—colorful, but factual.

I quickly found out that Max wasn't going to tongue-lash me as he did the others; instead, he chose to ignore me. Irving was instantly given a desk, a typewriter, and soon after a private office. I was told to find someplace to sit. It didn't matter where, Max said, since I would be out of the office selling most of the time. I found an old desk and chair in a bull-pen area and waited. Nothing happened. I waited two weeks and then went in and told Max that he hadn't assigned me to any accounts yet. I was eager to get started.

To do what? Max asked. He told me his agency's clients were there because they wanted to do business with him. Why should they want me instead? What could I do for them that he couldn't? Max had hired me to help, but he didn't know how to let go of anything. He didn't see me as his employee but as a potential rival. Luckily, I was an expert at survival. It was clear that Max would not pay me $10,000 a year for doing nothing. The only solution to the problem was for me to get new clients who wanted to do business with me. Max might resent the competition, but he wasn't going to turn down the chance to make a profit.

Max had only a handful of active accounts at the time, and he had not succeeded in getting much new business, not even Willy Novak's. So I began to look for business with my usual desperation, except that this time I had an edge. I was working for a well-known genius. The claims I made for his agency were credible. The agency was producing great ads for Doubleday's Literary Guild and other large clients.

I worked hard to get accounts. I got married as planned at the end of May, but I was afraid that if I took a honeymoon, it might mean the end of my job. I postponed the wedding trip, but it was the end anyway.

Just a few weeks later, after the July Fourth weekend, Max called me in to his office and told me that he had made an honest try to work me into his agency. He was paying me $10,000 a year, and I was not earning it. He hadn't understood what I did and still didn't. He only knew that he wanted me to leave. I was upset, disappointed, and frightened, but above all angry. He had recruited me from another job and made me give up the clients I had developed there. He had promised to teach me what he knew. He had offered me a future. How could I know what I should be doing if he didn't talk to me? How could he back down on a promise after so short a trial?

He said he didn't want to argue about it. It was over—it had been a mistake. I was furious. The whole situation was rotten: he knew I had just gotten married, he knew I wanted and needed the job.

I told him he was wrong—more wrong than he had ever been—and that I would prove it to him. When someone is fired, two things happen, I said heatedly. One is that he stops showing up, and the second is that he stops getting paid. He could stop paying me, but he couldn't keep me out of his office. Unless he got a policeman to arrest me or hired a bouncer, I was going to continue to come to work every day. I was going to fight him for the job. He looked at me as if I had gone berserk. I left his office, and as I went out I said, "See you tomorrow."

At the end of the week, I was taken off the payroll, but I kept coming to work and bringing in and managing new accounts. I was working for free—as I had done once before when I was the "vigorish" for Cap Pinsker. I needed the job, I wanted to learn from Max Sackheim, and I wasn't going to give up the opportunity. After a month of not speaking to me, he called me in to his office. "All right," he said, "you win." He was still not sure what I did, but he said he had never seen a man who wanted a job more than he wanted money. He put me back onto the payroll at $7,500 a year, the same amount he paid Irving. This time he promised he would try to help make it work.

He did. Max believed that mail order was the most convenient channel of distribution. It worked best when it created an ongoing customer rather than a onetime sale. He had learned that early in his career at Sears, Roebuck. A Sears catalog buyer was encouraged to become a continuing mail-order customer, not a onetime buyer. While Cap Pinsker believed the cost of media was the key to success, Max believed the key was creative copy and ideas.

They were both right. Cap Pinsker was good at making weak ads and marginal businesses profitable. He offered only one service: low-cost access to the public through cut-rate media. Max Sackheim, on the other hand, did everything he could to provide added value through creativity. He was able to imagine and dramatize new business ideas and distribution techniques, as well as write persuasive copy.

Max was a brilliant and demanding teacher. He was a famously creative copywriter, but he was also a practical businessman. He understood credit, costs, margins, management, and profits, and as our relationship developed, he was willing to share that knowledge with me. My curiosity stimulated him, and together we began to diversify the mail-order advertising business and bring it more up to date. Max's desk was covered with yellow legal pads, translucent pads of layout paper, and a container of ultrasoft graphite pencils. He didn't theorize about advertising. He just did it.

The only way Max could judge an idea was to write an ad for it. If the ad seemed convincing, it was a good idea. I didn't work that way. I started with ideas. The ads could express them later. He couldn't understand my way of working. He had been brought up in a world where a good account executive was called a "copy-contact man."

When I returned from visiting a client, Max would frequently look at my empty hands and ask what I had done there. Had I told jokes? I certainly hadn't written any ads. Carefully, I would admit that I hadn't written any ads, but I had discussed marketing strategy and analyzed results. Max may not have understood how I worked, but when he discovered that clients found my services valuable, he grudgingly let me do it my way.

I realized the only way to gain Max's respect was by acquiring the right kind of new accounts. About that time, I became aware of the Young People's Record Club through its advertising in *The New York Times*. When I read its ad, I knew this was a client I had to have. The Young People's Record Club was widely considered the best way to turn children into music lovers.

The business was owned by the well-known attorney Abraham Pomerantz and managed by musician Horace Grenell and record producer Lester Troob. Because I had some friends who knew these men socially, I heard that someone with neither direct marketing skills nor experience in selling club memberships was doing their advertising. The business was, unsurprisingly, only marginally successful. One night, I arranged to be introduced to Pomerantz at a dinner party. I told him how much I admired the Young People's Record Club and that I was an expert in mail-order advertising. I said that the club should be using advanced mail-order techniques and that it would be a great loss if such a good business idea failed because of mediocre advertising. Pomerantz spent the next three hours asking me what the Young People's Record Club should be doing better. He knew law, politics, and much more, but little about record club marketing. I told him I worked for Max Sackheim, who knew everything about book and record clubs and who, in fact, had started the Book-of-the-Month Club.

Pomerantz told me that if I could persuade Grenell and Troob to give me the advertising account, he would agree to change agencies. I spent the next morning analyzing their ads with Max. I wanted to be prepared to offer them some dynamic new ideas at our first meeting. But Max insisted it would be more effective if I asked to see their scrapbook of test ads with an analysis of the results. He said that would be the best indication of whether they were getting good service from their current agency. As usual, Max had gone directly to basics.

I went to see Grenell and Troob and did as Max suggested. I explained who I was and what our agency did, and I told them I wanted their account. I promised that our experience with clubs and response advertising could help them build their business, but I needed to study their split-run results book first. They wanted to know what a "split-run results book" was and why it was so important. I told them that a club had many leverage points. No one could know how to maximize their value without isolating and testing them through scientific split-run advertising. I showed them some of the tests we were then running for the Literary Guild and what the results had been. I explained that each factor in an ad—the price, the form of membership, the premium offered for joining, the headline, the layout, and so on—could leverage results by 15 to 100 percent. Together, these factors would determine success. After a hurried call to Abe Pomerantz, they agreed to hire us. Our "scientific" methods had won the day.

This was my first opportunity to work closely with Max on a potentially large new account, and I discovered that he was a virtuoso strategist. He drilled me in copy strategy, offers, and coupons. He insisted on getting the fundamentals right first and then going for the creative breakthrough.

Max eventually helped me design a series of split-run ads to identify the key response elements as well as the Young People's Record Club's fundamental business possibilities.

The first ad we tested was a winner. We bought a split run in the then-liberal *New York Post*. Half of that day's papers carried the control ad—the ad the club had been using. The old headline was NOW A WONDERFUL NEW WAY TO BRING THE ENCHANTING WORLD OF MUSIC TO YOUR CHILD. The rest of the papers carried our ad with a new headline, HELP YOUR CHILD DISCOVER THE ENCHANTING WORLD OF MUSIC. Ours was shorter and involved parents directly. Each half of the run cost $262.50. The old ad pulled thirty-nine subscribers, the new one, eighty-one—an improvement of 108 percent, a result later confirmed by further split-run tests in other newspapers.

In another split run, we tested a change in the coupon offer from an annual purchase of ten records, paid for in advance, to an ongoing monthly shipment, billed monthly. The improvement was 23 percent.

We soon discovered that the potential market for the Young People's Record Club was passionate but thin, limited to parents of children aged two to eleven, and its appeal was strongest to parents of children age two to five. Since the benefits of the club were best understood by parents who were well educated themselves, it looked as if the Young People's Record Club was never going to be worth advertising in mass media.

When we began our program of split-run testing, I was surprised to discover how volatile the results were and how much they could be manipulated. For example, changing the offer from a ten-record commitment to one that offered a membership that required no minimum order and was cancelable at any time increased responses by 158 percent. Changing the illustration so that it featured record jackets rather than large illustrations of children made a difference of 21 percent. Because the club didn't have mass appeal, the advertising had to be totally persuasive to the small number of prospects to be found in whatever medium we used. It was as if we were pinpointing targets with a high-powered rifle. To succeed, we had to hit a bull's-eye.

At the end of the first year, we had doubled the advertising results and made the business more profitable and predictable. We were ready to look for the "creative breakthrough." It came from a completely unexpected source. Horace Grenell had written a letter to Sergei Prokofiev in the Soviet Union, asking if he had composed any additional pieces for children besides the hugely successful *Peter and the Wolf*. Months later, a letter arrived from Prokofiev containing a score and lyrics for *The Ugly Duckling*, a new work that had never been performed in the United States. This was the breakthrough we had been seeking. We believed that now we could use mass-circulation media such as *Life* magazine. We did, and the offer was a major success. After that, the club began to grow rapidly.

Max was pleased. My ability to create good advertising and a winning strategy finally brought his praise. As a result, my job became more secure, and my income began to increase. A year later, I was promoted to vice president. Two years later, in 1949, I was earning a salary of $20,000. In 1951, I was appointed senior vice president. In 1956, I was made executive vice president and later chairman of the Plans Board at $50,000 a year. Max had finally understood what I did. I knew how to run an advertising agency. I could get and build accounts. I could recruit, manage, and stimulate employees. I could make profits. In 1958, we separated, but we had spent a productive twelve years together. Years later, when he wrote a book about his career, he sent me an inscribed copy with the inscription "To Lester, who wisely decided to be the first Lester Wunderman, rather than the second anyone else."

The years with Sackheim taught me how to use scientific testing to help make advertising pay. To this day, I believe that the most important tool available to the direct marketer is the ability to test, a form of pragmatic research that doesn't just tell you how a consumer *might* react to an ad but how consumers really *do* react. Direct marketing makes advertising totally measurable and accountable.

The Young People's Record Club was there when I most needed it. What I didn't know then was that getting the account was the first critical link in a chain of events that would eventually change my life. But that happened much later. The most immediate benefit was that Max began to assign important accounts to me.

7

God's Hearing Aid

One of the first accounts Max assigned me to was the Acousticon Hearing Aid Division of the Dictograph Corporation, an account that was notorious for hiring and firing its advertising agencies. It had gone through seven in just three years, among them some of the very largest. Since the purpose of Acousticon's advertising was to get leads for salesmen and to create retail-store traffic, the Sackheim agency seemed a reasonable choice. However, many of the Acousticon executives were not happy with our appointment. Each of them had a favorite agency, and we were not among them. We had been chosen by the chief executive officer of the company, an ex-lawyer named Stanley Osserman, because, as of that moment, we were his "hunch." When he gave us the account, he asked Max if he was afraid of the assignment. Max said he wasn't, but he told me that he was afraid of Osserman. And he was right. No client repeatedly fires good agencies unless its demands are unrealistic and wrongheaded or its internal politics make advertising the scapegoat for its own unresolved power issues. Max assigned the account to me. He was counting on my survival skills. The first test came very quickly.

Acousticon had a weekly advertising meeting to which the executives of all relevant departments were invited. I entered the meeting room to find that the chairs had been carefully arranged. Acousticon executives were seated along the walls around the room. I was alone in front of Stanley Osserman's desk. It was a setup for a third-degree interrogation. Osserman opened the meeting by welcoming me as the representative of the company's new advertising agency and said he hoped our relationship would be productive. This seemed normal enough, and I thanked him for his confidence. Then Osserman declared that it was time for "today's word." The word that day was "cybernetics." Luckily, I had been following reports of Norbert Weiner's work at MIT, so I knew what the word meant. But I wondered how many of the others did. I never found out. The names of the executives at that meeting are blurred in my memory, but what they said is not. Osserman turned to the executive to his right, the director of sales, and asked what he thought of the word.

His response was that it might be the most important word that Osserman had ever raised at their meetings. He hoped the new agency would be able to act on it. Osserman went on to the next executive, the director of advertising, and asked what he thought of the word. His reply was that Osserman once again had challenged them and that they would respond aggressively. But he had some doubts as to whether the new agency could grasp the challenge. I began to get the message. No one in that room, perhaps not even Osserman himself, knew what "cybernetics" meant, but they were all well trained to pass the buck. And so it went around the room. Everyone had the same two opinions: Osserman was right as usual, and the agency, as usual, would fail them. Finally, Osserman turned to me and told me that this was my first meeting and so far I hadn't measured up to his needs. I had said nothing. What did I plan to do about cybernetics?

Now I really had a problem. Hearing aids were a good example of cybernetics, which Weiner had defined as the study of self-regulating mechanisms or organisms whose performance is adjusted by means of feedback or by its own actions. The problem was not the word but the hostility in the room. If I said I knew what the word meant, I would antagonize the group further. If I said I didn't, Osserman would be all over me. I decided I had nothing to lose.

I paused for a moment, trying to think my way out of the problem. Then I looked at Osserman and told him that in three years he had gone through seven advertising agencies, most of them excellent companies. The atmosphere at this meeting suggested that he would soon go through another. I didn't think that was good for his company, so I wanted to suggest another word for that day's meeting. That word was "fire." I told him that he had already fired seven agencies and I thought it appropriate that he now fire the executives who had pre-

vented the agencies from helping him. I rose and pointed my finger at
every department head in the room in turn. Suddenly, there was pan-
demonium. Osserman turned pale and slumped down into his chair.
The others shouted at me. They pushed me into a reception room and
told me to wait. Had I lost the account before we even had a chance to
begin work on it? I thought this time it was not only the agency that
would be fired; I would be, too.

After about fifteen minutes, the door to Osserman's office opened,
and he summoned me inside. He was alone. "Lester," he said wearily,
"you have just done a terrible thing. You have upset me. You have also
upset all my key executives. And this was your first meeting. I have only
one question to ask." "What's that, Stanley?" I asked, resigned to my
fate. "Do you know what 'cybernetics' means?" he asked. "Yes, Stanley, I do," I replied.

Osserman looked at me strangely. I couldn't begin to read his mind.
He said I had taken a terrible risk, one that should cost my agency the
account. But he was not going to fire us just yet. He said he admired
intelligence and respected courage. But placing his finger inches from
my eyes, he warned me never to do anything like that again. Then he
smiled and told me to apologize to each of the people I had offended.
And while I was at it, I could explain to them what "cybernetics"
meant.

In the large cities where Acousticon owned its own retail centers, our
job was to bring customers into the stores. In the rest of the country,
our job was to produce leads for salesmen to follow up by visiting
prospects at home. The competition was fierce from companies that
sold their hearing aids more cheaply and whose devices were stocked
by a larger number of independent dealers.

Hearing aids were hard to sell. A key problem was that people with
poor hearing didn't want to confront their handicap. They would often
rather withdraw from life than deal with the typical hearing aid of the
time, a bulky microphone and amplifier connected to a speaker in the
user's ear. That made advertising difficult. Prospective buyers were
moved only by advertising that promised technological miracles—in
other words, invisible hearing aids. Acousticon itself made a device that
promised A NEW REVOLUTIONARY TECHNOLOGY NOW HELPS YOU HEAR
WITH NOTHING IN YOUR EAR. What the ad didn't say was that the aid
was worn behind the ear. What's more, the Federal Trade Commission

had forced almost every hearing aid manufacturer to stop making such dubious promises.

It was hard going. Excessive promises were censored by the lawyers who reviewed every ad, and ads that didn't promise enough didn't work. Osserman was relentless in his demands for results, yelling and growling when he became angry. His yelling was a kind of warm-up. His growling was the real thing. He called daily. Even before he said "Hello," I knew who was calling and what he wanted. I would pick up the phone and hear the yell or the soft growl, and I would answer, "Yes, Stanley, I'll take care of it." Whatever it was.

One Wednesday morning my phone rang, and Osserman growled, "Chicago." I asked what was wrong there. "Fix it," he said. He went on to threaten that if I didn't fix it by next week's meeting, I needn't bother to show up. The conversation was over, and he hung up. I called the company's director of sales and asked him what was wrong in Chicago. He had never forgotten or forgiven me for suggesting that he and the others be fired, and I could hear the hostility in his voice as he told me that he had just reported to Osserman that the ads we were running in Chicago had produced the worst sales figures in years.

I went into Max's office and reported the problem. He asked when I was leaving for Chicago. I asked if he seriously believed I should go. Of course, he told me, that's where the problem was. The problem wasn't in Chicago, I replied, it was in Osserman's head. There was trouble in Chicago because the market was dominated by Acousticon's strongest competitors. The sales manager was using this to get rid of us.

Max told me that I could either rewire Osserman's head or neutralize the sales manager's antagonism by finding a quick fix for Chicago. Those were the only choices. I told Max that I had never been in Chicago and didn't know what I could accomplish by going there. But he wouldn't listen and told me to fix the problem. He was beginning to sound like Osserman.

I flew to Chicago the next day, a Thursday, and went to the Acousticon retail center, where I learned that business was indeed terrible and that our ads were not working. Both Beltone and Zenith, the Chicago-based competition, dominated the market with expanded dealer distribution and lower prices. Acousticon was a fast-fading third in the market. The office manager told me that he desperately needed leads and traffic, and he expected me to find an answer—fast.

It was already late afternoon. I went back to my hotel and called Max. The problem was real, I told him, and I didn't know what to do next. The competition had equal or superior technology, better distribution, more credibility, and lower prices. I didn't know how to fight that. I wanted to leave. There was nothing I could do here. Think of something, he told me, and hung up.

I was stumped. There I was, in a strange city with no friends, no ideas and no one to talk to. I didn't have the feel of the market. I had to get to know Chicago better, and in a hurry. There are dependable sources of information in any city, among them taxi drivers and bartenders. They can tell you a lot if you're willing to listen. I saw a lot of Chicago in the next few hours. When it turned dark, I began a tour of the bars. There I learned that on Saturdays most men washed their cars, saw their girlfriends, went shopping with their wives, or listened to the ballgame on the radio. No surprises there. Sundays, some of them even went to church. So far, I wasn't any closer to the answer.

However, one bartender mentioned casually that there was a certain minister, Dr. Preston Bradley, whose Sunday sermons drew almost as many people to his church as the Cubs or White Sox did to the stadiums. Dr. Bradley was a Congregationalist minister and was respected by worshipers of every denomination. That rang a bell.

The following morning, I called on Dr. Bradley. I told his assistant that I was a stranger with an urgent problem and wondered if Dr. Bradley could spare me a few minutes. Before I knew it, I was face to face with one of the most charismatic people I had ever met. No wonder his church was filled every Sunday morning.

He asked what my problem was, and as I began to tell him, I realized he was the solution.

I told him I had an idea that might help a lot of people in Chicago who needed his help but who literally couldn't hear him. They were people whose deafness cut them off from many of life's blessings. I explained that I was in the advertising business and had come to Chicago because my client, Acousticon, a hearing aid company, wanted to reach out more credibly to the hard of hearing in the area. I believed that many of them would listen to him if he spoke to them in their homes— on radio.

I said that I knew that it would not be appropriate for a company to sponsor his Sunday morning service. But if he could deliver an abbreviated fifteen-minute version of it on Sunday night, on a major Chicago radio station, he and his message could reach almost every home in the area.

He didn't interrupt, but I could see that he had questions. He asked why I had chosen radio as a medium for reaching people who couldn't hear. I explained that a radio was like a large hearing aid. It was the only sound the hard of hearing could turn up. He then asked when I wanted him to broadcast. I said that Sunday nights seemed appropriate. His next question was the most difficult: How many commercials did I have in mind, and how "commercial" would they be? I said I thought we could open with just a brief statement of Acousticon's pride in being able to sponsor his program. There would be only one commercial, and it would be at the end of the program. Reprints of the program would be offered, and people would be invited to write for them and for more information about how Acousticon could help them. I waited for his answer.

He nodded and asked me when I would like to start using radio as God's hearing aid. This Sunday, I told him, if I could buy the time. All I needed was a letter from him agreeing to broadcast. I would do the rest. He told me I would have it, and our meeting was over.

I left the church and took a taxi to WMAQ, the NBC-owned radio station in Chicago. The general manager was in. I told him who I was, who my client was, and that I wanted to buy a fifteen-minute program for Dr. Preston Bradley on Sunday nights following network time. Dr. Bradley would broadcast live, and so would the commercial announcer. I believed Dr. Bradley had the makings of a star on radio. Broadcasting his Sunday morning sermons on Sunday nights could become very popular. He agreed. I wrote the commercial, ordered the time for that weekend, hired an announcer, and ran back to complete my arrangements with Dr. Bradley. Events had moved so quickly that I hadn't dared call Max or Stanley. They had sent me to Chicago to solve the problem, and I was doing the best I could.

On Sunday morning, Dr. Bradley's church was full. I was sure I was doing the right thing. But when the congregation prayed, so did I.

I spent Sunday afternoon reviewing the script with Dr. Bradley and working on the commercial. I wanted to be sure he approved. Dr. Bradley included in his Sunday night radio sermon a statement about how pleased he was to be able to reach those who couldn't attend his church or hear him in the usual way. The broadcast was transcribed onto the sixteen-inch glass disk used at the time, and early Monday morning I called Acousticon in New York. I asked that the regular Monday meeting be postponed until I returned from Chicago. I took the next plane home, guarding my fragile disk.

I had bought radio time without authorization from Max or Stanley. I had hired talent on my own. I had written and broadcast a commercial no one had approved. I had advertised to deaf people on radio, the one medium that required hearing. As the plane approached New York, I wondered whether what I had done was inspiration or desperation.

When I arrived, I called Max and told him the whole story. He was not pleased. Tuesday morning, I took my glass disk to the Acousticon meeting and asked that equipment be available to play a radio transcription. When the group settled down, there was silence. I said nothing. Osserman finally growled, "Chicago, did you fix it?" I answered that I wasn't sure. He demanded to know what I had done, if anything. He had told me what was at stake. They were all waiting for my report.

I tried to explain that I had created a new radio show. It had been on the air the past Sunday night, and Acousticon had sponsored it. I had the transcription with me.

Stanley began to shout. Who had given me permission to create a radio show and put it on the air? Who had approved of the sponsorship? Who would pay for it? This was unauthorized and outrageous! Had I completely lost my mind? I controlled myself as well as I could. I asked if they would just listen to the transcription before passing judgment. I put the record on the machine, and for fifteen minutes it played the vibrant, warm words of Dr. Preston Bradley. As I heard him, I said to myself, "You were right! You were right!" But when the record ended, the room exploded with accusations, covering everything from my ridiculous notion of advertising to the hard of hearing on radio to lawsuits, mental examinations, and so on. It was a lynch mob in full cry—a replay of my first meeting. Once again Osserman slumped into his chair, his face gray. This time, I had no defense. There was nothing I could say or do. Or was there? I took the glass record off the machine, and I smashed it on the floor. That got their attention. I told them they had said enough. They had sent me to Chicago to fix a chronic problem. They had known from the outset that it was an impossible task. They had lost the Chicago market years before and were covering up their mistakes by asking me to fix it in a few days. But perhaps I had. I demanded that someone call Chicago and get the results.

Osserman picked up the phone. He called his sales manager in Chicago and asked how business was. The answer stunned him. The retail centers were busy, the phones were ringing, mail was beginning to pour in. Yes, Osserman assured the manager, he had instructed Wunderman to put Dr. Bradley on the air on Sunday night. He was delighted it was working. As always, he was ready to help when problems arose. "Call me tomorrow and tell me how things are going."

It was time for me to leave. I got up amid a sea of smiles. "Good idea, Lester!" "You're our boy!" "We knew you could do it!" "Brilliant move!" "Have we got an exclusive on Dr. Bradley?"

Nothing succeeds like results. When you get them, you're a hero. When you don't, you're a bum. As it turned out, we put Dr. Bradley under a long-term contract, hired a producer for him, and created a special show in which he gave advice to people in trouble. Later, we put the show on television, where it worked even better.

The Acousticon account? We kept it for more than three years, longer than any other agency had. How did we lose it? I sold them another radio show, this time featuring Eleanor Roosevelt, then an official at the United Nations. She wore a hearing aid publicly and gratefully. But Stanley didn't like Mrs. Roosevelt or her late husband. The show was well reviewed, but the first results for Acousticon were poor. The program had gotten off to a slow start in the ratings, but I was sure it would improve in time. Osserman claimed that we didn't know how to buy radio or television. He wanted a new agency. Max offered Osserman a certified check for $25,000 as the agency's guarantee against the results we would produce. Stanley refused the check, and we were fired. It was time to go. But I had learned how to make radio and television pay. Our success with Dr. Bradley had also led me to explore religious magazines, which were read mainly by older people, the majority of the hard of hearing. So print also became successful for Acousticon. I learned a lot from that account and from Stanley Osserman, perhaps more than they learned from me. I learned how to get leads for salesmen in print, radio, and television. I learned how to create store traffic. But most of all, I learned that the only thing that counts is results.

8

The Virtual Store That Opened in *Esquire* Magazine

One of my clients at Sackheim was the John Blye Shop for Men. There were three Blye shops, one on Broadway, one in White Plains, and a "Fifth Avenue" shop on East Forty-fifth Street that actually had only ten feet of Fifth Avenue frontage. They sold chic, expensive menswear to young executives. Arnold Blye, the owner, was an ambitious merchant who wanted his business to grow faster.

The first mail-order ad we ran for him in *The New York Times Magazine* cost $400 and produced $4,000 in mail-order sales. The advertising budget grew from $12,000 in 1948 to $100,000 in 1950, a large budget for mail-order advertising at the time. The best medium was *Esquire* magazine, which consistently brought in $4 in sales for every dollar spent in advertising. In 1949, we placed sixteen one-eighth-page ads in *Esquire*.

One day Arnold told me that business in his Fifth Avenue store wasn't growing and he didn't know why. People from all over the world passed his shop, he was paying a high rent for Fifth Avenue traffic, but people weren't buying. I asked him if he knew how many potential customers passed his shop every month—men he was paying so much rent to reach. He had no idea.

I asked what he would do if I showed him a street where almost a million young, fashion-conscious, affluent men shopped every month. He said he would open a store there in a minute. I told him there was such a place. "Where is it?" he asked. "*Esquire* magazine," I replied.

I proposed that we approach *Esquire* and offer it not an advertising contract but a "lease" for what would now be called a "virtual store."

We would guarantee a full-page ad, a "store window" each month—twelve times a year—if they would create a special rate not for advertising but for a retail lease. We would guarantee a minimum monthly rent plus a share of sales. We would require the same position "up front" in the magazine each month, so that readers of *Esquire* would become accustomed to the location of the "store." I had not forgotten my media training with Cap Pinsker. We struck a deal—not quite what I wanted but enough to get us started. We would try to renegotiate later, when we knew exactly what we could afford to pay.

And so we opened the fourth John Blye store in the May 1950 issue of *Esquire* magazine. As *Tide,* the influential advertising newsmagazine at the time, reported in its March 31, 1950, issue:

JOHN BLYE'S STORE-IN-PRINT

How a New York retailer parlayed an advertising budget of $12,000 into a national campaign costing $100,000, from which he expects a mail-order return of over $250,000. When the May Esquire hits newsstands next month, its readers will be greeted by a black-and-white page announcing the opening of "The new John Blye mail-order store, to be permanently located on this page of Esquire." Lester Wunderman, Blye's account executive at Maxwell Sackheim & Co., (New York), explains the new campaign in Esquire as the equivalent of a fourth store for Blye. He figures a new store in any major traffic center would cost more in rent and overhead alone than the 12 pages a year in Esquire. And he also believes another shop couldn't get half the traffic.

We opened the store, and the results from the first ads were promising. But Arnold was uncomfortable with a merely "virtual" store. He wanted a piece of real estate. He continued to think of each month's page in *Esquire* as an ad instead of a store. And so the "virtual store" closed.

The problem with the single-page John Blye store in print was that it was only a store window. To succeed, we should have been able to show the entire inventory. Many years later, my client L.L. Bean successfully inserted catalogs as "stores in print" in selected Sunday newspapers at the peak of the Christmas shopping season. Television and radio commercials called attention to these catalogs, which were easy to use. Now consumers' mailboxes are crammed with such "virtual stores."

The John Blye experiment in 1950 was a promising effort to explore the possibility of creating stores in media, but it was too little and too early. However, I believe that a leased store in a magazine is an idea that still awaits an alert retailer and publisher to promote. Meanwhile, the Internet potentially offers even greater results.

9
The World's Largest Rose Grower

The advertising business is a constant battle to get and keep clients. When you don't have enough good clients, you worry. But when you have plenty, you worry that other agencies will try to take them from you. I remember meeting an old friend who, impressed by my success in what he thought was the glamorous world of advertising, asked if I didn't find every day exciting. He was disappointed when I told him that I went to work scared and went home knowing why. Advertising offers many rewards for success, but security isn't one of them.

Although Max wasn't very good at getting new business, he knew how to keep the clients he had. He did this by giving them so many new ideas and new ads that there was little chance that another agency could suggest ideas that Max hadn't already submitted. Max's way of satisfying clients turned out to be a good way for me to relieve my own anxiety about losing them. I, too, never went to see a client without a new idea in my pocket, and I do so even now.

Many of my first clients were too small to use all the ideas I gave them, but Max encouraged me to keep it up. One day I would find a client who would welcome them. In 1949, I found one. It was the Jackson & Perkins Company of Newark, New York, the world's largest rose grower, world-famous as creators of new, patented varieties sold by mail. We first heard from the company when Ed Schofield, its advertising manager, asked Max whether he would like to be one of a small group of agencies competing for its account. Max said "Yes," and Ed came to New York to meet us. Jackson & Perkins had been owned by the Perkins family for many years. Charles Perkins, the president and majority owner, was committed to building a very large horticultural mail-order business. He was tough, shrewd, and ambitious, and he had fired his previous agency because it hadn't helped his business grow fast enough.

The business of creating, growing, and selling new varieties of plants and trees developed rapidly after Congress passed a law in 1931 declaring that new varieties, like new inventions, were patentable—that anyone who invented a new variety of flower, vegetable, or tree owned it and could collect royalties from anyone else who wanted to grow it for resale during the seventeen-year life of the patent.

Charlie Perkins saw the new law as his opportunity to convert his business from growing standard nursery stock to creating new and better varieties of patented roses for which he could command higher prices. During the Depression, while other flower growers and farmers who grew commodity crops had gone bankrupt, Jackson & Perkins had thrived by selling its first great patented plant invention, "Blaze," the first "everblooming" red climbing rose. Instead of blooming only once in the spring, Blaze produced flaming red blossoms in spring, summer, and fall. It quickly became America's favorite "rambling rose," and its brilliant red blossoms were a familiar sight on fences and walls of houses and barns from coast to coast. Millions of Blaze rosebushes were sold, and Jackson & Perkins earned a royalty on every one.

In 1939, Jackson & Perkins displayed patented roses at the New York World's Fair and offered to send a copy of its catalog of new varieties free to anyone who left his name and address. This list of hundreds of thousands of interested visitors to the World's Fair became the foundation of Jackson & Perkins' mail-order business.

After World War II, Jackson & Perkins began to build its mail-order business in earnest. America was moving to the suburbs, and Charlie Perkins wanted to sell his roses to this large new market. Rosebushes had to be shipped in early spring, while they were still dormant, but catalog photographs could show the roses in bloom even in the winter, when homeowners began thinking about next summer's garden.

Good catalog copy and photography were the best way of explaining the unique characteristics of each rose variety: color, fragrance, hardiness, size, frequency of bloom, and so on. Retail garden centers, the other major channel through which plants were sold, displayed and sold packaged rosebushes. But all they could show was the bare stalks of dormant plants with pictures on the packages. Jackson & Perkins did not sell through these retailers under its own brand name, but other rose growers licensed Jackson & Perkins roses, paid the royalty, grew them, and sold them to retail garden centers.

We knew nothing about horticulture. Max was a good mail-order man who had once run the Jim Brown stores, which sold fencing and other products to farmers, but America's young homeowners were a different market and patented hybrid roses a unique product. Ed finished the briefing by telling us that Charlie Perkins himself would decide which agency could best make his mail-order business grow.

The Sackheim agency had no research department. We were too small, and Max didn't believe in it. All the research he needed, he said, was the ability to test ads until he found the one most consumers would respond to. This "research" worked well for clients, but not for prospects.

Neither Max nor I had ever done any gardening. We could study the nursery business and master the facts, but we couldn't discuss the feelings that made people buy plants. Since Max's strong point was not new business, I would have to carry the burden of the presentation. I suggested to Max that we take a risk. Charlie Perkins and his executive group were going to find out very quickly that we didn't know anything about roses or rose growing. So why not admit it? If we tried to hide our ignorance, any error would make them feel that they had discovered our weakness. Max agreed.

So we prepared for a presentation that would highlight our strength at mail-order selling, hoping to convince Charlie that we knew our business and could learn his. Would it work?

The day of our presentation approached. In 1948, you went to Newark, New York, by train from Grand Central Station. It was still dark when we arrived. The station was closed. Ed Schofield was waiting for us in his car. He was the only one in sight. "Welcome to Newark," he said.

Ed took us to an all-night diner, already crowded with farmers and rose growers on their way to work. I listened to the talk at the adjacent tables, trying to find some clue that would help me at our meeting. I knew Charlie Perkins would find us very different from his colleagues and neighbors. But was that good or bad?

Three agencies had been asked to present for the account. One had already done so the day before. The other was to precede us that morning. Ed drove us to the office, where we would wait while he joined the J&P group hearing the first presentation. Then it would be our turn. Afterward, the J&P executive group would choose. If a clear winner emerged, we would be told before we left Newark. If Charlie needed more time, we would be told in New York.

The office was not what I had expected. J&P's headquarters was a white farmhouse with a center hall furnished with two benches for visitors. To our left, what had once been the parlor was now a room full of women busily opening mail and typing orders, a familiar sight. On our right, the door to the dining room was closed. As Ed took his leave, he told us to make ourselves comfortable. The other agency was ready to present, and he would come for us in an hour or two, when it was finished. It was just 7:30 A.M. It was going to be a long day.

On a small side table next to our bench were Jackson & Perkins catalogs for the past two seasons, spring and fall. I went through them to make sure I was familiar with the names and colors of its featured roses. On the table were also copies of the magazines in which the company advertised: *Better Homes & Gardens, American Home, Flower Grower, Horticulture,* and so on. There were also some handsome professional journals, including some from Europe. In one of them I found an article by Eugene Boerner, J&P's head of horticultural research, who invented most of the company's new, patented varieties. It all seemed very technical. I began to worry even more about our lack of horticultural expertise.

At about nine o'clock the door opened, and the preceding group left. They were smiling. One of them wore a beard, and I assumed he was a professor of horticulture. As Ed led us into Charlie Perkins' office, my fear turned to panic.

We were introduced to Charlie, his two brothers, and Eugene Boerner. They, with Ed Schofield, would make the decision. They were all in shirtsleeves. Charlie, behind wire-rimmed glasses, looked about fifty. He was tall and a little ungainly, but his handshake was warm and firm, and he exuded such authority that I realized at once that the "they" who were going to make the decision was Charlie.

And so we began. Max identified himself and introduced me. I couldn't forget the bearded man. Instead of making the presentation we had planned, I admitted my fears. "Mr. Perkins," I said, "I'm a kid from New York City. I don't know anything about rosebushes, and I'm very nervous about that guy with the beard who just left." Charlie looked at me and said, "Look here, young man, we know about roses. What we need to find out is what you know about mail-order advertising." I fell for Charlie Perkins then and there. It was the first of many times he would help me over a rough spot.

On this unexpectedly supportive note, I decided to omit the presentation we had prepared about the work we had done for other clients and began to talk about J&P's catalog business. First, I asked the key mail-order questions: How big was the company's customer list? What percentage of customers reordered every year? There were a spring and fall catalog; did that mean there were spring and fall buyers? In what proportion? How did J&P stimulate additional purchases? Did it offer credit to old or new customers? What was the size of the average order? Were there records of exactly what each customer had ordered and when? When was each catalog mailed? Why then? Were there follow-up mailings after each catalog? If so, how many? What did they offer? Were they effective? What about inquiries? What did it cost to bring in a new customer? What was the best way of doing so? How long did the company keep an inactive prospect's name on file? Did new prospects get the same catalog and follow-up pieces as old customers? What percentage of inquiries was followed by orders? Were the percentage and size of sales the same from each medium the company used? Which media, if any, were more productive? Could the company track the ads' productivity?

Charlie was enjoying himself, and Max was in his element. He made notes of some of the questions and answers and began to sketch out some ads. He was about to do his "magic act" and produce copy and layouts on the spot. We were now animated. Everyone was identifying problems and hypothetical solutions. We discovered that J&P was missing a real opportunity by not asking its customers or prospects to recommend friends who might want catalogs. We told Charlie and his colleagues that "get-a-friend" programs were the lowest-cost and most productive way of getting new customers. This source alone could add as many as 15 percent more names to the list of J&P prospects. By exposing my fears up front, I had cleared the air. Charlie's encouraging response had converted the meeting into a work session instead of a new-business presentation.

Suddenly the noon whistle sounded. We had been together for three hours and were just getting hot, but Charlie stopped the meeting. He grinned and told us that he guessed he had begun work with his new agency that morning. We would have lunch and then return to the office to start solving problems that very day, thus I discovered that we had created the best possible new-business presentation by discussing J&P's problems rather than our own credentials.

When we returned to the office after lunch, we were officially appointed J&P's new advertising agency. I could hardly believe it. It was the beginning of a relationship that would last for years.

Learning about rose growing from Charlie Perkins was like learning about automobiles from Henry Ford. Charlie didn't want to be just the world's largest rose grower; he already was. He had a vision of a horticultural industry bigger, better, and more profitable than it had ever been. Beautiful new J&P roses would one day brighten the gardens and lives of tens of millions of homeowners who might never have grown a rosebush before. He wanted the rose to become America's national flower. He named roses for presidents and their wives and donated rosebushes to the White House gardens. Together we were going to change the way a whole industry did business.

The fundamental obstacle to J&P's growth was the nature of the product itself. J&P introduced new varieties of patented roses every year. For J&P to grow and be profitable, these new roses had to be "hits."

Each fall, after two years in the field, millions of mature hybrid roses were dug up when they became dormant for the winter. The following spring, they were packed and shipped to customers.

When I asked Charlie what he did with the unsold roses at the end of the season, he said, "We burn them." He saw that I was startled and added that in some years they burned their entire profit. It was obvious that they had to sell what they grew, and it was my job to see that they burned as little as possible.

Charlie took me through the warehouses in the fall after the roses had been put into storage. He wanted me to see the volume and variety of plants that for years had been carefully planted, nurtured, and prepared for sale. It was awesome. I was obsessed with the millions of rosebushes sleeping in the warehouse. Would they sell or burn?

Each year's crop was carefully planned two years before the rosebushes were to be sold. The proposed inventory was then planted. J&P didn't know how many customers it would have two years hence, nor could it know what they would order. The public was unpredictable; nature even more so.

So the trick was to find ways of selling the entire supply of each of the hundreds of varieties offered in the catalog. Most catalog companies plan a minimum inventory and then reorder when the supply runs out. At J&P there was no way to reorder. Other catalog merchants can hold inventory over from one season to the next or have an end-of-season sale. At J&P, when the season ended, there was no tomorrow: the unsold inventory couldn't be kept in stock or replanted.

My first job was to attract more new inquiries for the free forty-eight-page catalog. The largest and most productive general magazine J&P used at that time was *Better Homes & Gardens*. Cap Pinsker had taught me that the first three right-hand pages of a magazine were the most productive. These "preferred positions" were in constant demand by large general advertisers. J&P bought only one page each year in January, when most gardeners were beginning to think about their spring and summer gardens, but *Better Homes & Gardens* refused to give J&P pages one, three, or five. So I went to Des Moines, Iowa, to see Fred Bohen, the publisher. He told me that J&P's single full page didn't merit special attention. I argued that J&P was entitled to a preferred position in *Better Homes & Gardens* because it was the largest advertiser in the gardening field. The fact that advertisers such as General Electric ran larger schedules was irrelevant. The magazine had a responsibility to its readers to feature editorial and advertising material on gardening. I told him that if he did not place the J&P ad up front, he should rename the magazine "Better Homes & Lighting Fixtures." That annoyed him, and I was waiting to be thrown out. But instead, he replied he had two things to say to me: I could have the preferred position and would I like to work for him?

I thanked Fred for the position—and the compliment. He gave J&P an option for page three or five in each future January issue of *Better Homes & Gardens*. Charlie was delighted. But *Better Homes & Gardens* was just one part of J&P's complex advertising problem. What we needed was a strategic marketing plan. The idea for it came to me while Charlie and I were out fishing.

After a successful year, Charlie would celebrate by taking a small group bass fishing at Henderson Harbor on Lake Ontario. The first day of my first trip, I was in a boat with Charlie, Gene Boerner, Ken Tack (who had replaced Ed Schofield as advertising manager after Ed took a job with Stern's Nursery), and a guide. I noticed that our guide kept dipping a large cup into the lake and pouring water into the bucket of live bait. I asked what he was doing, and he told me that he was filling the leaky bucket, as if that explained everything—and suddenly it did. It was the image I had been seeking for J&P's business. I worked on the idea all day, and that evening at dinner I told Charlie that I had discovered a better way of thinking about his business. He was constantly filling a leaky bucket, I told him. He looked at me strangely. He knew it was the first time I had ever been fishing. He also knew I had had my share of good Canadian ale. He wasn't going to get in the way of my good time: if I wanted to think he was filling a leaky bucket, it was all right with him. I told Charlie I was serious; I wanted him and Ken to help me. I believed I had figured out the right approach to next year's total marketing plan. Now I had their attention. I explained what I had been thinking about all day. At lunchtime, while the guides were cooking our fish, I had sketched a bucket. Leaking from the bottom were customers who had stopped buying or inquirers who had never bought in the first place. The bucket itself was full of customers and new prospects.

I said to Charlie that each season his ads attracted 135,000 new prospects. About 10 percent became customers. That was the valuable new volume going into the bucket. In the bucket, too, were the customers who bought regularly as well as those who had stopped buying. Those were his three marketing variables. He could increase sales by putting more prospects into the bucket. While they were there, he had to sell them not just roses but a variety of other plants. Prospects who didn't become customers and customers who had stopped buying were an overhead expense. If we couldn't make them buy, we should let them leak out of the bucket as quickly as possible.

That evening, we started work on the basic marketing changes to make the business grow faster and more profitably. The system we created is now used by all good direct marketers. Today, we call it "database-targeted marketing" or "relationship marketing," and it was originally invented to fill J&P's "leaky bucket." Now the work is done with the help of computers, regression and segment analysis, and scientific modeling, but back then we had to make do with simpler tools. The essential problem was J&P's lack of information. Our mailings were not relevant to many of the customers because we didn't know what they had already bought and what, if anything, they were likely to buy again. Nor did we know the size of their gardens or what was already planted in them. We were marketing in the dark.

J&P was a mass marketer of new varieties of rosebushes and other plants. To deal relevantly with our customers as individuals, we would have to learn more about their needs. The first step was to stop identifying our lists as general "customers" or "prospects." We would have to classify them by the type, size, and frequency of their purchases.

We separated our customers by the date and size of their last purchase and discovered that after four inactive seasons (two years) it was more profitable to remove a name from the active file than to go on mailing to it. Now we could determine who bought roses and who bought perennials, fruit trees, and so on, and we began to create special new offers for each group. We separated gift buyers from gardeners and inquirers from orderers by season and size of order. In other words, we segmented what had originally been one large list. I proved to J&P that the more separate files we created and the more we learned about each customer, the more profitable the mailings became. Thus J&P created a dialogue with its prospects and customers long before the idea of interactive communication became fashionable. Customers got to know and trust Charlie even though they never met him in person, and he got to know his customers, if not by name, then by their buying habits.

Rose growers begin distributing spring catalogs in January, but their profit or loss is determined by what happens in the last few weeks of the planting season. Early mailings bring in a trickle of orders, but the orders flood in—or don't—when the season peaks in April. Roses have a built-in genetic clock that can't be stopped; they begin to bud even though the warehouse is kept cold and dark and the roots are bare of soil. So the planting season is the critical deadline for roses, the rose grower, and the home gardener.

The countdown at J&P began in March, when J&P executives would tally the daily orders received from each promotion. They watched sales and inventory as avidly as Wall Street traders follow the tickertape. Charlie's office, the order-processing center, and the warehouse were the three command posts, and Charlie moved constantly from one to the other, often with me in tow. At the center of this spring season activity, Charlie was like General Patton at the height of a battle, deploying manpower and inventory to maximize gains and cut losses. He would try to sell surplus varieties to garden centers or supermarkets. If orders were coming in faster than expected, Charlie would buy roses from other nurseries. Each week we placed full- or half-page ads in Sunday newspapers featuring the varieties we needed to sell, ads that not only paid for themselves but also supported our other promotions. We revised or created direct mail promotions at the last moment. We wrote commercials for radio and television. Charlie expected me to use all kinds of productive advertising, and I did.

One morning late in March, when the season was in full swing, I was in Charlie's office, waiting to join him on his morning rounds. He closed his door and told his secretary he didn't want to be disturbed. Uh-oh, I thought, this is not like Charlie. Something's bothering him, and it must be serious. I soon found out what it was.

He told me he saw a disaster coming. We had promoted his new varieties so well that people were not buying the older roses in the catalog. For years his main objective had been to create and promote new and better roses and sell them at higher prices. He had bet his business on that idea, and now he was afraid it had backfired. I was confused. I told him that as far as I could see he was winning. Sales for the new, more expensive roses were pouring in. The public had bought his idea. But I had never seen him so agitated. He stopped pacing, sat on the edge of the desk, sighed, and told me that I was right, but the public had done it too soon and he wasn't ready.

Charlie had spent two years growing the wrong roses. He didn't have enough of the new varieties his customers were ordering and had too many of the older ones that they weren't. He couldn't fill thousands of orders, and that meant refunding the customers' money. He was going to end the season with a bonfire of unsold older varieties. What could he do?

I had two ideas. The first was simple: he should immediately send a refund check to every customer whose order couldn't be filled. The accompanying letter would offer disappointed customers a priority on the next fall crop if they reserved the roses they wanted now. J&P would guarantee to deliver the reserved plants in time for fall planting and would include a chrysanthemum plant as a bonus. The letter would demonstrate Charlie's personal concern by providing the refund promptly with his regrets. The new offer would soothe his customers by offering a delayed shipment rather than a flat rejection. The free chrysanthemum plant would be the first free offer in J&P's history. I believed we might recover as many as a third of the rejected orders. Charlie agreed and instructed me to write the letter and work out the mailing system with Ken Tack.

But his most serious problem remained: What to do with the unsold inventory? I suggested to Charlie that he take a risk, that he make the most daring offer in the history of rose growing. He was interested. I knew he would try almost anything. I suggested he create assortments of four of the surplus varieties and calculate how many such assortments would clear out all the inventory. We would send a mailing to the hundreds of thousands of unconverted inquiries from recent years, offering an opportunity to try Jackson & Perkins roses without risk. The mailing would offer an introductory assortment of roses on approval. Customers would send no money, just permission to ship. When they got the roses, they would plant them. By June 10, when the roses were in bloom, customers could either pay for them or destroy the roses, notify J&P to that effect, and pay nothing. It was a credit offer, an approval offer, a deferred-payment offer, and a no-risk guarantee of satisfaction all in one. It would be irresistible, I thought. Charlie looked at me, grinned and said, "Write the letter."

The copy read, "Send no money now. Nor pay a penny when the plants arrive. We will enclose a memo bill with the shipment. By June 10, the roses will be thriving in your garden. If you are completely satisfied at that time, pay the bill. If your roses do not thrive as promised—if they are not satisfactory in every way—tear them out of the ground and pay nothing. Just return the bill indicating that you have destroyed the plants." I'll never forget the pained look on Charlie's face when I gave him the copy to read. Did they really have to tear the plants out of the ground? he asked. No gardener would do that. That, I told him, was the crux of the idea.

Within a week after the "send no money" letters were mailed, orders began pouring in as never before. Within a few weeks, the warehouse was empty. Now we would wait to see if the gamble paid off. Charlie's surplus inventory had been converted to potential accounts receivable.

Never did June 10 seem so slow to arrive. We wouldn't have to burn our surplus roses, but we might still have a bonfire of returned, unpaid bills.

In early June, payments began to arrive, many by airmail with letters telling Charlie how well the roses were growing. Then, by mid-June, checks began to flood in just as the orders had. By the end of June, we had collected almost 75 percent of the outstanding bills and checks were still coming in—a bonanza. The selling cost had been so low that J&P made more profit on the surplus roses than on the most popular new varieties. We had not only sold the surplus, we had created a revolutionary new sales technique. Gone was the fear of growing too many roses. Gone, too, was the danger of growing a mix of wrong varieties. Charlie saw the possibilities at once. He cautioned us to keep the results quiet. If competitors asked, we should say that the credit losses had been unacceptably high. Ken Tack told Charlie that nobody else would have the guts to make a "send no money" offer. Charlie said he knew that, but he didn't want his competitors to know why he would be buying all their surplus roses next year.

That was just the beginning of J&P's use of credit offers. We now had a better mail-order offer than other rose catalogs' and one that could not be matched by retail garden centers. But other problems remained.

Charlie had an ongoing conflict with the American Nurserymen's Association. Each year, an industry panel chose its All-American Rose Selections from the new varieties submitted for competitive testing. The winners were widely publicized and sold by all members of the association. J&P roses had won many AARS awards, but all at once they stopped winning.

Charlie was furious when a beautiful new J&P floribunda named "Spartan" failed to win the AARS award. He believed Spartan, with its brilliant orange-red blooms from spring right through fall, was the best floribunda rose of its time. He was so sure Spartan would be a winner that he had grown a large introductory crop. This, he said, was never going to happen again. With or without the AARS awards, his new products would succeed in the marketplace.

New horticultural products begin as a mystery to the public, which cannot see the blooms until after they are planted and sold. All anyone can see is a color reproduction in a catalog or magazine, which was why an AARS selection was so important. Garden editors wrote about the AARS winners, and the major nursery catalogs featured them. The problem was to create equal credibility and publicity for J&P featured roses, even without AARS awards. The answer, when it came, was simple. I suggested that we create the Jackson & Perkins Rose of the Year, chosen not by an industry panel but by a panel of J&P customers. So we created the Jackson & Perkins Rose Testing Panel. Members would be sent experimental roses before they had been named or sold. The panel would grow the roses, judge them, choose the winner, and propose names—and they would be asked to pay for the privilege of doing so. I was certain that J&P customers would buy memberships in the panel and that we could teach them enough about judging roses that the best plants would win. But could our winners match or exceed the publicity the AARS selections received? I suggested to Charlie that we create the first nationally advertised branded rose. We would treat each J&P Rose of the Year as a major new product launch. By dominating the media, we could top the excitement and publicity of the AARS selection. To pay for the extra promotion, I suggested that Charlie add 25 cents to the price of his Rose of the Year. I wanted to advertise the selection in national magazines and on radio and television, and get publicity as well. If we did it right, the Jackson & Perkins Rose of the Year, selected by home gardeners, could become a major annual media event. Charlie approved. If it worked, Charlie would solve the problem of awards, and I would double J&P's advertising budget.

The next season, we invited a limited group of the best J&P customers to join our Rose Testing Panel. Membership was $10 a year, and we promised to send four new roses for testing. The response was so good that we didn't have enough of the new varieties to go around, so we put many respondents onto a waiting list, which made membership even more desirable. The votes and suggestions for names came in just as we had hoped. The first Rose of the Year was called "Kordes Perfekta" after its creator, the great German hybridizer Rainer Kordes, whose American rights J&P had bought. The second Rose of the Year was J&P's own "Hawaii." Each year, we increased the size of the test panel. The $10 membership fees offset much of the company's research cost, and when the Rose of the Year was sold for $2.75, it provided, as planned, extra money for advertising and publicity.

J&P Rose of the Year selections sold well, and Charlie didn't have to offer them to his competitors, as he did AARS selections. J&P could now have exclusive best-sellers. The Rose of the Year became a successful and profitable annual event—a value-added product and service.

After a few years Charlie once again made his roses available to the AARS selection committee—only this time, he had the Rose of the Year weapon backing his entries.

In the third year of the Rose of the Year campaign, Charlie entered a rose he felt certain would win every worldwide prize, a beautiful coral-pink hybrid tea rose. Charlie offered his new rose to both the J&P Rose Testing Panel and the AARS. One day, he asked me how many roses I thought he could sell if his new hybrid tea rose won both prizes. The new coral-pink rose that grew in my own J&P-inspired garden was the most beautiful rose I had ever seen. I told Charlie that we could sell a million the first year if he could grow them, four times the sales any rose had ever achieved in its first year. I also felt that J&P now had the promotional resources to do so. The customer list was growing each year. The "send no money" mailings were going to as many as eight million new prospects each spring. We had expanded our advertising into general magazines and added radio and television. The new rose won both the AARS and the J&P Rose of the Year awards that year, the first ever to do so.

We chose "Tropicana" from the names suggested by our panel, and Charlie managed to grow a million of them. At 25 cents extra a bush, this gave us an additional advertising budget of $250,000, which we spent on full-color pages in *Life* and other major magazines. We also bought time on the *Today* show and got publicity from hundreds of magazines and newspapers. We had learned how to launch successful new "brand-name" roses. We also discovered that now we could almost double the number of new customers we converted from catalog inquiries.

Until Tropicana, J&P, like other mail-order nurseries, had sent catalogs in response to new inquiries, and we knew that about 10 percent of those who asked for the catalog would buy from it the first season. Now we tried something different. When J&P received an inquiry, we didn't send the catalog at once. Instead, we sent a letter that said the catalog would be mailed as soon as it was ready. We apologized for the delay but offered to send three of the prizewinning Tropicanas on approval for spring planting. It was our old friend, the "send no money" offer, but presented in a new way. The results were extraordinary. Eight percent of the inquirers ordered Tropicana from the letter. Then we mailed the catalog to everyone. We worried that the Tropicana offer would cannibalize orders from the catalog, but it didn't. The usual 10 percent still bought from the catalog for cash. Thus we increased our conversions from 10 percent to 18 percent, which totally changed the economics of J&P's mail-order business. I was learning how to sell roses, but, more important, I was discovering the business that I would later name "direct marketing."

We found that we could dramatically increase the share of leisure dollars a homeowner would spend on gardening. The Rose of the Year promotion and the "send no money" offers represented additional sales created by special promotions sent in addition to the catalog. I had learned that J&P customers had an almost insatiable curiosity about new varieties and that the customer list could be a gold mine if properly exploited.

In 1952, Charlie married an attractive southerner named Mabelle. She changed Charlie's life. She redecorated his house, replanted the gardens, and gave parties to celebrate every occasion—a strawberry festival, a rose festival, Halloween, a birthday. Mabelle could make an ordinary weekend an occasion for a gala. She also persuaded Charlie to spend time in New York City and Europe.

Mabelle liked lavender sachets. So Charlie began to experiment with lavender plants, which were grown widely in the south of France and the southern United States. But lavender was not hardy in colder climates. Almost no one in the northern United States had ever seen a lavender plant. That didn't bother Charlie. He developed a lavender plant that withstood freezing temperatures. He grew tens of thousands of them, but they sold poorly. As usual, Charlie asked me to help.

Most American gardeners didn't know what lavender plants were or how to use them. We ran beautiful photographs of them in a mailing that proclaimed that this fragrant plant could now be grown almost everywhere. The mailing, like the catalog listing, was a failure. Charlie couldn't accept this because he not only had to sell plants, he had to please Mabelle.

Then one day I had an idea. I bought some lavender perfume and applied it to the mailing, which I showed to several friends who gardened. They said the plants were beautiful and asked where they could get some. I had found the answer: lavender fragrance added the power of what researchers call "aided recall" and instant recognition. The difficulty was that scented inks, scratch-off scents, and other ways of putting fragrance onto paper in quantity had not yet been invented. It was late in the season, and Charlie pressed me for a solution. I asked a research chemist how I could add lavender scent to a million letters. He told me that it was easy enough to buy essential oil of lavender, but how to preserve it on paper long enough to reach the consumer was a problem. He promised to think about it. The next day, he called to say that gum arabic, better known as rubber cement, was the answer. I told him the letters would be printed in Rochester and delivered in bulk on skids to Newark for folding and inserting. He asked how many letters were on a skid. I told him thousands. He said he thought we could do it, that all we needed was to suspend the right amount of oil of lavender in barrels of rubber cement and paint the sides of the stacks of letters with the gummy fragrance. He believed the fragrance would last long enough for the finished mailings still to be scented when they reached the customers. Together we went to Newark, where he mixed the "goo" in one of Charlie's empty warehouses. The fragrance was overpowering. Charlie and I watched as the lavender scent was "painted" onto the sides of the stacks of letters that were to become part of advertising's first scented mailings. The letter began, "You undoubtedly noticed something unusual about this letter. IT'S SCENTED with the world's best-loved fragrance . . . lavender."

We had stumbled upon a principle made famous by the French artist René Magritte, who had painted a picture of a pipe and then written below it, "This is not a pipe." Of course it wasn't, it was a picture of a pipe. And so it was with our photographs of lavender plants. They weren't lavender to the gardeners until we added another sensory clue. Without knowing it, I had stumbled into the world of semantics and semiotics, where a word is a "signifier" and the product is the thing signified, and the signifier gives meaning to the signified. Many years later, this idea would help me land the biggest client of my career. Direct marketing would have to make things real if it was going to sell through images rather than the products themselves, which were physically present only at retail. And so another season ended successfully for Charlie—and along the way, I had discovered new possibilities for direct marketing.

After the lavender success, Charlie searched for more plants to sell. In late fall, we offered amaryllis bulbs from South Africa, which bloomed indoors at Christmas, and Christmas roses, which bloomed outdoors from November to March, even in the snow. We sold exotic lilies, tulips, and daffodil bulbs from Holland. But Charlie was not finished. There was more to come.

One fall day, he took me to the small airport at Newark. I knew we were going somewhere, but he didn't say where or why. I was sure that wherever we were going, there was a problem for me to solve. I was right. We flew for about ten minutes until we were over some of Charlie's more distant growing fields. They were aflame with dazzling bands of color—white, red, yellow, bronze, pink—all in long, brilliant rows. I asked Charlie what they were, and, as I expected, he said that they were my new assignment. Below were tens of thousands of chrysanthemums, new varieties that Gene Boerner had been hybridizing and growing for several years. He had named them the "Bird Series," and they were now ready for market.

Having sold warehouses of surplus roses and greenhouses packed with lavender plants, I now had to sell miles of mums. It took a while, but we solved the mum problem by offering buyers a new and yet-unnamed mum with their purchase of six chrysanthemum plants. They would be the first in their neighborhood to grow it. The mailing was a success, and it became the eighteenth in J&P's annual cycle of special promotions. We had sold Charlie's "miles of mums," and once again I learned that a successful premium needn't be merely a bribe if it also offers a unique benefit. Years later that knowledge would help me sell millions of magazine subscriptions.

In fewer than ten years, the J&P promotion calendar had grown from a catalog and two follow-up mailings to an arsenal of promotions and offerings that had increased sales to the average customer by more than 300 percent. Whether it was mums, roses, lavender, Christmas roses, dahlias, lilies, dianthus, or Holland bulbs, J&P had become a unique source of information as well as of plants and, as a result, a much larger and more profitable company. We were no longer meeting in the farm-house dining room. Charlie had built a large, modern office building for J&P facing the display garden, the largest of its kind in the United States and a popular tourist attraction. Hundreds of thousands of visitors came to Newark each spring and summer to see the roses in bloom. Newark, New York, was now the "Rose Capital of America."

J&P's fourth Rose of the Year, "South Seas," sold out in the spring, as did the lavender and other perennials. We were prepared for fall with tested promotions. It was time to go fishing. Despite our differences in age and background, Charlie and I were now friends. Charlie faced each day with courage and optimism, and I thought of him as the archetype of the men who had built America. He enjoyed risk, challenge, and "doing the impossible." Charlie never doubted the correctness of his instincts. If something "felt right," he acted on it. These instincts were soon going to get him into deep trouble, but we didn't know that as we enjoyed peace and camaraderie at Henderson Harbor on Lake Ontario.

One night after dinner in the fishing camp, Charlie asked me what I thought the most important functions of a business were. The question took me by surprise. I told him that I had never thought about it because I had been too busy surviving. Charlie told me that he was certain I knew the answer by the way I approached what I did. I was a little baffled, but he went on. He said that the main purpose of a business was not to make a profit but to satisfy its customers' needs, as I did for him and helped him do for others. Next he said that a business must continue to grow; if it stood still, it would start to die. Most important, a business must endure. I told him I understood; I had been struggling to survive and grow all my life. Every time I had felt I was standing still, I had begun to worry that I wouldn't make it. As for satisfying customers, he had taught me more about that than anyone else had. Over the years, I have reflected on that evening countless times: "to serve," "to grow," "to endure." I have never forgotten it.

The next morning, we were out on the lake fishing with our guide. It was a beautiful day. Ours was the only boat in sight. Lake Ontario looked as untouched as it must have to the Native Americans who had fished it long before we did. Charlie's brother Ralph was with us, and as he cast his baited hook, a gull swooped down and took the bait before it hit the water. The bird was caught on the hook, and Ralph began to fly it like a kite. The bird circled the boat, trying to escape. The sight of Ralph flying the hapless, bewildered bird was unforgettable. Fortunately, he was able to reel the bird into the boat unharmed, remove the hook, and release it. Ralph had enlivened the morning, but he had done more than that: he had given Charlie an idea. At lunch Charlie sat next to me and told me Ralph had caught a big bird with bait meant for a small fish. Perhaps we could learn something from that. He thought our ads, which offered free catalogs to prospects, should also be catching big birds, not just small fish. Though J&P was selling to many more people season after season, only 135,000 new prospects responded to our advertising for the catalog each year. The business would grow a lot faster, he said, if we could attract more inquiries. I told him we were doing the best we could. I should have changed the subject, but it was too late. The next day, Charlie asked Ken Tack to join us and told us to go after one million new inquiries the next season. He thought we could find a way to do it. That was the end of my peace of mind for that trip and that year. Nobody had ever produced a million inquiries for a rose catalog—but then, it's possible that nobody had ever caught a gull with a fishing rod before.

Direct marketing advertising consists of two parts: the so-called front end, which is the initial result received from the advertising, and the back end, which is the orders and reorders received from subsequent promotions sent to those who respond. The success of the front end is judged by how many first-time customers or prospects each dollar of advertising attracts. The success of the back end is determined by the number of customers who buy, how much they spend, and how long they remain active before they stop buying. Most direct marketers are content to break even or lose money on the front end to attract new customers, because profits come from back-end orders. The first sale is only the beginning. The fundamental franchise of all direct marketers is the nature of the ongoing relationship they build with their loyal customers. The quality of the relationship is what motivates customers to buy repeatedly over long periods of time. When the relationship is good, a special bond of loyalty develops between buyer and seller. As the size and productivity of the customer list increase, they provide the sales and profits required to support the advertising used to attract new prospects. Good direct marketing is an endless spiral, never a straight line.

By asking for a million new inquiries, Charlie was right, as usual. If he had asked for a 10 percent increase, we could have achieved it by making minor changes in our traditional techniques. By asking for a million inquiries, he made us come up with an entirely new idea.

For the previous two years, our agency had been experimenting with business reply cards bound into magazines. Magazines had been using such cards for their own subscription offers. They thought of their cards not as advertisements, but as a convenience to their readers. But I knew how helpful a business reply card could be to a direct mail effort, so I called a friend at *Time* magazine and asked him how the cards they put into their magazine were working. He said they were a terrific success. I then tried to persuade a large magazine to sell us a bound-in reply card with our ad. The publisher resisted the idea as "intrusive." Intrusive was, of course, just what I wanted. Eventually, I persuaded a few small publishers to accept a postcard insert, but first they wanted us to buy the two pages surrounding the card. That way the card would not detract from other advertising or editorial matter. Our first cards were hugely successful. We then began to persuade other publishers to accept cards and teach them how to produce and charge for them. Bound-in reply cards were potentially a great source of revenue for publishers. We suggested that the card be priced at the equivalent of the rate for a half-page of space, so that a two-page ad with a card would cost as much as two and a half pages of space. The advertiser would pay the full cost of printing the card. Early results indicated that this unit would create enough additional responses to be more than worth its cost.

We also tested an even more radical concept, a four-page advertisement printed full size on light card stock and bound into the center spread of *TV Guide,* then the country's largest-circulation magazine. A record club and a vitamin company had successfully used insert cards to sell subscriptions and pills, but they had never been tried to promote a free catalog offer.

I believed the insert card could get Charlie his million inquiries, but I had no idea whether such a mass of inquiries would convert to customers. Nevertheless, the time seemed right for combining all of J&P's new back-end promotion ideas with a more dynamic approach to attracting new inquiries. I had some new ads designed with the new format, two-page spreads with a card in the center. The left-hand page was a black-and-white ad offering the free Jackson & Perkins Catalog of

Roses and Perennials, and bound between the two ad pages was the postpaid business reply card. The right-hand page, in full color, announced the Jackson & Perkins Rose of the Year. I took the new layouts to Newark and showed them to Ken Tack. I also showed him the advertising schedule, which called for a very much larger advertising budget. We then showed Charlie the layouts and copy, and I explained that the page announcing the Rose of the Year would be paid for by the special budget we had created for the purpose. Making that full-color ad part of a two-page spread would provide J&P with a dominant advertising unit. Both pages would receive extra attention. The insert card would make it easier for the readers to reply, and the card was bulky enough to make the magazine open to the spread. I then showed Charlie the ad schedule, which called for two pages and a card in most of the magazines we had previously used, plus the four-page card-stock ad in *TV Guide*. New inquiries at the time were costing J&P 60 cents each. The proposed budget for new inquiries was more than $500,000. But the goal of a million inquiries seemed achievable.

Charlie looked at the ads and the advertising schedule. He was silent for a while, and then he asked if I believed in it. I told him I did. "Okay, let's catch the gull," he said.

That January, a flood of new inquiries came in to Jackson & Perkins. *Better Homes & Gardens*, which had never produced more than 32,000 inquiries from a full-page ad, pulled 150,000, and *TV Guide* produced 275,000, far more than we had planned. We easily achieved our one million inquiry goal and were prepared to convert these inquiries into sales. Many of these new prospects bought from the Rose of the Year mailing, which was sent out before the catalog. Others bought more familiar varieties from the catalog itself. Everyone received each of the eighteen powerful direct mail promotions we had already developed. By the end of the year, we had added almost 200,000 new customers to J&P's base. The aggressive advertising and promotion attracted new customers and stimulated old customers to buy more.

By 1960, J&P had become a very large business. I believed in the efficiency and convenience of marketing directly to the consumer, but I knew that there was a large additional market of prospects who preferred to shop at retail garden centers close to home. The heavily advertised J&P brand could create sales there as well, so I persuaded Charlie to change his policy and offer his best varieties at retail, featuring the J&P name, trademark, and guarantee on the package. I was certain we could double his business.

J&P's aggressive and revolutionary advertising, marketing, and distribution helped build the entire nursery industry. Charlie took the spectacular growth in stride and kept pushing the boundaries of the business forward. But he had a new concern: where to grow all the roses he now needed. The property he owned in Newark and the land he leased in California weren't enough. He began to look elsewhere. His instincts led him to Arizona.

On a visit to Phoenix, Charlie noticed how well cotton and citrus grew in the hot, clear days and cool nights. The soil was sandy, which forced plants to put down strong roots. Arizona had everything but water, and that was available underground if you knew where to look for it. As usual, Charlie didn't wait for research or expert opinions. He had a hunch that Arizona was the place to be. Land was still cheap, and so was farm labor. Charlie bought several large parcels just outside Phoenix. He was going to sink wells and grow the largest, strongest, and most beautiful roses in the world at low cost and without the losses from bad weather he had experienced elsewhere. He predicted that in Arizona, superior giant roses would spring into bloom at the first touch of sun and water.

It took Charlie a year to find water, and he finally planted his first large crop. The desert sun really did turn those roses on. Charlie was ecstatic and asked me to join him for an inspection of his first crop. At the airport in Phoenix we rented a car, and, with Charlie at the wheel, off we went at ninety miles an hour toward the new J&P rose ranch. Charlie couldn't wait to show it to me—and when we arrived, I could understand why. There were miles of the most vigorous, healthiest-looking rosebushes I had ever seen. Charlie was more excited than ever. As much as he loved marketing, selling, and problem solving, he loved the land and growing things even more. As we toured the fields, Charlie kept pointing out the number of large, multibranched bushes. He had never before seen so high a percentage of number-one-grade plants and said that the long, straight root systems would make the plants easier to pack into shipping cartons. Also, the deep roots would survive winter freezes better because they would extend below the frost level.

But it was not long before the first disaster struck. Warmed by the hot sun and watered by ample irrigation, the roses were growing furiously, but as fast as the roses grew, so did the Johnson grass, the western equivalent of crabgrass but more pernicious. It was suffocating the young rosebushes, but any chemical strong enough to kill the Johnson grass also damaged the roses. Hand weeding was impossibly expensive. No one had grown roses in Arizona before, and no one could have foreseen the disastrous weeds. The roses, the Arizona project, and even J&P itself were suddenly in serious trouble. Charlie asked his managers to think of a solution, but no one had an answer—until a small, weathered Mexican field hand named Jesús came to Charlie one day and told him that he knew something that loved Johnson grass. What was it? Charlie wanted to know. Since boyhood, Jesús said, he had raised geese. Johnson grass, he assured Charlie, was their favorite food.

Within a week, thousands of geese were waddling through the rose fields. They not only ate every bit of Johnson grass as it grew but converted it to fertilizer. The crop was saved, and Charlie was happy again. He seemed to have clear sailing to the best rose harvest in J&P history. When fall came, the rosebushes were lush and strong, with beautiful, intensely colored blooms. As soon as they became dormant, the bushes would be dug up and sent to the cold warehouses in Newark, and next spring America's gardeners would be planting superroses, plants that would be better and stronger than the finest number-one grade.

But the roses didn't become dormant. The wonderful Arizona sun and the fertile, well-irrigated soil just kept them growing and growing. Once again a call went out to agricultural chemists, this time to provide a defoliant that would hasten dormancy. But science failed again. The crop and the company were once again faced with disaster. Finally Charlie went to Jesús and asked for another miracle—and got one. Jesús told him that the answer was sheep. Everyone knew that sheep ate every leaf they could find. Soon the sheep had eaten every leaf off of every rosebush in sight. It wasn't chemicals, science, or the experts but Jesús's two simple tips that saved the company. The roses were harvested, and the following spring, giant, healthy J&P-brand roses from Arizona dominated not only the mail-order business but retail garden centers as well.

The last time I saw Charlie Perkins was when I stopped by Phoenix on my way to California to attend another client's planning meeting.

Charlie had become a rancher as well as a rose merchant, raising roses, geese, and sheep for market. He was seventy-two, and I wondered how long he could go on working and playing so hard. The next day, he returned to Newark and I went on to Palm Springs. Two days later, I received a call from Ken Tack, telling me that Charlie was dead. I mourned him then—and I still do.

Years later, I learned that Charlie's love of Arizona had created serious financial problems for J&P. Beautiful roses did grow there, but at an unacceptable cost. Charlie's instincts had finally failed him, and the company was sold soon after his death.

I loved Charlie Perkins, his roses, and the way he did business. Charlie lived on the edge of possibility and encouraged me to join him there. He made me feel that if I stepped off the edge I wouldn't fall—I would learn to fly.

A significant part of my life had ended. But by that time, I had other clients and other problems to solve. I had learned from Jackson & Perkins that direct marketing, applied with imagination, is an advertising and selling force of enormous power—and that there is always more to learn. I had learned new ways of attracting great numbers of responses for a specialized catalog. I had also learned better ways of converting them into buyers. For the first time, I really understood the importance of segmentation of customer and prospect lists and how to use it to create a database that identified the best prospects for further promotion. I had learned the value of credit when it was used as a real customer benefit. I had also found that relevant premiums used as rewards are stronger than discount coupons or financial bribes. Most of all, I had learned that the real objective of direct marketing is to convert sales to relationships, because the relationship bonds the customer to the company and the brand is the total of all that. I had also learned that it takes a good client to help an agency create good advertising.

10
The Power
of Clubs

The Young People's Record Club had faded away as a client, but its key personnel quickly helped build a new club, the Children's Record Guild, for the Greystone Press. We became the advertising agency for the new club.

John Stevenson, the principal owner and chief executive of Greystone, a large and diverse marketer of books, book clubs, book series, and records, was a talented, aggressive businessman. Born in England, he had learned newspaper promotion on Fleet Street, then the most competitive newspaper marketplace in the world—British publishers gave away china, bedsheets, or whatever else it took to get new subscribers. Stevenson had worked for a while in Australia. Then, in New York, he had used his considerable circulation skills for the *New York Post*. After a brief stint at Doubleday, he had founded Greystone.

Building on his newspaper experience and what he had learned about book clubs at Doubleday, he started the Fiction Book Club, which sold low-priced popular fiction with the kind of bold offers he had used to build newspaper circulation. He also published one-volume how-to books on sewing and home decorating, which he advertised on the back pages of local and national Sunday newspaper supplements. Another Stevenson invention was the book "continuity series," which provided a book a month to a member until the series was complete. The first series, a fourteen-volume illustrated *Encyclopedia of Gardening,* sold more than two million sets. It was followed by other series on animals, home repair, photography, decorating, and so on. Some sets contained as many as forty-four volumes. Greystone sold tens of millions of continuity-series volumes. Stevenson was a brilliant risk taker who spent millions of dollars on advertising each year; we became the agency for most of it.

When I began to work on his account, John told me how he thought we could best work together. We would meet for a full day each week to review the results of every program, every ad, every split run, every medium, and every offer. We would seek new businesses and create advertising schedules, headlines, promotions, and new tests. It was the same kind of work I had done years earlier with Eric Eweson of Ballco Products. However, this time I was working with the most adventurous entrepreneur in the mail-order business. John Stevenson knew how to use offers, follow-up mailings, and collection techniques to get the most profitable return on advertising investments. But for Stevenson, advertising was only the first step in marketing. How long a customer stayed and how much he spent were the keys to promotional decisions. Like Charlie Perkins, he taught me that the main objective of mail-order advertising was not just to make a sale but to build long-term relationships with customers, who would buy again and again as new products were offered to them. He developed a large data bank of his best customers, who became the foundation of his business.

The Children's Record Guild was an instant success. The price of the monthly record sent to club members was $1 plus postage, and since John was a firm believer in distributing mail-order products through retailers as well as directly to customers, Children's Record Guild records became best-sellers at retail, where they sold for $1.19. John then repeated his success with recorded "Living Language" courses, which he sold for $9.95.

Stevenson found business opportunities everywhere. His apartment at 1010 Fifth Avenue overlooked the Metropolitan Museum of Art. One cold Sunday morning, he looked out his window and saw people shivering as they waited on line for the museum to open. He wondered how many of them might prefer to receive art at home.

Stevenson then called Harry Abrams, the leading publisher of art books in the United States. Abrams had begun as the advertising manager of the Book-of-the-Month Club and understood mail-order publishing and selling. Stevenson bought from Abrams the rights to a series of sixteen art portfolios that hadn't sold at retail.

In exchange for taking the sixteen portfolios off Abrams's hands,

John persuaded him to expand the series to thirty, so that his subscribers could eventually have a complete library of the world's greatest artists. Stevenson planned to convert the failed bookstore series into a successful mail-order continuity program in which buyers would receive a portfolio each month, plus a lesson from an art appreciation course, for $2.95. We named the program "Art Treasures of the World" and began to create test ads for it.

We took nothing for granted; everything was tested, and some of the results were surprising. We immediately learned that because people were not accustomed to collecting portfolios of art, they were reluctant to make a firm commitment to buy until they were convinced they would be satisfied. We learned from our first split-run tests that the initial offer was the most powerful lever for successful ads. The tests also showed that:

- The offer was very price-sensitive. A premium offer of two portfolios for $1 was 274 percent as effective as one that offered the same two portfolios for $2.95.

- An offer that required no minimum purchase attracted 461 percent more members than one that required a commitment for the purchase of a minimum of four additional portfolios.

- An enrollment premium of the portfolios of van Gogh and Toulouse-Lautrec attracted 49 percent more members than a premium of works by Renoir and Degas did. Later, we found a successful way of offering Degas prints when I wrote the headline WOULD YOU GIVE AWAY THIS MASTERPIECE JUST BECAUSE IT CREATED A SCANDAL? It was the first time in the club's history that copy made a difference.

- The last-mentioned headline was 66 percent more effective than the headline that asked, CAN YOU ANSWER THESE QUESTIONS ABOUT ART? We discovered that people were interested in learning stories about art that they could repeat to their friends.

- An ad that showed a print in full color was no more effective than an ad in black and white.

The club was successful for years and made a great deal of money for Stevenson, Abrams, and Maxwell Sackheim's agency.

While we were fine-tuning Art Treasures, Stevenson had another idea. He had learned a lot from the success of the Children's Record Guild and a series of recordings of American classical music called "American Recording Society." In 1953, John sensed the potential of a major new mail-order business in records. The continuity club form, which offered subscribers a new product every month, was as suitable to classical records as it had been for books, art portfolios, and children's records. So we developed another club called "Music Treasures of the World." Stevenson realized that the most famous conductors, soloists, and orchestras were already under contract to major record companies, but he believed he could get some of the great European orchestras such as the Vienna Symphony to record for him if he agreed not to use their names. He was right, and he commissioned his first "anonymous" recordings from among them.

To determine whether the concept would work, we made the following copy test. Half the split run named no artists, and we made this a virtue. The copy read:

> You will note that we list no names of conductors, orchestras or soloists. This is because other contractual arrangements and our low royalties require that they remain unnamed. But if you have a trained ear—or if you have a friend who is a musician—their names will be revealed in their performances, as clearly as one's own signature.

The copy used in the other half of the test named the conductors:

> Music Treasures of the World selections are not low-priced reissues of old "flat" performances which were recorded on old-fashioned equipment for 78 r.p.m. shellac pressings. Music Treasures selections are new performances, played by internationally-famous orchestras, under the batons of such acclaimed conductors as Otto Ackerman, Walter Goehr, Paul Hupperts, etc., and recorded on the very latest equipment that captures the beauty and brilliance of every tone of the thrilling live performance with thrilling high fidelity.

Both ads produced a large and equal number of orders. Music Treasures of the World was an instant success. Our first wave of advertising attracted 500,000 members for as little as $1 each. Another early test revealed some interesting additional information. The test priced the Beethoven-Schubert premium record at different levels: $1, 10 cents, and free. The $1 price, a credible bargain, attracted the best and most profitable members. The 10-cent offer produced 30 percent more responses from members, but these didn't buy much or pay well, and most of them dropped out immediately. Surprisingly, the free offer attracted the fewest members. Early in my career I had learned that "free" is the best selling word in advertising, but in this case the perception was that "nothing good is free."

My work for Stevenson taught me about clubs and continuity series. What I learned from him was the catalyst for the next and most meaningful step in my career.

11

The Birth of the World's Largest Club

On a rainy day in March 1955, I was at my desk working on one of Charlie Perkins's emergency projects when the phone rang. Sackheim's receptionist announced that I had two visitors. I wasn't expecting anyone, so I asked who they were. She told me they wouldn't say. I was certain they were media salesmen or fund-raisers, so I went to the reception room to send them away.

There, I found two impeccably dressed men in their early forties. I asked who they were and why they had come, and their answer was that they would talk only in my office. Once there, I asked again for their names and the purpose of their visit. Their answer added to the mystery. They said they had been investigating me and wanted to ask a few questions. They were not then prepared to tell me any more, but they assured me it would be worth my patience.

I was intrigued. They asked intelligent questions about the mail-order business, mainly about clubs. They also asked about my education and my knowledge of literature, art, and music. Turning back to business, they wanted to know if I had ever done advertising in support of a sales force. Their questions were incisive and well organized. They had something in mind, but I couldn't guess what it was.

Finally they stood up, shook hands with me, prepared to leave, and said they would be back. I was frustrated and felt I was being set up, but I didn't know for what or by whom.

Less than a week later, I received a call from one of my anonymous visitors, asking to see me again that afternoon. This time I was determined to find out what they were up to.

That day, they opened the conversation with a new question: Could they depend on me not to discuss what they were about to tell me with anyone? That would be difficult, I answered. If the subject was business, I would need to talk to my boss, Max Sackheim. If it was personal, I wanted to be free to seek advice. They didn't think any of that would be necessary. They had a sensitive business problem to discuss, but they required total confidentiality to protect their company. They assured me I was not at risk. It was only their business that could be seriously damaged if our conversations leaked prematurely.

They then identified themselves as James Conkling, president, and Goddard Lieberson, executive vice president, of the Columbia Records Division of CBS. They apologized for having been so secretive, but they had a potentially explosive problem to solve. They had recently returned from a nationwide series of meetings with Columbia Records dealers and distributors. At each one, they had heard worried talk about record clubs. The independent clubs such as Stevenson's Music Treasures of the World were doing well. The Book-of-the-Month Club, *Reader's Digest,* and other large mail-order companies were approaching the major record companies and their recording artists, asking for the rights to sell their records by mail. They showed me a headline from *Billboard* magazine that read, RECORD CLUBS CLOBBER RECORD COMPANIES.

They had to deal with the record club question and act quickly. They wanted Columbia to take the initiative, but they didn't want their distributors, dealers, competitors, or the press to discover that they were talking to a mail-order advertising agency—not just yet.

They told me what was on their minds. For security, they wanted to talk to me personally, but not officially to the agency. They suggested a thirty-day consultancy. If I could solve their problem, they would then consider hiring the Sackheim agency. If I failed, they would pay $5,000 and that would end the matter. However, during the thirty-day consultation period, I was not to discuss the assignment with anyone but them.

I told them that I was flattered by their offer, but that they would have to let me tell Sackheim that I was going to be spending thirty days working on a confidential project for Columbia Records. I believed I could persuade him not to ask any further questions, but he would have to know what I was doing. They agreed. There was, however, a more serious obstacle. I was helping John Stevenson market the largest of the record clubs that were "clobber[ing the] record companies." Obviously, they knew it. It was my experience with record clubs that had led Columbia to seek me out, but that very experience would most likely prevent me from working for them. As a matter of principle, an agency could not accept work from a conflicting client without the approval of the existing one. I couldn't consult with Columbia Records without getting John Stevenson's permission.

That did disturb them. John was a member of the Recording Industry Association of America. He knew all its key people. He was friendly with the top executives of the Book-of-the-Month Club, which was seeking mail-order rights to classical records. Besides, his record business had a great deal to lose if Columbia started a record club that offered the best popular and classical recording artists.

How much would I have to tell him? they wanted to know. I said that, at the very least, I would have to say that a major record company had approached me with a consulting assignment. I wouldn't have to tell him the name of the company, nor would I have to provide details. I could ask Stevenson to protect the confidentiality of the assignment, but there was no assurance that he would do so. I told Conkling and Lieberson that I trusted Stevenson's integrity—but that he would be a fool to let me work on a project that might put him out of business.

We had reached an impasse, and they said they would have to reconsider the problem before making a decision. They left, and I was certain our discussions had ended. Putting myself into their position, I couldn't believe they would let me talk to a competitor about so critical an issue. Even if they could accept the idea, I saw no reason for John Stevenson to agree to it. It seemed a shame. It was just a matter of time before major record companies and their artists made their recordings available to clubs. I had been offered an inside track to a very large new business opportunity, but I couldn't exploit it. If Columbia or its major competitors found a way to start a record club or to offer their recordings to other clubs, they could destroy Music Treasures of the World, one of my largest clients. Once again I found myself threatened, but I had pledged to speak to no one, and I didn't.

Later that week, Lieberson called again. He asked if I could come to his office that evening. I said "Yes" and spent the next few hours wondering what to expect. At seven o'clock, I was at 799 Seventh Avenue, the Columbia Records headquarters. In the reception room I saw photographs of Bruno Walter, Isaac Stern, Rudolf Serkin, Leonard Bernstein, Frank Sinatra, Paul Weston, Benny Goodman, Louis Armstrong, and other CBS artists, a dazzling assembly. Conkling and Lieberson had adjoining offices separated by a small, private reception area furnished with Mies van der Rohe's Barcelona chairs and sumptuous leather armchairs by Charles Eames. This was Columbia Records, the fastest-growing record company in the world, a division of CBS, then the world's most imaginative and powerful radio and television network.

I entered Lieberson's office. He was surprisingly warm and cheerful. We chatted for a few minutes, and then he told me that they had considered their alternatives and I was the one they wanted for the job. If I had to talk to Stevenson, they would trust me to be circumspect. If I could persuade him to let me do this assignment, we could go to work. I was flabbergasted. I floated out of his office, forgetting for the moment the difficulties I would soon confront. It was wonderful to be wanted by Goddard Lieberson and CBS, but I was earning my living with Max Sackheim and John Stevenson.

The next morning, I went to see Max and told him what had happened and that I had promised to keep it confidential. I would need Stevenson's approval before going forward with Columbia, but he would have to depend on me to do nothing that wasn't in the best interest of the agency. Max created no problems. We had been working together for eight years. He trusted me.

I went to see Stevenson and told him that I had been approached by a major record company whose name I had promised not to disclose. It had offered me a thirty-day consultancy on the subject of record clubs. I would not accept it without his approval. I'll never forget his answer. He told me that we had come a long way together. He had made a lot of money from what we had accomplished. He would say nothing to anyone. All he asked in return was that I not divulge his advertising results or his future plans. He went on to say that we would continue working together as usual. I couldn't contain my excitement or my gratitude.

I returned to my office, phoned Lieberson, and told him that I was free to go to work. That evening, we met again. When I arrived, Lieberson and Conkling told me they wanted to include Al Earl, their next in command, in our discussions. He would be my day-to-day contact. We got right down to business.

Again they told me about their recent nationwide trip. Dealers everywhere had raised the club question. They were unhappy that clubs were getting an increasing share of the classical record business. They worried that Columbia, RCA Victor, and Capitol Records would soon make their records available to a third party such as the Book-of-the-Month Club. That would cost them even more customers.

When Columbia Records had invented the light, unbreakable, easily mailed LP record in 1948, record clubs had become inevitable. Lieberson and Conkling asked me to consider the following possibilities:

- They could try to help their seven thousand dealers set up a record club, but that would be difficult, if not impossible.

- They could license Columbia Records to a third party, such as the Book-of-the-Month Club. While that would earn additional profits for them, the lion's share would go to the Book-of-the-Month, and the record dealers would get nothing.

- Columbia Records could start a record club of its own, using its own repertoire. But its dealers would be furious. Columbia was then the largest record company in the world. No one could predict the outcome if Columbia challenged its own dealers.

Conkling was in favor of putting the dealers into the club business. Lieberson preferred to go it alone. Earl said nothing but looked worried. They told me I was free to recommend anything, no matter how novel or revolutionary. It was exhilarating to be invited by a powerful company to influence the way its whole industry did business. Mail-order advertising had attracted an important new player, and I had thirty days to invent the game.

I went to work on the problem at once. Regardless of the differences expressed by Lieberson and Conkling, it was clear that Columbia Records wanted to start a record club. But their dealers would fight any direct mail-order relationship between a record manufacturer and the consumer. So the problem was how to start a successful record club without provoking a war with the dealers.

I knew that when the Book-of-the-Month Club had begun, it had been attacked by booksellers. Lawsuits and requests for government intervention had gone on for years. Book-of-the-Month was a third party, buying books from all publishers, but Columbia was the prime manufacturer in its field and thus would be even more vulnerable to attack.

Launching a record club for Columbia was something like sailing a ship over Niagara Falls. No boat had ever survived it, but a woman in a barrel had. I spent two weeks trying to create an insulated "barrel" for a club the dealers could not destroy. Once over the falls, it would be clear sailing.

I had already used up half of the thirty days I had been given to solve the problem when an idea began forming in my mind. I knew the finished product didn't have to be a consumer marketing plan, merely the presentation the Columbia Records sales organization would make to its dealers. If Columbia thought the presentation was credible, I would then work on the design of the club itself.

I called Lieberson the next morning. I told him I had an idea that I liked and that I would present as promised at the end of thirty days, but I needed help. I wanted his permission to ask Ed Ricotta, then senior art director at Maxwell Sackheim & Company, to work with me. Lieberson agreed and wanted to know what I had come up with. I told him I wasn't quite ready to tell him yet but would give him a preview just as soon as I was. Ricotta and I then began working on a dealer presentation we hoped would persuade Columbia Records that it could launch a record club its retailers would accept.

In early April 1955, I was ready to give Lieberson the preview I had promised. I told him I believed the rewards of starting a record club were greater than the risks. A successful record club would help the record industry; record club selections would become best-sellers at retail, just as book club selections had. I had researched the correlation between book club selections and best-selling books at retail. I found that it wasn't necessarily best-sellers that became book club selections but often the other way around. A book advertised as part of a "Three Books for $1" new-member offer in a newspaper would frequently catch fire in the stores at full retail price despite the fact that new members could get it from the book club for just 33 cents. Book clubs spent millions of dollars each year advertising books and the pleasures of reading; publishers spent relatively little. The same could be true of a record club. The independent record clubs selling recordings of unknown artists were already outspending the major record companies, and it was advertising that worried dealers. What Columbia should do was launch a record club before its competitors or some third party did. The tactical problem was how to win dealers' acceptance of the idea. Lieberson interrupted me. How, he wanted to know, were we going to do that?

I unwrapped my presentation announcing the Columbia Records Dealers' Record Club. Columbia Records, in response to its dealers' needs, was going to create the first mail-order club designed specifically for retailers. Columbia Records would create a club headquarters, which would help track all of its complex data. It would advertise the dealers' club at its own expense. The advertising would advise people to apply for membership at their dealers. Dealers would forward the applications to headquarters for fulfillment. Columbia would pay for the free bonus records that would be offered to new members. The club headquarters would sell and ship members' records and allow members to buy on credit at the company's risk. The dealers would be paid a 20 percent commission on all sales made to members they enrolled. Since they would have no overhead or inventory, they would make more profit than they usually made on sales through their shops. The 20 percent they would earn on sales to club members would continue for the life of each membership.

It was a radical concept, the first attempt to combine retail traffic and in-home, mail-order selling. I believed dealers would accept it despite their historic suspicion of clubs because this club was created for them. It would provide sales and profits night and day, seven days a week—and give them commissions even if their customers moved or shopped elsewhere.

I could see that Lieberson was pleased. His only reservation was that the deal was too good for the dealers. It offered them more than he thought they deserved. He then proposed that I present it to Jim Conkling, Al Earl, and Hal Cook, Columbia Records' director of sales.

That would be a more difficult audience. I believed that Conkling and Earl would go along with Lieberson, but I was worried about Cook. He was responsible for the Columbia Records distribution network. The dealers and distributors were his customers and friends. He was good at his job because he thought like a dealer. He knew better than anyone else that while the record dealers talked a lot about clubs, what they really wanted was for them to go away. Dealers couldn't imagine a club that would be on their side.

As I walked to the meeting, I remembered a story, probably apocryphal, from the days when our office had been on Union Square, the site of political demonstrations, some of them pro-Communist. One day, as the police were roughing up some demonstrators, one yelled, "Stop, I'm an anti-Communist!" "I don't care what kind of Communist you are!" the policeman responded and continued to beat him.

I worried that Hal Cook would say, "I don't care what kind of a club it is, I'm against it." I was nervous. If Columbia Records management said "Yes," my life would change. Columbia Records was the most respected company in a highly visible industry. I was thirty-five years old, and this was my big chance.

Conkling opened the meeting by telling Cook that he and Lieberson sensed that the company was facing an enormous opportunity. They had engaged me to try to work it out. No matter how the meeting turned out, we were all sworn to secrecy.

As I went through my presentation, I never took my eyes off Cook. He paled when I began, and I knew what he was thinking. He was in an impossible position. Conkling and Lieberson were gambling with the company's profits, but Hal Cook's career was at stake. Conkling and Lieberson nodded enthusiastically to each other as I talked. Al Earl looked uneasy. Finally, we all turned to Hal Cook, who said, "I don't believe I'm saying this, but I'm for it. It's a great idea." He would have second thoughts later.

Everyone had questions: When could we launch it? What equipment would we need? Who would run it? How was a fulfillment system set up? How much would it cost? Who would do the financial plan? How could we keep it secret? Who would do the work?

So far, all I had was an idea, not a club. I told them that I would get to work on the rest of the plan but that I would need one of their people to work with, ideally the person who was going to run the club. They promised to appoint someone. Then Lieberson said the club would have to be launched by August 15 or it would be too late for the fall and Christmas seasons. Could I do it? It was now April 15; I said yes.

But what about John Stevenson? I had promised to tell him if there was going to be a next step. Now there would be a half step. Once again I needed Lieberson's permission. John was my client; I couldn't agree to do any more work for Columbia unless he said I could. Conkling and Lieberson had little choice. If they wanted my services, they would have to trust me and Stevenson. I went to see John and told him that the consultancy I had previously discussed with him had now resulted in a tentative decision by a major record company, whose name I still couldn't disclose, to launch a record club. It wanted me and the Sackheim agency to help them do it. While the possibility existed that its management would refuse permission, I had to begin to work. Stevenson understood what was at stake for me, him, and the record business. He said he believed it was inevitable that the major record companies would soon enter the club business. He would have to find solutions of his own. He also said, to my surprise, that for the time being, he would keep his account with our agency. Not many clients would have acted as decently, but there were very few men like John Stevenson in business—or anywhere else, for that matter.

My next task was to create the record club. I had assumed that the Columbia Record Club would be similar to the Book-of-the-Month Club, but it wasn't that simple. The twelve-inch long-playing record could hold an hour of entertainment for almost every musical taste. But the record market had become extremely segmented. Therefore, we couldn't choose one "record of the month." When I looked into Columbia's research, I discovered another major difference. A person who bought a book felt he was doing "a good thing for his family." A record buyer thought he was doing "a good thing for himself." I concluded that a record-of-the-month club based on the book club model wouldn't work.

But how could the club satisfy all musical tastes? No such club had ever existed. Searching for a helpful metaphor, I thought of a department store. A department store stocked goods for different purposes and needs. All the departments were under one roof. No matter which department you used, you entered the store through a common entrance. What I needed was a "department store" of record clubs.

My "department store" would be named the Columbia LP Record Club. Its departments would be called "divisions": "Classical Music," "Broadway Shows," "Jazz," and a category called "Listening and Dancing." Others could be added as needed. There would be one coupon or application, and the member would specify the appropriate division. A monthly club selection would be made for each division, but the member could refuse any selection or choose records from any other division. The concept of this multidivision club was a revolutionary change in club design. I was certain that a club that appealed to diverse tastes would attract millions of members.

I created sample ads for Lieberson's approval. The ads listed twelve of Columbia's hit records, three for each club division, and offered any one free to members who joined the club and agreed to buy four additional records during the first year. For every two records they bought, they would also receive a free bonus record. By fulfilling their commitments, members would buy a minimum of four records and get three free. That still left problems of cost for Columbia. So I suggested raising prices. Other experience indicated that a small charge for postage and handling would be acceptable to members because of the convenience of home delivery. The most controversial question we faced was which bonus records to offer. I wanted members to choose their bonuses from the regular Columbia Records repertoire. Hal Cook said the dealers would object unless we created special bonus records for members that were not sold in stores.

Arguments continued throughout May. I was certain that the club would help the retail record business, but Cook now feared that it would ruin it. He began to create additional obstacles. He argued that the only way he could sell the plan to his dealers was if Columbia Records agreed never to accept direct members. Conkling agreed with Cook. He had originally wanted a club only for dealers, and he still did. We created yet another financial model to prove that to make a reasonable profit, Columbia Records would have to enroll at least half of the members direct, free of commission. I was certain that no matter how cooperative dealers would be at the outset, their interest in the club would soon wane. Lieberson agreed. While we debated the issues, the clock kept running.

Something dramatic had to be done to break the impasse, and I wrote a report showing that the independent record clubs had already signed on a million members. By the first quarter of 1955, they had accounted for 35 percent of all classical records sold in the United States. They paid no commissions to dealers, and they would continue to grow if they remained unchallenged. I argued that they, or somebody like them, would soon try to sign Columbia's well-known classical artists and orchestras. They already had enough sales to guarantee large royalties. If some important Columbia artists signed with them, we could find ourselves preempted. To succeed, we had to launch our club at once and establish the principle of enrolling members directly. We couldn't fight a marketing war without weapons. My report refocused everybody's attention. They put aside their differences and prepared to meet the August 15 deadline.

In May, Goddard Lieberson told me that he had chosen Norman Adler, Columbia's in-house lawyer, to run the club. I was dismayed. I thought of how much I was going to miss John Stevenson's professionalism and experience. In 1955, there were no computers. The club I had created in theory might turn out to be impossible to operate in practice. The good news was that Norman Adler didn't know it. He told me that Goddard had assured him that I would teach him all he had to know about the mail-order business. But would there be time for that? We agreed that we would confer daily. Since our respective telephone operators were to know nothing of our plans, we established a secure, direct, private telephone line between our offices.

Despite my adverse initial impression, I quickly discovered why Lieberson had chosen Adler for the job. While he had no experience in marketing, advertising, record clubs, or mail order, he knew how to ask the right questions. As we became better acquainted, I discovered that he was not only intelligent but eccentric, humorous, forthright, and stubborn. He would not be diverted or satisfied until he knew the whole answer.

Though there were times when I thought him slightly mad, there never was a moment when I wasn't grateful to be his associate and friend. Every working day began with a call on our private line. Neither of us could have succeeded without the other's help. The task was too complex and the time too short. On June 1, the commitment to launch the club by August 15 was made.

When Norman later spoke about that period, he said, "Two days before Memorial Day 1955, I was called in and told that I was to be relieved of my legal duties and that I was to launch a record club (whatever that was) by August 15. When I asked about staff, premises, budgets, fulfillment organization and the like, I was told that I had an advertising agency and that if I went and talked to a Mr. Wunderman,

I would find out everything I needed. It was like driving a locomotive at full speed while laying track in front of it."*

As soon as we got the signal to go ahead, Norman went into action. He rented and furnished office space, hired and organized a complete staff, put into place a fulfillment system equipped to serve a tidal wave of members, ordered data processing equipment, created and printed hundreds of forms, and started a monthly magazine.

I, too, had a daunting agenda. I had eight weeks to produce and print more than fifty different kinds of dealer sales aids; prepare a national advertising campaign to break in every major newspaper and magazine; make radio and TV spots; and create a series of four-page ads for the trade press as well as the complete direct mail campaign for dealers, distributors, and distributor salesmen—all in total secrecy. For those eight weeks we lived on the edge of disaster.

All calls between CBS and the agency had to go through the private phone lines we had installed. Since we couldn't risk seeking competitive bids, I chose suppliers I trusted, battling their prices down to what I thought was fair. We pledged all of them to secrecy as a condition of getting the work. We made them hire special messengers whose only job was to pick up and deliver our material. We used a code name, "Alabama Hit Record Club," that had the same number of letters as "Columbia LP Record Club." We set type and placed orders in that name. We told the printers, binders, and engravers we had selected that for eight weeks they could do no work but ours. It was the only way we could make the deadline.

The dealer presentations, which Ricotta and I had created, were now put into production. They came to fifty-eight tons of top secret printed matter, all sent to subdepots under guard. On August 15, Western Union would deliver the presentation to Columbia Records dealers all across the country at 10:00 A.M. local time.

Our most difficult problem arose when the magazines and newspapers we had selected wouldn't accept our ads without knowing who the advertiser was. I went to see Fred Gamble, then president of the American Association of Advertising Agencies, and took him into our confidence. Gamble let us use his name and title on each publication order,

---

*Speech to Direct Mail/Marketing Association Annual Conference Oct. 12, 1960.

something he had never done before. We asked publishers not to spec-
ulate on the identity of our client. Gamble assured them that it was an
advertiser whose business they would be proud to carry. We checked
the closing date of every publication we were going to use. All of our
materials were shipped as close to the actual printing time as possible.

More than a million dollars for promotion was committed without
tests or margin for error. When I saw the finished material collated and
packed for shipment, I was terrified. Could we protect our secret? What
would we say or do if it leaked? How would the club be perceived by
the dealers—and the public? Would the ads bring in enough members?
Could we convince the dealers to accept a distribution revolution?
How would the trade press handle the news? What would we do if our
multimillion-dollar promotion bombed? Could the orders, if they
came in, be fulfilled? What if there were too many—or too few? Our
success would depend not only on what we did but on the precision
with which we did it.

The final schedule was as follows:

- *Wednesday, August 10:* All Columbia Records district sales managers would be brought to Chicago for a briefing. Each would receive a complete set of the promotional material we had prepared.

- *Thursday, August 11:* All Columbia Records distributors would be
  briefed by Columbia's district managers.

- *Friday, August 12:* Materials would be delivered nationwide to
  every Columbia Records distributor, so that they could brief their
  salesmen that day. Special kits would be mailed to the distributors,
  and complete folders would later be distributed to every Columbia Records distributor salesman. (We held off on the salesmen so
  that we could introduce the club to the retailers.)

- *Saturday, August 13:* A press conference would be held for wire
  services, the trade press, newspapers, and other interested parties.

- *Monday, August 15:* At 10:00 A.M. local time, complete presentations would be put into the hands of Columbia Records retailers
  all over the country by Western Union messengers.

- *Tuesday, August 16:* Columbia's distributor salesmen would deliver "Action Packs"—store display material too large for the original Western Union delivery—to every major Columbia Records

dealer. They would then answer the dealers' questions. They were prepared to explain the club concept and operations in detail.

- *Wednesday, August 17:* A saturation campaign of radio commercials would air in every major city in the United States.

- *Thursday, August 18:* Four-page trade paper ads would appear.

- *Sunday, August 21:* Every major newspaper in the United States would carry a full-page ad announcing the Columbia LP Record Club to the public, and from then on, nearly every day thereafter, a national magazine would carry the announcement ads. Two-page spreads would break in *Life, Look, Saturday Evening Post, Time, Newsweek, Collier's,* and thirteen other major magazines. Beginning August 17, we hoped that tens of thousands of prospects would pour into Columbia Records dealers with requests to join the club, and that the dealers would be ready for them. The dealers would forward membership orders to club headquarters, which would process them quickly.

That was the plan—and there were only a few mishaps. A driver of one of our printers' trucks in New York reported that a package of dealer manuals had fallen off his truck—but he didn't know where. We sent teams of men over the route the truck had taken, and they found the package unbroken and unopened. Lucky. Any "leak" or premature disclosure might have alarmed the dealers before we had explained the merits of our radical plan.

Despite our precautions, rumors began to leak the week before the launch. I received a call from the record editor of *Billboard* magazine, the main trade journal of the record industry. The editor was my cousin. He told me he had heard I was helping Columbia Records start a record club. I had to deny it. Nothing was actually published but the report of the rumor. Not a single leak of any consequence occurred. Not a delivery, not a shipment, not an ad went wrong—except one.

Our original newspaper ads suggested that people could join the club at their dealer or send their coupon directly to the club if there was no dealer nearby. The day after the ads were sent to the papers, Conkling and Cook, still worried about the dealers' reaction, told me to substitute new copy that would provide for enrollments only at dealers. I was told to call every advertising manager of every newspaper personally to be sure that the change was made. Only *The New York Times* got it wrong. It published an apology and ran the corrected ad without charge the next day, but its error, which showed that we had originally prepared an ad offering the alternative of direct enrollment, caused a furor. That was only the first of our problems.

The data processing equipment Columbia had ordered was not delivered on time, so the space built for it had remained unfinished. When the equipment finally arrived, the ceiling was still being plastered, and wet plaster fell into the keypunch equipment. Adler called down all the powers of darkness on the heads of the building contractor and the company that had sold CBS the equipment. Nothing helped, so he made alternate arrangements. For the first months after the club was launched, the data processing was done at night by the Drydock Savings Bank in New York.

We had known from the outset that our success or failure was in the hands of the record dealers. If they didn't rebel—if they could sell enough memberships to sustain their interest in the club—we would make a revolutionary retail entry into the mail-order business. My plan from the outset was to force the dealers to cooperate by flooding them with customers.

And that's what happened. No sooner had the dealers received the promotion materials than our advertising brought masses of customers to their shops asking to join the club. My gamble was that the dealers would accept the business—and in the main they did. We had given up 24 percent of our income to buy the dealers' and distributors' cooperation. We had presented them with a club of their own as a response to the growth of the independent record clubs. By concentrating our marketing efforts on the dealers' role in the club, we had successfully camouflaged Lieberson's main strategic purpose, which was for the Columbia LP Record Club to dominate the market.

As the dealer war came to an end, the battle for the consumer began. We had budgeted a $4 cost per member, but the first advertising campaign brought in members at $10 because the newspaper ads directed potential members to their dealers. To attract responses, advertising must be simple and allow prospects to respond when their impulse to buy is strong. The gratification of receiving things by mail is always deferred until the merchandise is delivered. Joining a record club at a record shop was a gratification twice deferred. First, you couldn't join the club from home, and then, when you went to the dealer's shop to enroll, you left without any records.

I knew that Cook and Conkling's "dealer coupon" would depress membership, and, as I had suspected, the club could not be profitable as launched. To succeed, we would have to find a way to encourage prospects to mail their coupons directly to the club. To do so, we invented a new form of enrollment that was to revolutionize the business once again.

The new enrollment form was a pure mail-order offer with one simple addition that read, "If you want this membership credited to an established Columbia Records dealer authorized to accept subscriptions, fill in his name and address here." The ad was now easy to respond to, and our customers could respond when they felt like it. They could also decide which dealer, if any, would be credited. A few dealers protested, but the direct memberships very quickly grew to 250,000. The cost per member was now less than our budgeted $4. Fewer than 10 percent of the new members filled in a dealer's name.

Dealers no longer feared the club promotions. Their major worry was that when their customers joined, they would remain in the club for life and stop buying records at their shops. We found that only half the members remained in the club more than a year, and the members who left the club became the dealers' most active customers. Even those members who remained for longer periods of time continued to buy at retail. The club was, in fact, what its research described as "a greenhouse for record buyers." We shared the good news with the retailers. As a result, in the fall of 1964, when we finally stopped using the dealer fill-in coupon in our ads, there were few objections. We also discontinued paying dealer commissions. The dealers had helped us launch the club, and, as it grew, they learned to live with it.

For the first two years, Columbia Records had the club market virtually to itself. The independent clubs couldn't successfully compete with Columbia's artists. Meanwhile, its major rivals, RCA Victor and Capitol, lost valuable time debating whether or not to risk starting their own record clubs.

12

Discovering the Magic Ingredient: Choice

The innovation that helped the Columbia LP Record Club serve constantly changing musical tastes was the concept of one club with many divisions. Had we imitated the Book-of-the-Month Club and selected one record of the month for all musical tastes, the club would have failed. By having members choose a division that reflected their main musical interest, we learned how best to serve them. As music technologies and audiences changed, the club continued to merge, drop, change, and rename divisions.

We discovered the importance of choice early in the history of the club. Our first ads offered members one record free for joining from the twelve records offered in the ad. While the ads were successful, they were not as productive as I had hoped. My original design for the club was to give members Columbia's best-selling records as bonuses, but the sales department protested. In 1956, we tested hundreds of ads and offers, but not until late in that year did we make a breakthrough by offering three hit records free against a commitment of four additional records in the first year of membership. This new offer was hugely successful. Membership grew so fast that Adler worried that as the club surged toward its first million members, it would outgrow its fulfillment systems. I argued that while we were still without competition, we might never again be in so favorable a position. I wanted to use the Columbia LP Record Club's profits and size to make competitive entry as costly as possible. Norman finally agreed. We expanded the advertising to attract all the members we could get.

By 1957, the club had a million active members, more than double the membership of the Book-of-the-Month Club, which was then thirty years old. Columbia opened a modern fulfillment center in Terre Haute, Indiana. In its first year, it shipped seven million records and processed more than twelve million pieces of mail. The postage bill alone was more than $1 million—and the club was just beginning to hit its stride.

The enterprise was becoming so large and complex that Adler recruited Cornelius F. Keating, another Columbia lawyer, as his second in command. Keating became a key player just as RCA Victor and Capitol Records were about to enter the club market. But we had learned something that RCA Victor and Capitol couldn't yet know: the critical element was a greater choice of product.

I discovered a new way to leverage that knowledge in 1957, when, after eleven years at Sackheim, I took my first real vacation—a month's tour of Europe, my first trip abroad. This made Adler nervous. I planned not to call him and had asked him not to call me unless there was a major crisis. I wanted to forget business. I made it through France all right, but by the time I reached Rome, Norman called and said, "I hope you're having as good a time in Rome as Nero did. While you're fiddling around Europe, our results have gone to hell, and there's no one here who can fix it." Norman told me to return at once. I said "No." I had, indeed, been fiddling around, but I hadn't stopped thinking about the club. In fact, I had had an idea in Italy that I thought could revolutionize the club's advertising. He wanted to know what it was. I told him it would have to wait till I got back. Norman was furious, but I was adamant. I asked him to be patient. For Norman that was an impossibility—but there was only one week of my vacation left.

What I had discovered in Italy was antipasto. Almost every restaurant offered it as an individualized first course for lunch or dinner. The idea of so many choices intrigued me, and the larger the selection, the longer the line at the antipasto table. Restaurant owners seemed to know this, because antipasto carts and tables were usually displayed prominently at the entrance. I made a point of counting the number of individual antipasto choices people took in relation to the number that were offered, and I discovered that they helped themselves to about the same number of dishes no matter how many were set in front of them.

I believed that the free records we were offering to new club members in our ads should be our "antipasto." Our first ads had offered one record free from a selection of twelve. Now we were giving new members three free records, but we still offered only twelve records to choose from—not enough. In fact, since the club had four divisions, each member had only three records from each division to choose from, and this was hardly any choice at all.

As soon as I got home, I saw Norman. He was ready to explode. After an abrupt "Hello," he demanded to know what I was going to do to improve the advertising results, which had fallen by 20 percent while I had been away.

I told him I had found the answer in Italy. "What is it?" he demanded to know. "Antipasto," I answered. I told him we had only to increase the antipasto to improve results. His face reddened. "Did you lose your mind in Italy?" he sputtered. "What does antipasto have to do with records?" He had learned that RCA Victor and Book-of-the-Month were about to offer all nine Beethoven symphonies, conducted by Arturo Toscanini, free to new members, and who knew what offer Capitol would make? Columbia needed a big new idea, and here I was talking about antipasto!

Finally, he let me explain. But he gave in grudgingly. He agreed to test an ad that increased the choice from twelve to thirty-two records. We tested it that fall, and our results almost doubled. The test ads were so effective that we decided not to use them at once but to wait until they could blunt the initial offers that were about to launch the RCA Victor and Capitol clubs. Although we had originally decided not to advertise in those issues of the magazines and newspapers that our competitors were going to use for their announcement ads, we now decided we should go on the offensive and compete ad for ad. We ordered the adjacent pages to RCA's and Capitol's ads for our "antipasto ads." It stopped them cold. Nineteen fifty-eight was the best year in Columbia's history.

Choice remains the key to the club's success today: current ads offer a choice of more than four hundred records. As it turned out, however, Columbia couldn't supply all the choices members wanted.

13
More Choices— From Outside

At a semiannual planning meeting in California, Norman Adler asked me a typically incisive question: If I were RCA or Capitol, what would I do to keep Columbia from continuing to dominate the club business? I told him I would organize an all-industry club that could choose the best-selling records from all companies.

He then asked what I thought Columbia could do to protect itself. I believed the problem was probably hypothetical. When RCA and Capitol launched their clubs, they were almost certain to follow the precedent we had set.

Norman summed up the conclusions of our discussion as follows: An all-label club would be the strongest competitive entry, but it wasn't likely to happen. RCA and Capitol would probably do what we had done and launch clubs offering only their own repertoire. If these sold only their own labels' repertoire, that would represent more than 60 percent of the records sold and would preclude multilabel clubs. Therefore, the right answer was obvious: if Columbia, RCA, or Capitol could arrange to offer its own share of hit records plus the independents' 40 percent share, such a club would become the predominant mail-order marketer of recorded music.

We decided to do nothing until RCA and Capitol committed themselves to single-label clubs. Then we would attempt to sign exclusive agreements with smaller independents.

In 1958, more than two years after Columbia launched its club, RCA, in partnership with Book-of-the-Month Club, entered the market, offering only its own recordings. Capitol did the same in partnership with John Stevenson, who had stopped marketing his own private-label clubs. Once they were committed, Columbia began negotiating and signing exclusive contracts with the independent labels.

By 1963, we had so large an advantage over our competitors that the industry encouraged the Federal Trade Commission to charge Columbia with unfair competition.

The lawsuit was one of the best things that ever happened to the Columbia Record Club. As long as the case remained unadjudicated, Columbia and its competitors were locked into place. Columbia's contracts with the independent labels remained in force, and RCA and Capitol couldn't approach those labels until the lawsuit was decided. Since Columbia had nothing to gain from a quick decision, its lawyers let the litigation drag on for years. Neither RCA nor Capitol could compete for Columbia's exclusive contracts.

Eventually, RCA and Book-of-the-Month ended their partnership and RCA gave its franchise to *Reader's Digest*. That didn't work either. Finally, RCA started its own club. Capitol, a division of a British conglomerate, took its club back from Stevenson and started its own, but Columbia remained out in front. It had the best product, the best people, and superior marketing. In 1962, Norman Adler became executive vice president of Columbia Records and Neil Keating replaced him as head of the club.

Neil was very different from Norman. Norman was refined and intellectual, with a subtle sense of humor, while Keating was Rabelaisian. He hated barbers, tailors, shoe-shine boys, manicurists, and nail-brushes. Among the well-tailored, well-groomed, sleek vice presidents at CBS, Neil looked like somebody's country cousin. That impression disappeared the moment he spoke. He would argue his point of view with anyone—and he was most often right.

Neil was also a generous, loyal friend. Over the years, the record club had many directors of advertising, some talented, some neurotic, some fools, egomaniacs, or incompetents. Many of them wanted to "get rid of the agency." They felt we had too much power and that they were not free to run the advertising department as they wished. Neil defended us. Without his support, we would have been fired.

Years later, when Neil Keating was asked to account for the club's ongoing success, he said:

We were always at the cutting edge, and Lester's agency was right there with us. We had the best people. CBS always gave us the investment money we needed. There was no mean-spirited, penny-pinching parsimony. The advantages we brought to the marketplace—guidance, choice, intelligence, the ability to have a charge account, convenience, shopping at home—were important. From the outset we created an environment in which people accepted that buying at home provided at least as good a bargain and better service than buying at retail.*

---

*1970 speech at Columbia Record Club Business Review Convention.

14

Inventing New Direct Marketing Media: "Gold Boxes"— Insert Cards— Newspaper Inserts

The Columbia LP Record Club had an insatiable appetite for media, an appetite that conventional direct marketing media practice couldn't satisfy. By 1958, the club had exploited all the media then available to direct marketing advertisers, including huge quantities of direct mail.

Most magazines, newspapers, and direct mail lists couldn't support more than one or two club ads a season. We could advertise in January and use our best mailing lists and publications again in late February, but then we had to rest them until July and September. We found that repeat messages dilute the medium, often by as much as 50 percent. General advertisers have a different point of view. They believe that the more they advertise, the greater their brand share. But direct marketing is wholly accountable, and our results tell us when a medium becomes fatigued. The club used full-page and two-page ads and lavishly printed mailings, but by 1958 we found we couldn't expand our sources of new members. At a million members, the club was very profitable, but we didn't want it to stop there.

I searched for clues to the more effective use of magazines. Even before we had done it for Jackson & Perkins, we had sought to place post-paid insert cards in mass magazines. Since I knew the publishers of all the major magazines, I began to persuade them to sell us space for the inserts; the card would be both the ad and the coupon. There were many objections: "Our presses can't handle it." "The post office won't accept the unit as part of the magazine." "Other advertisers will object." "It breaks the book so that it opens only at the card." "Our readers will be annoyed."

Because we now had large mail-order advertisers such as Columbia and J&P, I was able to persuade a few publishers to accept—and others soon followed. The card unit increased responses by as much as 500 percent. In time, we taught every major publisher of magazines how to produce and bind the inserts into their magazines. It was good business for them, as the ads were using unsold "airspace." Soon the Columbia LP Record Club was on its way to two million members.

As I had done years before with comic books, we now contracted with publishers for the insert card space and persuaded them to give us an exclusive option on the same position year after year, unless we canceled it. Our exclusive agreements held for a while, but publishers and other advertisers soon found that we were onto a good thing. Insert cards soon became a conventional media format.

But if we could put cards into magazines, why couldn't we create other new formats? Why couldn't we use magazines and newspapers as flexibly as we did direct mail? Direct mail advertising could be any size, shape, color, format, or texture we chose, as long as it was mailable.

We inserted a full sheet of gummed "value stamps" in *Life* magazine. Each stamp represented the cover of a record album, a whole *Life*-sized page of record album stamps that a customer could choose from and affix to a postpaid response card. We placed four- and eight-page glossy stock booklets in magazines. We discovered that newspapers could mechanically insert extra advertising sections into their Sunday editions. We printed four- and eight-page special inserts for them. These were precursors of the FSIs (freestanding inserts) now so widely used by packaged-goods advertisers. We were the first to use an "answer card" in newspapers. The "answer card" was a prepaid postcard, lightly gummed and affixed to the back page of a Sunday newspaper supplement.

Most of these formats succeeded, and some multiplied responses by as much as tenfold.

Because we printed these ads ourselves, we could use the media for testing by changing the ads on every second, third, or fourth sheet. Since publishers bound our ads in the exact sequence in which they were provided, we were able to create a new test medium in which only we knew the number and sequence of the test ads—and, most important, their results. These new media techniques expanded and intensified our advertising. We could now acquire millions of additional members.

One day at Idlewild (now John F. Kennedy) Airport, I noticed that the *Encyclopaedia Britannica* had installed a display unit that contained small, four-page, couponed card-stock ads called "take ones." I took one and showed it to our clients at Columbia as an interesting new medium. With some reluctance, they allowed us to print fifty thousand "take ones." We distributed some of them in the New York and Chicago airports. Nothing happened. After several months, Leslie Klemes, then the club's director of advertising, told us we had better find another way to use the booklets.

We got lucky. Our booklets were exactly the size of *TV Guide*, at the time America's fastest-growing magazine. *TV Guide* had a different edition for each city, listing local programming. The editorial section, in the front of the magazine, carried national advertising. This was followed by the local television listings, printed in black and white on very inexpensive paper. We asked *TV Guide* if it would staple our fifty thousand "take ones" into the center of the Baltimore edition, which had a circulation of fifty thousand. Again, we were buying "air rights" by inserting our ads between the pages of the magazine.

Thus we happily disposed of our nonproductive "take ones." What we didn't expect was that the inserts would produce more orders per thousand readers than any other medium had. When we examined copies of *TV Guide*, we understood why we had stumbled onto an advertising gold mine.

TV Guide looked like a magazine, but it was really a directory. People referred to it whenever they chose a television program to watch. Our four-page, full-color insert printed on heavy card stock, inserted in the middle of the magazine, was like a tollgate. Readers had to get past it every time they used the guide. To retest our results, we then used 250,000 inserts in several cities. Once again, we were flooded with responses. At the time, *TV Guide* was sold mainly in supermarkets and on newsstands. Subscriptions were discouraged. Therefore, much of the readership changed every week. Based on the results of our two tests, we ordered seven national, full-circulation center spreads for the record club with the option to buy them every year. Our stubborn search for a way to dispose of an embarrassment had led us to a bonanza. At its peak, *TV Guide* sold almost twenty million copies a week. It became Columbia's most profitable medium.

Because more than 50 percent of the club's members were lost to attrition each year, the secret of growth was the continuing discovery of new ways to acquire an increasing number of members. We called one of these ways the "Gold Box of Colorado." We created it in 1974 for an off-site planning meeting at Snowmass, Colorado. After Keating, an avid skier, replaced Adler, it became a tradition to spend half the day working and the other half skiing. The air at 8,100 feet was thin, but the atmosphere was free, congenial, and creative. It led to a solution to a problem that had been nagging us.

In 1972, the Columbia LP Record Club had decided to support its print advertising with television spots and had hired McCann-Erickson, a large general advertising agency, to create them. The commercials asked for no response. It was an unproven belief that people who saw the television commercials would be more likely to subscribe when they saw the club's ads or mailings. The club didn't know whether the commercials were successful, because it was difficult to measure the results accurately. McCann had sold the club an idea for television that it had accepted in the absence of a better one.

I was furious. If the idea was a good one, why hadn't we thought of it first? I believed that you never let a client "date" another agency for fear they will fall in love. We had to get rid of both the idea and McCann.

Peter Rabar was my partner on the Columbia LP Record Club account, as well as on Jackson & Perkins. Preparing for our next Snowmass meeting, I told him we would have to devise a better form of support advertising in time for the meeting. Nothing stimulated me to produce ideas like a deadline or a competitive challenge.

The week before the Snowmass meeting, I asked Peter to join me in my office to talk about "support" advertising. It could be justified, we agreed, only if it could be proven that it made more people look for a specific ad in a specific medium and if it increased the response. To be effective, it had to stimulate measurable action, not just awareness, as general advertising did.

Suddenly, I had an idea. What if we hid a secret "buried treasure" in the coupon of our print ads? And what if we showed on television where the treasure was hidden? Would it make more people look for and respond to the ad? Now the solution was only a step away. I told Peter that all we needed was to print a "gold box" on the ad. To the unknowing, it would look like a design element, just a yellow bar at the bottom of the coupon, until a television commercial revealed it to be a special "Gold Box." The commercial would also state that anyone who found it could get an additional free record. Only viewers who saw the TV commercial would recognize the Gold Box as a special offer and write the number of an additional free record on it. The free record would be sent along with the regular offer. We could safely print the yellow bar in all of our ads because it would have no meaning or value except in those cities where we chose to test the commercial and measure the effect of television support. All we had to do was count the number of coupons that came in with the Gold Box filled in, and we would then know exactly how many people who responded to our print ad had been motivated by the television commercial. We could test various levels of TV support in different cities and measure the value of the incremental TV responders.

And so, in 1974, the Gold Box of Colorado was conceived. It was to earn millions of extra dollars for Columbia and a great deal of extra advertising for us—but not all at once. We took one of our standard ads and asked our art department to put the yellow bar into the coupon. Then we wrote a commercial that told the "secret of the Gold Box," and took the ad and the storyboard with us to the Snowmass meeting. When it came time to discuss support advertising, we told the group that we had a new idea, a way of measuring the effect of support television for the first time and making it fully accountable. We presented the idea of the Gold Box and our ad and storyboard. I talked of the potential effectiveness of "buried treasure." The Columbia people didn't get it. They were disenchanted with support television and believed we had developed a competitive idea only to encourage them to fire the other agency.

In 1975, most of the club's advertising was unprofitable, and Columbia was worried about the next season. I again insisted that our

Gold Box was a revolutionary idea. It wasn't just support advertising, it was a fuse that could ignite ads in all media. My persistence was again written off as competitive spirit in high gear.

Not until December 1976, almost two years later, were we allowed to test the Gold Box against McCann-Erickson's efforts. Our Gold Box commercial was assigned to thirteen test markets and McCann's to thirteen others. The club agreed not to tell McCann about our tests. Each agency was given a month's time to spend whatever it thought appropriate for each of the markets it had been assigned. Thirteen additional markets would receive no television support of any kind. *Parade*, a Sunday supplement appearing in the test cities' newspapers, and local editions of *TV Guide* were chosen as the print medium to be supported.

McCann bought 300 to 400 gross rating points in prime television time in each of its markets. We bought far fewer, and our buys were in the less expensive fringe time. As a result, McCann outspent us by 400 percent in their markets. Moreover, our efforts were accountable, while theirs were the usual "creative" spots. The results were far better than our most optimistic forecasts. Even though we spent far fewer TV dollars, our Gold Box spot increased the results for the print ad by 80 percent in our markets, while McCann's spots increased the results in theirs by 19.5 percent. Every market supported by the Gold Box was profitable. In some markets, responses increased by 140 percent. That ended the competition.

What follows is part of the Columbia Record Club's internal analysis of the results of the test:

> Based on this data, it is apparent that the Wunderman campaign is the most cost-effective method for stimulating application response. Notice that the overall cost per estimated application (non–TV supported) is $18.60, while the overall cost per incremental application (due to TV support) is only $4.00. Not only did the Wunderman campaign increase application response, it did so at a lower overall cost per application.
>
> On the other hand, the McCann campaign is less cost effective than no TV support in stimulating application response. The overall cost per estimated application (non–TV supported) is $17.87 compared to overall cost of incremental applications (due to TV) which is $28.01. While the McCann campaign did increase overall application response, it also increased the overall cost per application.

The following season, every Columbia ad in all media included a Gold Box in the coupon. We produced better commercials, and in January we began to buy television nationally. The Gold Box became a national treasure hunt. The effectiveness of the campaign was startling. In 1977, none of Columbia's ads in its extensive magazine schedule had been profitable. In 1978, with Gold Box television support, every magazine on the schedule made a profit, an unprecedented turnaround.

I learned a lot from the Gold Box. I had found a way of getting our ads and mailings read. Furthermore, the Gold Box had made the reader/viewer part of an interactive advertising system. Viewers were not just an audience but had become participants. It was like playing a game. Later, we used similar techniques for Time-Life Books and other clients, and they worked just as well. Still later, our offices in Spain, the United Kingdom, West Germany, and France applied the idea to their markets with equal success. The Gold Box created readership; the offer led to action. Both are the lifeblood of direct marketing.

Game playing via media would be offered as a media revolution years later, when billions of dollars would be spent creating interactive television and computer data systems. We had accomplished the same thing by using our primitive media tools and a Gold Box.

From the beginning the Columbia LP Record Club has been a laboratory for direct marketing experimentation and a school for training experts. So has our agency. We have worked together using the best analytical tools available. Over the years, for example, we discovered that response "levers" can be engineered. They can be in the offer, the method and time of payment, the way a medium is used, or how a product or service is presented. Some ads contain as many as eight levers in the offer section alone. Some years ago, *TV Guide* began to offer two insert cards in each issue: one up front, in the editorial section, and one in back, in the program section. Conventional advertising practice has it that ads located in the front of a magazine always do better than ads at the back. In *TV Guide,* we had our choice. We opted for the back insert because it was in the program section, and when we tested both, the back insert was 18 percent more effective than the one in front. The general advertisers with cents-off coupon ads for their packaged-good brands bought the front position, in accordance with the rules of good response advertising. They wasted money because they didn't see the need for testing.

· · ·

But in spite of our success with Columbia, we also made mistakes. Keating and I were troubled by the "Teen Hits" division. We felt that there were people who liked the music the division offered but were not teenagers. We sought a better name and came up with "Today's Sounds." It was a good name, we tested it, and the tests were very positive. They showed that the name change didn't affect the number of people who joined the club, but it did change the mix of members. The ads we had been using enrolled 50 percent of our new members in the "Teen Hits" division. With the test ad, which carried the name "Today's Sounds," 72 percent were enrolled. So we changed the name of the division. A year later, we realized that we had made a costly error. Members of the "Today's Sounds" division didn't behave the way "Teen Hits" members had. They bought fewer records, returned more of them, took longer to pay, and canceled faster. Though the new name was attractive, it misled many members, who weren't offered the records they really wanted—the category was too general. We calculated that by making the name change in our offer, we had, in one year, cost the club $5 million in sales and $1 million in profits.

Another problem had surfaced when we began with four divisions and immediately discovered that the behavior of members in each division was different, even though they all joined the club from the same ad in the same medium. In the early days, the "Jazz" division attracted many members who didn't pay their bills, and the club wanted to drop this "deadbeat" division. Later, we found that a division that attracted bad members helped us quarantine them. We kept the "Jazz" division but restricted the credit offered to its members until we learned which of them might become delinquent. Later, "Rock & Roll" was the leading "deadbeat" division: Chubby Checker single-handedly attracted more members who didn't pay their bills than any other artist did.

The really bad times came when all the divisions became "deadbeat" divisions. That could have meant the death of the club. So far, we had made most of the media work by imposing credit limitations to control bad debts. We had learned that coupons written in pencil were more apt to be delinquent. So were those in which not all the questions asked in the coupon were answered. We hired graphologists to analyze handwriting as predictors of creditworthiness. We devised new credit questions. The easy ones didn't reduce responses, but neither did they reduce credit losses. Tough questions such as: What is your phone number? Name of employer? Name of bank?—each reduced the number of responses by 20 percent, but they didn't stop the bad debts. Eventually, as many as 65 percent of our new members never paid their first bill. They kept the records offered for enrollment and any additional records they received, but they never paid. We learned that records appeal to the very young, the unemployed, the disadvantaged, and those who simply like to get something for nothing. Soon the situation had become critical. Our acquisition "levers" were still working, but the more new members we enrolled, the more money the club lost. During the late 1960s, bad debts became almost the only subject we thought about or discussed. For the first time, the club, which had grown every year, began to cut back on its advertising and shrink its membership. We were using the income from good old members to offset the losses from bad new ones.

We began to think of everything in our experience or anyone else's that we could learn from. The book clubs couldn't help us; they didn't have the same problem. Books appealed to older, more upscale members. They didn't use mass-media advertising. Their major medium was direct mail, which permitted the clubs to select lists of prospects who were proven good credit risks. Columbia did that, too, but we needed more media exposure to sustain growth. Columbia was not the only record club that was suffering. Weighed down by bad debts, the Capitol Record Club eventually went out of business, and the RCA Club also cut back its efforts. Once again, we were called on to solve a difficult problem.

As I thought about it, it occurred to me that the only solution would be to make new members pay cash in advance for the enrollment offer. There must be a number of records, I believed, that could be offered at a price so appealing that new members would pay for them in advance. The problem had always been to collect the first payment. It not only qualified the credit but also offset some of the cost of enrollment. It was radical medicine. No club had ever demanded payment in advance. We tested some ads and found that asking for payment in advance cut the number of responses by more than 50 percent. That was disappointing, but the offer also significantly reduced the percentage of bad debts. We had identified payment in advance as a key lever, and now we had to find a way of using it profitably.

The solution, when it came, was revolutionary. We created an ad that contained three different cash offers by which new members could join the club. They had the choice of paying $1, $1.86, or $5.95 for a different number of enrollment records, but the terms were all cash in advance. Those who chose to pay only $1 were subject to more rigorous credit screening, but 50 percent paid $5.95. All these new members were of superior quality, and we could invest much more in advertising to attract them. For example, when we offered credit in *TV Guide* we could afford to spend only $4 a member in advertising, and that was barely profitable. With our new cash offers, we could afford to pay 600 percent more, or $28 per member, and make an acceptable profit. Once again, we could afford to attract millions of new members each year. The offer had restored the club's profit and our advertising budget.

The Columbia LP Record Club and I learned the general principles of direct marketing together. Over time, we learned that members will take many kinds of actions: reject or return records, cancel their membership, ask for bonus records, get friends to enroll, and so on, and each of these actions affects profits and teaches something. Each ad, each medium, and each group of members has different performance characteristics. The current costs of advertising, the immediate results achieved, and the future sales anticipated can now be predicted by experts who have mastered a very complex set of tools. There are at least twenty-one different ways of controlling the results achieved by any aspect of an ad, ranging from the offer itself to the way it is presented. Is the premium delivered at once, or is it deferred? Does the ad ask for cash or offer credit? How many products are provided for the prospect to choose from? What are they? Are there credit questions to be answered? What are they? What is the size of the ad? One page? Two pages? A special section? What does the headline promise? How often does the copy repeat the commitment? How is it worded? Does the ad make more than one offer? If so, how many? How large is the coupon? Where is it positioned in the ad? Is prepayment encouraged or made necessary in the coupon? If the ad is a television commercial, how long is the toll-free number shown on the screen? Is it stated as a number or as a word? And so on.

Each of these elements and more have dramatic effects on both the number and quality of the responses received. If you don't know what they are and how best to use them, you probably won't maximize the potential results. Every good direct marketing ad or offer wears out—sometimes in a few months, more often in a few years. Unless you know how to create and test new ideas and measure their effectiveness, you are likely to get lost. Small changes make large differences; even no changes make differences. But good ideas can be unbelievably rewarding. Only direct marketing experience can create good direct marketing professionals. I have seen talented general advertising practitioners fail at direct marketing time and again—not for lack of talent but because they don't know what levers to use. Direct marketing works best for those who know what they are doing.

Today, the music club has fourteen divisions from which members can choose. These divisions change as musical tastes diversify. In January 1982, the club started a videocassette division. While many believed that few people would pay a high price to buy videotapes, which could be rented inexpensively, the video club has grown at a surprising pace—and very profitably. By 1996, it had more than five million members.

Neil Keating, who was Columbia's CEO until he retired in 1994, attributed much of the success of the club to the way it handled new technologies. "We always got an after-boost from technology. When something new came out, we were always at the cutting edge."* The Columbia Videocassette Club was again first in the market.

Courage, imagination, and innovation have paid off for Columbia. Today, it has more than thirteen million members and is the largest in the world. It sells $1.5 billion worth of audiotapes, CDs, and videotapes a year.

*Speech to Direct Marketing Idea Exchange 1982.

15

The American Express Card

In April 1958, I became involved in another secret project, this time with American Express, which wanted to change the way Americans paid their bills.

Ralph T. Reed, then the chief executive officer of American Express, was an old-fashioned autocrat. He had passed retirement age but remained as CEO. A short man who wore elevator shoes, he was sensitive about his age and appearance. When he made public appearances, he refused to be photographed. Pictures of a younger Mr. Reed were available from his public relations office.

I met him first in his office at American Express. To my surprise, we were alone. He explained that his company's stock was publicly traded and that if the financial community heard prematurely about the arrangement he was about to discuss with me, the price of the company's shares would become volatile. I soon discovered, however, that he had another reason for secrecy: he didn't want anyone else to know what he was doing until the crucial decisions had all been made. I had lived with similar restrictions three years earlier with Columbia Records, so I was not unprepared to maintain secrecy.

Mr. Reed spoke softly, even though we were behind closed doors. Later, others told me that his quiet manner masked a terrible temper. But as we talked, I found him charming and articulate. He told me he had always wanted "his company" to create a new form of money—so powerful, so prestigious, so ubiquitous that it would become an international currency. He wanted it to be a secure currency like the popular and universally accepted American Express Travelers Cheques, one that if lost or stolen would not be useful to anyone other than its original owner. It was this new financial instrument that he wanted me to help develop for American Express.

He already knew what he wanted, but before he told me what it was, I had to understand the American Express Company. He explained that millions of Americans traveled domestically and internationally for business. He believed that this traffic was going to grow as business and leisure travel became more international. American Express already arranged reservations for business and pleasure trips. It conducted group tours. It arranged for the rental of private automobiles with or without guides and drivers. It helped its customers secure passports and visas.

As he spoke, he communicated his enthusiasm for and pride in his company and its relationship with the people it served. I saw why he was reluctant to step down from his job: not only was he the leader of one of the world's most powerful companies, he had a vision and a mission. I liked that. The assignment he had in mind was likely to break new ground.

Mr. Reed went on to describe his company's financial services: American Express Travelers Cheques, sold by banks, travel agents, and American Express offices and spendable as cash worldwide; American Express Money Orders, which protected any financial transaction by mail; and many other banking services offered through the company's overseas offices. The company also had shipping services for commercial goods and personal effects.

As Mr. Reed spoke, I began to anticipate what he had in mind. American Express was in the service business. It protected its affluent and powerful clients' time, pleasure, money, and property. He wanted to expand the services American Express offered to this select segment of the American public.

Finally, Mr. Reed paused and seemed to wait for me to speak. I wasn't sure what I was supposed to say. I really wanted to say, "Mr. Reed, this is a nice company you have here—now let's get to the problem." But I understood the protocol. I was being guided to a point of view he wanted me to share. It was crucial that I understood that this was American Express, and anything it did would have to be done differently and better. It would also have to be what Ralph Reed wanted.

I answered carefully. I told him he had told me that American Express already provided more services to businessmen who traveled than any other company in the world but that there might be a way to serve those executives in a new way, that American Express was just a step away from being an even more comprehensive executive service business.

He looked at me the way a professor focuses on a promising student and asked what I thought that step would be. A new kind of travel and entertainment charge card, I guessed.

"Ah, just so," he answered. Then he handed me a paper that contained six questions:

1. Should the American Express Company market a charge card?
2. What kind of services should the American Express Company make available through a charge card?
3. At what price should the American Express Company sell such a card? Should the price be presented as an annual fee or a monthly activity charge?
4. How should such a card be marketed?
5. How many charge card customers can the American Express Company enroll by December 31, 1958?
6. What would be the approximate cost of the required promotional activity?

He wanted answers to those questions in thirty days. If he liked my answers, I would have an assignment.

When I asked if I should talk to anyone else at American Express, his voice turned cold. He told me not to talk to anyone without his permission. Again, I asked if I should at least be in touch with Mr. Howard Clark, who I knew had recently become executive vice president of American Express. He answered bitterly in words I have never forgotten: "They forced me to hire him, but they can't make me talk to him." What Ralph Reed didn't know was that Howard Clark would succeed him in two short years and go on to be one of the most successful and respected CEO's of American Express.

I had met two Mr. Reeds: the visionary and the despot. I wondered which of them I was going to be dealing with. On my way out, I stopped in his personal men's room. The urinal was full of ice. I was not surprised.

I couldn't begin to answer the six questions until I understood the market. First I had to know who was already serving the market and how. In 1958, there were two kinds of charge cards being marketed: single-service and multiple-service. More than 5,000,000 single-service cards had been distributed by gasoline companies such as Texaco (1,700,000 cards), Hilton Hotels (850,000 cards), American Telephone & Telegraph (1,500,000 cards), airlines (800,000 cards), and so on. These cards were issued without charge, except for the airline cards, which required a prepaid deposit. It was clear that the number of free, single-service cards would grow enormously—as would the wallets required to carry them.

There were, at the time, two multiple-service billing cards: Diners Club, which had entered the field in 1950 and whose members paid a $5-a-year membership fee, and the Esquire Club Card, marketed by *Esquire* magazine and similar to the Diners Club Card; both of them offered mainly charge privileges in restaurants. The key fact I discovered about the Diners Club Card was its accelerating growth. As of March 31, 1958, it already had 560,000 cardholders and was aiming to have 760,000 members, who would charge $150 million by April 1, 1959. Ralph Schneider, the chairman of Diners Club, said in a public statement, "We are nowhere near the saturation point—our membership growth is limited only by our capacity to handle the influx." At the time, no bank cards existed.

My first task was to identify the market, then devise a better way for American Express to serve it. I had no doubt that with the right services American Express, with its reputation and marketing power, would eventually dominate the market. The service we would create should flow from the unique facilities and character of the American Express Company. If we could accomplish that, it would be relatively simple to develop better ways to find the right audience.

We had to find out who bought Diners Club Cards and why—and what would induce them to buy a new card. We also had to know why people did not join Diners Club. What did they want that Diners Club didn't offer? I hired Crossley, S-D Services, a major research organization, to help me find the answers.

Despite Mr. Reed's initial insistence that I talk to no one else at American Express, he finally understood that I needed someone to work with on a daily basis. It was then that I met Robert Mathews, whom Reed had chosen to manage the charge card if and when it was launched. With his help, we created a list of potential services for the American Express Card. I knew that some American Express executives worried that too many services would entail a serious credit risk. (They would later turn out to be right.) Others worried that the charge card would cannibalize the travelers cheque business. I wanted to create two lists of services: one that would serve the needs of people similar to those of Diners Club members, another for senior executives of well-rated companies. For working purposes, I called the first proposed product the "general card," and the second the "executive card."

The lists of services we developed and researched covered a far greater range than had ever been offered by a single charge card, a range that only American Express had the means of offering. We created the basic list in 1958. It was meant to serve both the general and executive cards, but a credit limit of $100 a month would be imposed on general card members. Executive cardmembers would have no credit limit. The services were:

- Reservations and tickets through a specified local office for plane, train, steamship, cruise, and bus travel
- Hotel rooms (including advance reservations)
- Motel accommodations
- Restaurants and nightclubs
- Chauffeur-driven limousines
- Drive-yourself car rentals
- Fly-yourself plane rentals
- Baggage shipment services
- Gift shops
- Florists
- Liquor stores
- Telegrams
- Gasoline and oil

Our research showed that 46.5 percent of the Diners Club card-holders who had been interviewed were willing to pay more than $5 a year for these services, while 36.7 percent of consumers who had free single-service cards said they would buy the new service and pay more than $5 a year for it.

We also showed the list of services planned for the executive card to presidents of substantial corporations. Again, the results were positive: 45.7 percent said they were very likely to buy a card for themselves and their key executives, and 41.7 percent said they would pay more than $15 a year for it.

Other information we gathered helped us plan our promotional copy: 77.8 percent of Diners Club cardholders said the card was valuable for keeping tax records and itemizing expense accounts. They also pointed out that with the card they didn't have to carry cash. The Diners Club Card was being used for business by 89 percent of its cardholders.

When I finished writing the first rough draft of the proposal, it was time for another meeting with Mr. Reed. He was eager to see me.

Before I began, I told him I wanted his approval for some key points. The first was that American Express should offer a prestige card to give members the sense that they were joining a select group. The second was that it should offer more services than any other card. This would expose American Express to an increased credit risk but would help position the American Express Card apart from and above the others. The third was that American Express should charge more for its card than Diners Club did. As Mr. Reed himself had said, American Express was highly respected and world-famous. Copying the competition's price would suggest weakness. He asked how much more American Express should charge. I told him I wasn't sure, that the pricing strategy would be psychological and not based on cost. Price would have to become part of the American Express image. I was not as concerned about the exact price as I was about setting the right precedent and market position.

I then read three fundamental positioning points I had drafted for the report: "The American Express Card provides the most universal charge card service in the world: more services available in more places." "The American Express Company . . . can add a new dimension of authority and respectability to the charge card field." "Don't carry more money than you can afford to lose is as meaningful a position for the charge card as it is for Travelers Cheques."

He agreed with these positions but was concerned that I had said nothing about the card being for the special people that the American Express Company was uniquely in business to serve. I was still working on that part of the report, but I read it to him from my longhand draft:

We believe that the American Express Card should be a prestige instrument, which will appeal to the ego of the user and influence suppliers of services as well. . . . We believe that this image will be enhanced if American Express Card members seem to be appointed by recommendation only—just as if the member were being accepted into any other exclusive group.

At that point, he asked if he had heard me say "members." Yes, I told him; they should be members. I read further: "These people are not going to buy a card as a product. They, as members, are going to become eligible to receive services as part of the special relationship that you and they will build together." He answered with enthusiasm. What I had just read to him was exactly what he had been trying to explain at our first meeting.

I knew I had made a sale. His agreement was all we needed; the others would follow his lead. When I left his office that day, I didn't know I would never see Ralph Reed again. I finished the report and delivered it to Max Sackheim, and then I felt depressed. An exciting new world of marketing was being born, and Max Sackheim's mail-order advertising agency seemed an unlikely midwife. Columbia Records and American Express had demonstrated that America's largest companies were going to be involved in this new world—a world I wanted to be part of—but Max and I didn't share the same view of the future. I decided it was time for me to explore these new possibilities on my own.

When the American Express Card was launched on October 1, 1958, I was already gone. I did no further business with American Express for the next twenty-eight years. American Express entered my life again in 1986 and went on to become my agency's largest global account—but that story is a few chapters away.

16

How to Start an Advertising Agency

A ugust 19, 1958, was a hot, steamy summer Tuesday. New York was experiencing what weather forecasters call an "air inversion," a system that keeps the bad air in and the good air out. I thought it was an odd day to have cold feet, but I was nervous. Max's company was suffering from an "ownership inversion," which I felt was keeping bad people in and good ones out. I was going to do something about it—that day.

I had decided to resign from Maxwell Sackheim & Company. It wasn't a sudden decision. I had been thinking about it for a year. When I left my suburban home that morning and said good-bye to my wife, Liljan, my six-year-old daughter, Karen, and my nine-year-old son, Marc, I wondered whether I was doing the right thing. After I resigned, life would be more difficult for all of us.

Max and I fundamentally disagreed on many things. As I drove toward the city, I reviewed the events of the past year. We saw the future differently. He thought his advertising agency was mature and stable. He was spending half his time in retirement in Florida, trying to run the company from there. I didn't think that would work. He wanted his two sons to succeed him, and I didn't think that would work either. I believed then, and still do, that an advertising agency is a service business that has only the talents of its people to sell. To grow, it must attract promising professionals and constantly upgrade their skills. It must also attract new clients. Agencies that stop growing and changing die. No advertising agency has a secure franchise. Employees are always free to leave, and the contracts the agency has with its clients have ninety-day cancellation clauses. Even the most successful advertising agency has earned only the right to do its clients' next campaign.

A year earlier, in June 1957, I had tried to resign when Max showed me a reorganization plan. The plan was that the Sackheim family would retain control of the business after Max's retirement. I couldn't accept that. Max then asked me for a counterproposal. With the help of an attorney, I gave him my objections in writing.

The following month, Max, with his lawyers and his two sons, met with Ed Ricotta, Irving, and me. I was not concerned about the stock percentages to be made available to each person. The key issue was control of the agency, its personnel, and its strategy. Max told me that he and his family rejected my suggestions, and I said I'd resign. Ed and Irving also said they couldn't accept Max's plan. We had another stormy meeting on July 4 and agreed on a compromise, one that said that upon Max's retirement, Ricotta, Irving, Max's two sons, and I would select a new president by majority vote.

On July 11, I sailed for Europe on that long-deferred vacation with assurances that the arrangement we had agreed to would be written and ready for signature when I returned. But on my return the papers did not conform to the agreement we had reached. They included a two-year restrictive covenant, which I couldn't accept. This stated, in effect, that if I left the agency for any reason, including being fired, I couldn't work for any of the agency's clients for two years. The covenant was also to apply to Irving and Ed Ricotta, but not to Max Sackheim or his sons. This looked like a trap. Obviously, Max couldn't face a future in which neither he nor his sons had complete control of the business, and I had no confidence in a future in which they did. And that was the way matters stood. We had an uneasy truce, but no one believed we had seen the end of the problem. It was no way to run a business or a life, and a year later I decided to break the stalemate.

I was thirty-eight years old, and I had choices. I was the best-known young executive in the growing field of direct response advertising. Most people thought I was Max's partner, but in fact I owned no shares in the agency. I had received other job offers regularly, but I had not been interested. I loved my work, but at the moment I didn't like my job.

I wasn't driven by the need for money or power. I had other things on my mind. A line from Spinoza haunted me: he had defined freedom as "the recognition of necessity." From childhood on, I had been forced to do what was necessary out of fear and insecurity. Now it was time to rethink my necessities. I felt ready for another kind of freedom, the freedom to follow my own vision. And this meant I would have to resign.

I told Irving, Ed Ricotta, and Harry Kline, one of Sackheim's account supervisors, of my decision. They said if I resigned, they would too. I couldn't have stopped them if I had wanted to—and I didn't. Our interests had been joined by the pressure of our negotiations with Max, his sons, and their lawyers. We were "the others," who had been dealt with as outsiders in the negotiations. Our reactions were the same. We didn't want to work for Max as an absentee owner or for his sons.

We didn't know what we would do after we left Maxwell Sackheim & Company, but we all knew we couldn't go on as we were. When we had objected to Max's plan for reorganization, we had known that Max would get rid of us, one at a time, as soon as he found replacements. Morale in the agency was low, and some clients were beginning to feel uncomfortable about the agency's unresolved problems. Something had to be done.

It was eleven o'clock when I entered Max's office. I sat down, looked at him, and thought of the twelve years I had spent with him. He had fired me once, and I had refused to leave. Now I knew he would accept my resignation without comment. We had been successful colleagues, but our interests were no longer the same.

Max looked at me without expression, waiting for me to speak. I swallowed hard and told him I had concluded that the best thing I could do was resign. He seemed neither shocked nor surprised and asked who was leaving with me. I said I didn't know. It was over. No handshake, no drama, no protests, no recriminations. Within the hour, Ed Ricotta, Irving, and Harry Kline also resigned. Max accepted their resignations without comment, and the four of us went to lunch. Having resigned, we were free to discuss the future, including the possibility of starting an agency of our own. When we returned to the office, we found that we had been locked out. The receptionist said she had instructions from Mr. Sackheim not to permit us to enter. My files and possessions had been "impounded." I understood the need to protect the company records, but I didn't understand why my personal belongings were being held. I needed my desk diary, phone book, brief-case, tax records, and personal papers. Max even had my winter ga-loshes.

Maxwell Sackheim & Company was then located just across the street from the Hotel Winslow. I registered there, taking the least ex-pensive room at $30 a day. It contained a single bed, two chairs, a small desk, a bathroom, and, most important, a telephone.

It was Wednesday afternoon, August 20, the first day of my new life. Irving, Ed, and Harry joined me in my "office" at the Winslow. Our combined assets were about $60,000. We had no real office, no com-pany, no credit, and no clients. And we would have to live on our cap-ital until we had some income.

I assigned each of us to a task. Ed Ricotta was to design stationery for our new agency, which we decided to call Wunderman, Ricotta & Kline, Inc. Irving and Harry Kline were to find inexpensive office space to sublet—we would move in at once. My lawyer would draw up pa-pers of incorporation and hire an accounting firm experienced with ad-vertising agencies (it would help us choose a bank). And my task was to call clients, who I hoped would give us work.

First, I called Ken Tack at Jackson & Perkins. He said that Max Sack-heim had called Charlie the previous afternoon and told him that I had "gone crazy and quit." Charlie was very upset. He didn't want Max and me to break up. Charlie was going to fly down to New York to play peacemaker. Ken then put Charlie on the phone. He asked me to meet him at La Guardia Airport that night. I said I would.

Since Charlie was not due to arrive until late, I met Harry Kline for a drink at the Saint Moritz Hotel on Central Park South. Edward Van Westerborg, the owner of Facts on File, joined us there. (He had been my client for fifteen years, first at Casper Pinsker's and then at Sack-heim.) He said he had some advice for me, and some business. First, the advice: He had watched me grow as a professional and as a person. He believed I could build a successful business, but I would have to learn to be more patient and thorough. Then he asked if we had any clients. Not yet, I told him. He wanted to know if we had chosen a name for our new company. Wunderman, Ricotta & Kline, I told him. He raised his glass and said, "I am proud to become the first client of Wunderman, Ricotta & Kline. You have my account as of now." And so we had our first client before we had an advertising agency. The rest would not be so easy.

I left Harry and Ed at the Saint Moritz and drove to La Guardia Airport to meet Charlie. I knew I had given him a tough problem. He and Max were contemporaries. Their wives were friends. They had much in common. I had helped Charlie build his business, but I had done it as Max Sackheim's employee. I knew Charlie would be fair, but beyond that I didn't know what to expect.

Charlie arrived, shook my hand, and asked if I was as crazy as Max had said. I told him I thought I had done a very sane thing. He asked me to tell him about it as we drove to his hotel. He asked questions all the way in. He had had no idea that Max and I were having problems. I told him everything. I described the offers Max had made and why I couldn't accept them. Since Charlie was Max's age and had two sons of his own, I worried that he would identify with Max and his family. We arrived at Charlie's hotel, went into the bar, and talked past midnight. Finally, Charlie turned to me and asked if I trusted him. I answered with an unequivocal "Yes." He then said that he wanted me to do whatever he asked of me, even if we had to argue like hell about it. I promised I would. Charlie said he had arranged to visit Max first thing in the morning. He would call me at the Winslow and tell me what happened.

It had been a long, taxing day. I drove home but was too nervous to sleep. In a few hours, I would have to be back in New York. There was so much to be done.

The following morning, I got to the Winslow early. I tried to reach Norman Adler and found him at the Columbia LP Record Club's headquarters in Terre Haute. He had already heard from Max and had made an appointment to meet him later in the week. Norman didn't want to discuss my resignation on the phone. He said we would talk when he got back to New York. He sounded cool and distant.

I then called other clients. Their reactions didn't help my morale. Al Dorne, head of the Famous Artists Schools, was furious with me. Why hadn't I told him earlier that I was leaving? I couldn't, I answered, because I had been advised that it would have been premature and illegal. He said angrily that now I was being legal, but I was still premature. He didn't want to do business with four out-of-work guys in a hotel room. This worried me. Dorne had been brutally frank. I had believed he would give us some work. Both Harry Kline and Irving had been key men on his account. All Al wanted from an advertising agency was ads that paid. He knew we could create them, but he was not going to wait for us to get organized. I was beginning to understand how hard it would be to start an agency.

My spirits were sinking fast when the phone rang. It was Charlie Perkins. His call didn't give me any comfort, either. He had seen Max. Now it was my turn, he said. I should arrange to see Max, apologize, and ask for my job back. I was not prepared to do that. Charlie reminded me of my promise to do what he asked. Charlie was going back to Newark. He asked me to call him at his office on Monday to tell him how things worked out. What Charlie was really telling me was that he didn't want to change agencies or personnel. He wanted things to stay the way they had been. He wasn't going to decide anything now.

I knew Charlie: if I didn't do as he asked, I wouldn't get his account. But if I went back to my job at Sackheim, nothing would change. I realized that the only way to have my own business and get Charlie's account was to force Max to make a mistake.

What had begun as a resignation on Tuesday had become a high-stakes poker game by Thursday, and I was playing with a weak hand. Norman Adler was back in town. We spoke on the phone. He was all business. He told me he had arranged to see Max late that afternoon. That didn't help matters. I knew that if I saw Max first, he would withhold his cards until he knew what Charlie and Norman were going to do.

I decided that my only chance was to bet everything on a bluff. I called Max and told him that Charlie had suggested we meet. I asked if I could see him at two o'clock. He agreed.

When I walked into the familiar reception room of Maxwell Sackheim & Company, I felt strange. I went into Max's office, and said, "Max, it's cold outside." He was unresponsive. I played my bluff. I said that Charlie had asked me to reconsider my decision to resign and I had. I apologized for the trouble I had caused. I offered total and unconditional surrender. I would return without any preconditions. As I had hoped, Max was not prepared for me to give up so easily and didn't accept the offer. He asked me to call him at home on Sunday.

He was going to see Norman Adler that afternoon. I was certain that he would confer with his lawyers and his family over the weekend before he gave me his answer. I left his office determined not to wait until Sunday. I was not going to let him decide my fate. It was only Thursday, and I had things to do.

On Friday, we filed the certificate of incorporation for Wunderman,

Ricotta & Kline, Inc. We were now a business under the laws of New York State. I called Ken Tack at Jackson & Perkins and told him I had seen Max and had asked for my job back, as Charlie had instructed. Ken told me that Max had also called that day. He had asked Charlie to leave the J&P account with him regardless of the outcome of our conversation. Charlie had not given him an answer. I knew then that Max was, as I had hoped, determined to turn me down. We were going into the weekend holding what seemed to be the same cards, but the momentum had changed. No matter what happened, I was determined not to go back to work for Max. That part of my life was over. But neither Max, his sons, nor his lawyers knew that. I was certain that if I appeared to be in a weak position, Max would not take me back, and his sons, in any case, would not let him. My return would be bad for them—and they were the issue.

That weekend, the stockholders of Wunderman, Ricotta & Kline spent Saturday looking for office space and Sunday making lists of things we had to do to get ready to do business. We needed an office, furniture, stationery, money, a bank account, a credit line, a financial system, a bookkeeper, telephones, art supplies, and the many forms required to order media and bill clients. We were like adopted house cats that have suddenly been put back into the alley. We had to learn survival all over again.

Sunday, I called Max. Our conversation was brief, and, as I had anticipated, he said he wouldn't reconsider. It was too late to make a deal—we should go our separate ways as good competitors. My bluff had worked.

First thing Monday morning, I called Charlie and told him I had done everything that he had asked. I had apologized and I had asked for my job back, but Max had turned me down. Charlie told me to wait for his next call. He convened the board of directors of Jackson & Perkins. They voted unanimously to give their account to Wunderman, Ricotta & Kline. The little room at the Winslow echoed with the sounds of our joy. It was going to be all right. We had our first large client.

Things then began to move quickly. On Monday, August 25, we held our first meeting. Not to repeat the error Max had made, I retained only 45 percent of the stock for myself. Thus I could be outvoted by the other stockholders.

Two days later, we signed a ten-month sublease on office space at

345 Madison Avenue. The same day, Harry Kline brought in our third client, the Alexander Hamilton Training Institute, a well-known correspondence school for executive training. It was one of the most prestigious business-to-business accounts of its time.

By the following week, the Columbia LP Record Club decided to give us its account. Now we had four clients: Facts on File, Jackson & Perkins, the Alexander Hamilton Training Institute, and the Columbia LP Record Club.

Soon after, we were also awarded the accounts of Harry Abrams, the art book publisher; Basic Books, which owned several small book clubs; and the Grolier Society, publishers of children's books. We were starting with seven clients, very little capital, a substantial overhead, and no prospect of immediate income. Because of the way advertising agency contracts worked, we would have to be able to provide complete agency services to our new clients beginning about September 1, but would earn nothing from that work until December and January. And we didn't have enough capital to survive the waiting period.

We didn't realize how serious a problem this would be until we received our first order from Jackson & Perkins. It was for a small catalog inquiry ad in the garden section of *The New York Times*. The ad would cost less than $200.

When we received the order, we believed we were ready to conduct business, but we soon discovered otherwise. We had moved into our new offices and hired a secretary and a typist-receptionist. Peter Rabar, with whom I had worked on Jackson & Perkins and the Columbia LP Record Club, had come over from Sackheim in early September. We had the core of an expert staff, each of whom was an experienced professional. But getting work produced under our own banner was daunting. First Irving and then Peter tried to write the copy for the small J&P ad. They had written hundreds of ads like it before. But now they froze. All the ad had to do was to offer a free Jackson & Perkins catalog, but it took them days to write it to their satisfaction. Then Ed Ricotta had trouble designing the simple layout. It took us a week to produce an ad that should have been finished in a half hour. The next step was to place it in *The New York Times*.

Formats for buying newspaper space were made available by the American Newspaper Publishers Association and the 4A's (American Association of Advertising Agencies). We hadn't yet printed any. I called the advertising department of the *Times* and told them I wanted to place an order for an ad in their Sunday garden section. They wanted to know who I was. I told them I was Lester Wunderman, president of Wunderman, Ricotta & Kline. What's that, they asked? I took the ad, walked across town to the *Times'* offices at West Forty-third Street, and took the elevator to the advertising department, where I was directed to a salesclerk. Once again, he went through the "Who?" and "What's that?" routine. He seemed unimpressed by my answers. I angrily replied that the paper's own advertising columnist, Carl Spielvogel, had announced the formation of our agency in the *Times'* advertising column of September 3. On September 8, he had written that we had won the Columbia LP Record Club, Jackson & Perkins, and the Alexander Hamilton Institute as clients. Don't you read your own paper? I demanded of the clerk. He never read the column, he replied. What he read was the authorized list of agencies entitled to credit, and he didn't find our name on it. If I wanted to place the ad, I would have to pay cash or provide a certified check. I was exasperated. I ran over to our bank and back to the *Times* with the cash. This time the clerk recognized me. I thought I was safe. It turned out I wasn't. The payment was all right, he said, but he couldn't pay us the commission. Why not? Because we were not on the list of recognized advertising agencies, he replied. I felt like Alice talking to the Red Queen. I asked to see the advertising manager. Happily, he had read Carl Spielvogel's column and he knew me by reputation. I still had to pay cash, but I did get to deduct the commission. I slunk back to our office, realizing that we weren't going to be in business until we were authorized to receive credit and commissions from media, and they weren't going to recognize us for credit unless we had enough capital and income to satisfy their standards. We had little capital, and it was going to run out soon. I hadn't given much thought to the business of starting a business; I had been too excited creating one.

The prospect was exhilarating. Wunderman, Ricotta & Kline, Inc., was going to be my business, and I was going to organize and manage it my way. Sackheim had been Max's business and it had never been much fun. Max was too serious, too tough, too inflexible, and too distant.

Max had once accused me of being a snob because I didn't spend much time with anyone I didn't think was creative or capable of having ideas. What he didn't see was that I believed that most people could have ideas if they were encouraged to do so. I was determined to build a totally creative business, rather than a business served by just a few creative professionals. I believed an advertising agency was in the business of creating and selling effective ideas. Everything else was details. If we created advertising that paid, the results would speak for themselves and also for us. Everyone in advertising claimed to be creative, but few could prove it. I wanted WRK to be first among those that could. If I could have written a small classified ad for WRK, it would have read RESULTS FOR SALE. That was my vision. But visions were not going to pay the rent.

We opened a bank account at the New York Trust Company with all the money we had, $60,194.56. If and when it was spent, we would be out of business and broke. Our monthly office rent was $1,145. That seemed high in those days, but we needed a Madison Avenue address. We also had to pay ourselves enough for our families to live on. I told Ed, Irving, and Harry that our pay would not be proportionate to our share of the business. Each of us would take what his family needed, regardless of his shares or the size of his investment. We took only a fraction of our previous salaries. Our total expenses for September, our first month, were $7,730. At that rate, our $60,000 was going to disappear if we didn't get some business quickly. We also needed to add to our capital if we were to be "recognized" for credit and commissions by the media associations.

On September 4, we filed our application with the American Newspaper Publishers Association. We estimated that our clients would spend $1,299,000 for media over the next year. Our commissions would be $194,850. We would make a profit—if we could survive the first few months. We filed similar applications with all other media associations. The cover letter from our accountants that accompanied the applications contained the following paragraph:

> Please note that we are not including a copy of the agency's contract and order forms because they are still in the process of being printed. However, we wish to advise you that the agency will be using the Standard AAAA Insertion Order Form. We further wish to advise you that this agency is immediately issuing orders for future insertions and will be a heavy user of national newspaper and magazine space.

Included with our application were our biographies and a list of our first clients. Because WRK had no history as a business, we worried that no media would approve our applications. To ensure that they would, we promised to send them regular statements of our assets and liabilities, as well as our profits or losses.

With such a critical audience we didn't dare lose money, even for a single month. I didn't want to lose the media's confidence. We would have to earn immediate fees for whatever work we could get. It was like the early days of the Coronet Advertising Service, but this time I knew what to do.

My goal was to build fee income for the first three months that was at least equal to our overhead. Afterward, our media billings would begin to produce commission income. The plan worked. To our surprise in September, our first month, we covered our expenses and made a net profit of $5,122.69, all from fees. We were on our way.

We wrote collection letters for the Columbia Record Club. We created marketing reports for a new division of CBS. We consulted on new products for Grolier's children's book club. We also began to write direct mail, something the Sackheim agency didn't do except as an accommodation to Jackson & Perkins. In direct mail, we discovered a new source of ongoing income.

At that time, advertising agencies didn't do direct mail because printers, list brokers, letter shops, and so on wouldn't pay commissions. But we wrote direct mail precisely because it wasn't commissionable. We needed immediate fee income, and direct mail provided it. Direct mail became a growing part of our business.

Despite our fears, or perhaps because of them, Wunderman, Ricotta & Kline was a success from the start. We quickly had almost everything a business needs: a group of core clients, a talented staff, and a vision. What we also needed was momentum. We had to be known as a going business. That happened quickly.

The media associations promptly granted us recognition, and we were then entitled to receive credit and earn commissions. Our original clients authorized us to place substantial media schedules for them in December 1958 and the first quarter of 1959.

We made a small profit in September, October, and November and were able to hire additional staff without depleting our capital. Learning to work as a team during those first difficult months created a special morale that became part of the WRK tradition. We thrived on accomplishing what other agencies couldn't or wouldn't attempt to do. Nothing was impossible. Everyone at WRK worked at full throttle, whether in media, accounting, client services, or creative work. As we built our staff, our small quarters at 345 Madison Avenue became crowded, and that also helped. No one had a private office, so everything was shared. We were a commando squad of problem solvers. And the more problems we solved, the more we felt like winners.

Harry Kline was in charge of publicity. I wanted the industry to learn the name Wunderman, Ricotta & Kline as fast as possible and to understand what we did. Thanks to Harry, the *Times* ran twenty-two items about WRK during our first three months in business. It wasn't long before our phone began to ring with offers of business and help. In our first ninety days, we gained five more new accounts. Our clients and staff began to feel like charter members of a successful team, and they were. We moved up in a hurry—but there was no margin for error, as we were soon to find out.

Our clients' advertising budgets for December 1958 and the first quarter of 1959 were larger than we had anticipated. Included in the Columbia LP Record Club's schedule was a two-page ad in the year-end issue of *Life* and a three-page "gatefold" in the January *Reader's Digest*. Each of them cost more than $100,000. Happily, we sent out the media orders. As I was mentally adding up the 15 percent commissions, the phone rang. It was the credit manager of *Life*.

He told me he knew we had been recognized by the Magazine Publishers Association, but *Life* had never been asked for $100,000 worth of credit by a new agency whose total capital was $60,000. He couldn't take the risk. I hastened to assure him that our client the Columbia LP Record Club was a division of CBS and was surely good for the money. He agreed but pointed out that it was Wunderman, Ricotta & Kline that was legally responsible for the bill. He offered me a way out. He would accept the order if the Columbia LP Record Club would assign it directly to *Life* magazine. *Life* would bill CBS for the space, and when the bill was paid, the commission would be rebated to the agency. I knew I couldn't accept that solution and told him I would call him back quickly with a better answer.

My problem was that Norman Adler had recommended us to his

management as his agency, based on my promise that we could provide all of the usual agency services. I didn't want to embarrass him or us by saying that media wouldn't give us the usual credit terms.

I called our accountant for advice, but before I could reach him, my phone rang again. This time it was the credit manager of *Reader's Digest*. He had the same problem and said that he wanted to be cooperative but the magazine didn't know us yet, and so on. Couldn't we get the client to guarantee payment? I promised to call him back. Our early credit problem with *The New York Times* had been a matter of $200. This time the problem was $200,000, and now I couldn't pay cash. I couldn't turn to CBS for help. Either we were a recognized agency—offering professional services—or we weren't.

I called Harry, Ed, and Irving into my office and told them what had happened. They advised me to go to CBS. I told them I wouldn't. Once again, it was time to "put up or shut up." They said they had already put up every penny of cash they had—they had nothing left. Yes, they did, I told them. They had their good names. We were going to have to guarantee payment personally. We all had houses, cars, and other personal possessions. We would pledge it all. They agreed. Now it was my job to sell the solution.

I called the credit managers of both magazines. I told them I couldn't go to our client for the guarantee; I would rather cancel the orders and buy less costly space. However, if they wanted the business, there was another way. The four owners of Wunderman, Ricotta & Kline would personally guarantee payment of the bills collectively and individually. This meant that when Columbia paid its bill to us, we would pay *Life* and the *Digest* before we paid any other creditor. The credit manager of *Life* said that no agency had ever offered such an odd proposal, but he would accept it. The *Digest*'s credit manager told me that we had guts and hoped we also had money. He accepted, too. We had the personal guarantees drawn up and forwarded that day. When January came and CBS paid us, I personally took our checks to the two magazines and recovered our guarantees.

The year 1959 had started with a bang, and things got even better as the year progressed. We had successfully started an agency; now we had to build a business. Within fifteen months we had acquired a list of good clients. They were:

Alexander Hamilton Training Institute, New York, executive training courses

American Paper Specialty Company, New York, greeting cards

Around the World Shoppers Club, Elizabeth, New Jersey, gifts

Basic Books, New York, book club

Britannica Press Division of the *Encyclopaedia Britannica,* Chicago, publishers

Columbia LP Record Club, New York, record club

Columbia LP Record Club of Canada, Toronto, record club

Damar Products, Inc., Elizabeth, New Jersey, household accessories

Facts on File, New York, news service

Grolier Society, New York, First Book Club

Harry N. Abrams, Inc., New York, publishers

History Book Club, Stamford, Connecticut, book club

International School of Photography, New York, correspondence course

Jackson & Perkins, Newark, New York, rosebushes and perennials

Library of Science, New York, book club

Natural History Book Club, New York, book club

Reader's Subscription, New York, book club

Rudder Publishing Company, New York, publishers

Science Book Club, New York, book club

Science Materials Center, New York, science equipment

Scott Mitchell House, Yonkers, New York, mail-order merchandise

Standard Camera Corporation, New York, camera equipment

Tropicoco, Inc., New York and Puerto Rico, soft drink

University of Michigan Press, Ann Arbor, Michigan, publishers

U.S. Health Club, Inc., Bergenfield, New Jersey, health aids

By the end of 1959, Wunderman, Ricotta & Kline had become the world's largest agency specializing in mail-order advertising. We were hot—fast-growing and talented. Our profits were greater than I had anticipated, and I used them to strengthen our capital base. The founders were now being paid what they had earned at Max Sackheim's, but now we were being paid by a business we owned.

We had started the agency frenetically, afraid to fail. Now we would have to build it patiently. We were going to select our clients carefully. We wanted clients from whose businesses we could discover new direct marketing techniques. I wanted to represent and learn only from the best. Getting such clients would take time, but now we could afford to wait.

. . .

In 1960, we won our first account from Doubleday, the largest book club advertiser. It offered us a moribund project called the Paint-It-Yourself Program, which had once been popular but, like all fads, had led a fast life and met a sudden death. Doubleday offered us the project as a test and a peace offering. It had been Sackheim's first and largest account and had been angry with us when we left. We accepted the assignment. I knew it was no use modifying the ads or changing the price or the other terms. We needed a new and better business idea. The early success of painting by numbers had revealed America's increasing love affair with art, and this romance, I believed, was not limited to a particular product. Museum attendance was growing. John Stevenson's Art Treasures of the World had been a great success, and now coffee-table art books published by Harry Abrams were becoming popular. I decided to convert the Paint-It-Yourself Program to an art appreciation course: one lesson each month about a different great artist. Along with the monthly lesson, members would receive everything necessary to copy a masterpiece by that month's famous painter. The copy would suggest that the best way of learning about and enjoying a painter's work was by copying in detail a work by the master himself. We also offered new members a choice of receiving a lesson each month or one every other month, since copying a painting would take time. Members should work at their own pace. We presented the revised program to Doubleday. It bought the idea and the ads and, a few months later, so did the public. We had turned a loser into a moneymaker, and I knew that more business was sure to follow. It did, but later.

Nineteen-sixty also brought us our first large business-to-business client and our first subscription magazine. It was *Nation's Business,* the official publication of the U.S. Chamber of Commerce, a prestigious addition to our client list.

Then we got lucky. We had done so well for the Columbia LP Record Club that CBS gave us the rest of the Columbia Records account—trade advertising to dealers and consumer advertising for Columbia's artists and their new releases in newspapers and magazines and on radio and television.

I wrote an ad about Isaac Stern for *The New York Times Magazine.* Over a photograph of the great violinist at play with his small son, the headline read THE JOY OF BEING ISAAC STERN. It was the first of a series about Columbia Records' great recording artists. The series won an award for creative print advertising. The following year, we won our first award for creative television. My tool kit was expanding.

Schuyler Chapin, who was now head of advertising for Columbia Records, asked me to write a long article for Goddard Lieberson on the entertainment value of records as part of an eight-page Christmas advertising section for Columbia to appear in *The New York Times*. The assignment worried me. Writing about the record business for Goddard was like writing about composing for Richard Rodgers. But Goddard made only minor changes. I was delighted. I was beginning to enjoy myself.

Al Dorne, the head of the Famous Artists Schools, finally forgave us for leaving Sackheim and gave us the account of a new business, the Famous Writers School, a correspondence school headed by a faculty of world-famous writers. The secret of writing successful copy for a correspondence school is to make the reader empathize with the satisfactions of being a professional. My brother, Irving, wrote great ads for the school. The most successful one was a full-page editorial ad signed by Faith Baldwin. The headline read IT'S A SHAME THAT MORE WOMEN DON'T TAKE UP WRITING. They soon did. The ad and the school were an instant success. Our creative momentum was growing.

Nineteen sixty-one was a vintage year. WRK was expanding, and so was my world. Advertising was challenging and exciting. Good advertising worked, and I could now see that mail-order advertising was becoming more sophisticated, more creative. It was also attracting new kinds of clients to WRK.

The year ended on a high note. We applied for membership in the prestigious and influential 4A's. To qualify, we had to have been in business three years and prove that we were providing quality professional services for our clients. We had to be of good moral character, and the agency itself had to satisfy the association's stringent financial criteria. In our case, the admissions committee discovered a problem. It was Irwin Zlowe, then head of the admissions committee and president of his own agency, who came to see me and explained that the 4A's couldn't accept our application without a special investigation.

I knew that mail-order advertising was still on the wrong side of the tracks, so I was fearful when I asked him what was wrong. Most general advertising agency executives didn't yet understand or respect what we did, but I wasn't prepared for what was on his mind. He said our agency was making too much money. The committee didn't believe that we could both provide good service and make as much of a profit as we did. I was aghast. Had I heard him correctly? We were being investigated not for a lack of capital, talent, clients, or management skills—but because we might be too successful!

Zlowe and his committee investigated us for weeks. I gave them access to our clients, our books, and our work. I presented case histories of successful work. I explained our "results department" and how and why we bought media. I proved that our ads created accountable and measurable profits for our clients. We were highly paid because we could prove that the advertising we did worked.

When Zlowe returned to my office with his final report, he began with an apology. He thanked me for letting him look at our business in detail. Everyone on the committee had learned something.

I asked what it was. He said they had learned that advertising that paid off for clients also paid off for the agency. I'll never forget his parting words. We would be recommended for membership, but the association would, of course, have to examine our balance sheet regularly—with envy. On November 14, 1961, WRK become a member of the 4A's. It was a significant turning point in the growth of direct marketing. We had finally been accepted, not only by our clients but by our peers.

In 1962, we moved to 575 Madison Avenue, a modern building at the corner of East 57th Street. We took an entire tower floor and designed it ourselves. We were becoming an "uptown" agency in every sense.

In the fall of 1963, at the end of our first five years in business, we had built a well-financed, profitable business. We had recruited and trained a unique, specialized staff. We had acquired as clients many blue-chip mailorder advertisers. We had helped them expand their business by creating better marketing, which made it possible for them to advertise more profitably in more magazines and newspapers. We had not lost a key client. We had built a powerful business machine. After five years our challenge had changed from how to survive to how to manage growth.

I made a list of tasks for our second five years. They were:

1. Continue to learn the direct marketing business from the best clients and the best practitioners.

2. Explore and invent what no one else yet knows.
3. Improve the quality and knowledge of our staff.
4. Acquire more key direct marketing clients and expand the number of new advertisers who would explore the discipline.
5. Expand the range of media direct marketing clients could use.
6. Expand and enhance the awareness and image of direct marketing: By writing and speaking at industry meetings—ours and others.

That list of priority tasks became our corporate program for growth. I added two items to my personal copy. They were:

1. Relax—have more fun!
2. Expand your vision! Read more, study more, learn more, know more. Experience everything you can.

During the next five years, we gained new clients from a wider variety of businesses, each of which helped us understand the changing trends and needs of the business marketplace and consumer culture.

One of the important new clients we helped build was Consumers Union, the publisher of *Consumer Reports,* the voice of the consumer movement, which began to grow dramatically in the mid-1960s.

Another was Dow Jones, which asked us to create circulation for *The National Observer,* its unsuccessful attempt to publish a weekly national newspaper. Although Dow Jones stayed in the business for years, the idea was ahead of its time. Years later, *USA Today* would become the first successful national newspaper. It would be printed in color, and the editing and marketing would be better. Our advertising, however, told us something we didn't know about middle-class women. We had been using a control ad directed at men. It featured the contents of the newspaper, and the headline read 17 THINGS I LEARNED FROM THE NATIONAL OBSERVER. The results were only average. But a variation of that headline directed at women, which read 17 THINGS I LEARNED FROM MY WIFE WHO READ THE NATIONAL OBSERVER, was an astonishing success. The growing power of educated middle-class women at home and in the workplace surprised us and would continue to do so.

In 1964, an old friend, Jerome Hardy, formerly of Doubleday and then publisher of Time-Life Books, visited me. At the time, Hardy was using Time Inc.'s traditional advertising agency, Young & Rubicam. He had already published several very successful single books and two continuity book series, the Time-Life World Library, a travel series, and the Time-Life Nature Library. The World Library had been a great success, the Nature Library less so, and he was about to announce a third series, the Time-Life Science Library. Jerry told me he had a problem. He didn't know whether he could take the Time-Life Books account away from Young & Rubicam, but he wanted to give us a chance to do a test. He had already ordered a three-page gatefold back-cover ad in *Reader's Digest*. The cancellation date had passed. He had to use the space. If he assigned the space to us, "Which library would you run?" he asked. If the ad were successful, he would let us continue to do the advertising for the series we had chosen.

He gave me no time for reflection. I had to choose immediately. The World Library was a proven success. The Nature Library was a mediocre performer. Jerry believed that the Science Library was going to be hot. I thought fast. I wanted my decision to provide enough leverage to get us the entire account. If I chose the World Library and it succeeded, so what? it was already successful. If I chose the Science Library, Jerry would attribute success to an exciting, new product. The Nature Library had to be my choice. A success with this mediocre performer could be attributed only to our ad. Jerry was surprised by my choice, but he kept his word. Our new ad was so successful that Nature became Time-Life Books' most profitable property. We were awarded the entire account. We beat Young & Rubicam because even the best general agency didn't know how to write a mail-order ad.

In 1965, the U.S. Post Office decided to introduce a five-digit ZIP code. It failed, even though the new system had behind it the authority of President Lyndon Johnson and the U.S. government. The ZIP code was becoming a national embarrassment when the president and the Post Office Department turned to the Advertising Council for help. The Ad Council asked us to volunteer to advertise for the ZIP code.* They believed that a direct marketing agency would better understand and explain the ZIP code's benefits.

---

*The Advertising Council, one of America's most powerful public service institutions, is made up of representatives of industry, media owners, and advertising agencies who contribute a pool of newspaper and magazine space, radio and television time, and outdoor advertising boards for public service use. It recruits an agency to provide the necessary work without charge except for out-of-pocket costs of production, such as artwork, film, etc.

We soon learned that businesses with large mailing lists resented the additional expense of ZIP-coding their huge databases. We also found that the public didn't want the extra bother of looking up the ZIP code number whenever they sent a letter. Our campaign showed postal workers drowning in mail. To their rescue came a cartoon character named "Mr. Zip." The campaign appeared in newspapers and magazines and on radio and television. We also redesigned the signs on the U.S. Post Office trucks. The ZIP code was harder than anything else we had ever done, and we were doing it for free.

We launched a campaign with almost $18 million of the Ad Council's media bank the first year and discovered that we could accurately track our results. Each post office branch kept a record of the number of ZIP-coded envelopes it processed, which let us measure how our ads increased the percentage of ZIP-coded mail. Our campaign turned out to be one of the most successful ever done by the Ad Council. After three years, the ZIP code became a familiar, accepted, and useful part of the postal system, and I was thanked for my contribution by President Johnson in the White House Rose Garden.

We also won the account of the country's largest insurance company that sold by mail, the Government Employees Insurance Company (GEICO). GEICO was the first insurance company to offer special rates to a low-risk segment of the population, and the headline we wrote for it started a whole new trend in the insurance business. Our research showed that the average policyholder believed all insurance rates were the same, which is why our headline was IT PAYS TO SHOP FOR LIFE INSURANCE. Not all insurance rates were the same. GEICO's position as a seller of low-cost insurance to low-risk government and other white-collar employees was persuasive. The company grew and prospered for years using variations of our original advertising theme.

A year later, in 1966, we learned an even better way of selling insurance by mail from Michael Fields, an insurance expert and marketing genius. Fields had a vision of a new kind of insurance policy marketed directly to consumers. He knew that the cost of hospital care was rising faster than the benefits paid by health insurance policies. More and more people were being discharged from hospitals with bills greater than their policies would pay. What Fields had developed was a supplementary health insurance policy to cover the costs not covered by a primary health insurance policy. He began testing the concept in direct mail in 1964 with great success.

In 1966, he asked us to translate his direct mail success into a full-page newspaper ad, and as a result a new industry was born. Our full-page newspaper ads, written by my brother, Irving, were spectacularly successful. The headline we used was LEAVE THE HOSPITAL WITH EXTRA CASH IN YOUR POCKET. We then took another step and recommended that Fields try a preprinted, freestanding newspaper insert, the media form we had pioneered years earlier. Each insert cost twice as much as a black-and-white page but produced four times as many applications.

Fields's supplementary policy was a breakthrough in insurance practice; and our long-copy, preprinted ads describing insurance in a way that was easy to understand were a breakthrough in direct marketing. Fields became one of our largest accounts, and we soon became experts at selling insurance directly. Once again, we grew and profited from a talented client who helped us expand our repertoire of direct marketing techniques.

17

How I Discovered Direct Marketing

Direct marketing did not enter my mind full-blown. I was learning it during the years I worked for Max Sackheim and even before. It was and remains an unending process of discovery.

I first used the term "direct marketing" publicly on October 1, 1961, in a speech to the Hundred Million Club of New York, an organization of leaders in the direct mail business. I wanted to describe my discontent with "mail-order advertising" and its lack of creative thinking and forward planning, and for the first time I described "direct marketing" as a "new frontier." I said, in part:

> We live in an age of convenience retailing—what is more convenient than to shop at home? . . . Is there any more scientific method of merchandising than the scientific copy, price, and market testing available to the mail-order advertisers? Competition for shelf space at retail is becoming ever more fierce and costly—yet sales access to the home by mail grows more efficient each year. The din of advertising becomes louder and louder, and it costs more to make a consumer remember the advertising he saw, heard or read when he makes a buying decision. Isn't it logical to sell him at the point of his greatest conviction, when he has just absorbed the sales message? That's what a great mail-order ad or mailing piece does. For these reasons and many others, I am absolutely convinced that the future of our industry lies with the large, highly competitive manufacturing companies which must increasingly bring their selling and marketing influence closer to the consumer. I believe the next ten years will see a continuing decline of the mail-order business as it has been defined

in the past. It will be replaced by Direct Marketing—a new and more efficient method of selling, based on scientific advertising principles and serviced by increasingly more automated warehousing, shipping and collection techniques.

I had identified direct marketing and defined the role it could play in the larger world of general marketing and advertising. Though no one paid much attention at the time, I had set the future agenda not only for Wunderman, Ricotta & Kline but for the advertising industry itself.

In 1961, when my colleagues and I were beginning to do direct marketing, Wunderman, Ricotta & Kline had become a 4A agency, part of the mainstream. I went regularly to meetings and conventions of the 4A's but no longer attended those of the mail-order advertising groups. I got to know the leading figures in general advertising and learned about the revolutionary changes taking place in the marketplace of the 1960s. Business was changing, and so was the culture. Abstract expressionism, the rock and roll generation and their music, intrigued me. I took courses in cultural anthropology, linguistics, psychology, and research; I read widely on marketing, management, and social and economic trends. I studied and later lectured on creative thinking at New York University, Columbia University, and the New School for Social Research. I was appointed the "Executive-in-Residence" at Boston University, counseling graduate students and faculty. The world was changing, and I was determined that we would be in the vanguard.

However, I didn't reach the next milestone on my path of discovery until 1967. It was one of those bright late-September days in New York when the air holds the first cool promise of fall. I had moved back to the city and as I walked the fourteen blocks from my apartment on Seventy-first Street and Fifth Avenue to my office on East 57th Street and Madison, New York looked particularly handsome. There were no crises on my calendar that day. This was going to be one of the easy ones, I thought.

Then the phone rang. It was the head of the Boston chapter of the American Marketing Association. I took the call, and my caller got right to the point. He wanted me to speak at their November meeting at MIT. Normally, he said, about three hundred corporate members and professors attended such meetings.

He said his organization had heard that our agency was practicing a new form of advertising, and he wanted me to talk about it. He suggested I provide a few detailed case histories and describe the advertising and the strategic plans behind it. He then said that his academic members—business school faculty from Harvard, MIT, Boston University, and other local universities—were particularly interested in the theory behind the practice.

I wanted to be certain I understood him. He wanted me to explain what we did? He agreed but repeated that his members expected to hear speakers talk about the philosophy of their work. They wanted to know not simply what we did but why we did it.

I agreed to speak. He thanked me and asked me to send an outline of my remarks in about two weeks so that he could announce the program. He said there would be a good turnout, particularly by the professors. We said good-bye, and I went into a deep funk.

Platform speaking had always made me nervous, so much so that years earlier I had studied at the American Theatre Wing, which at the time taught theater techniques to public speakers as well as actors. With its help, I had learned to use my anxiety to become a more creative and effective speaker. It wasn't so much the platform as the prospective audience at MIT that concerned me. My talk in New York to members of the Hundred Million Club hadn't changed the perception that mail order was a second-class business. I was sure that the professors of marketing and advertising at Harvard and MIT would agree.

What should I say to them? I had spent most of my working life in mail-order advertising. It worked because it was pragmatic and result-driven, but no one had ever provided a theoretical argument for it. I was the best-known practitioner of mail-order advertising, but what did I really know about its theory—assuming there was a theory? My day had begun peacefully, but it ended with troubling questions.

For weeks I tried to write the speech, but I couldn't until finally I saw how the social and economic changes we were living through had made me think of marketing in a new way. My theme would be the contradictions we were seeing between people's individual needs and the mass solutions they were still being offered, a pattern the advertising and marketing community had not yet noticed.

I had agreed to talk about the work I did, the kind of advertising others still knew as mail order or direct response. I would explain why general advertising for the mass market was becoming increasingly irrelevant. I would predict that such advertising and the production and distribution systems it served would eventually give way to something new and much more complex. Some of the best social scientists and other writers were saying that we had become a society in which human beings had become mere objects in a system of mass production and consumption. We were producing and consuming faster and faster at the expense of human values and individual desires. We were no longer the beneficiaries of the Industrial Revolution but its victims. We had forgotten Immanuel Kant's warning that man—or in our case customers—must be treated as an end and never as a means, and from Martin Buber's *I and Thou* I had learned the importance of intimate dialogues.

These ideas and others had led me to conceive of an advertising, marketing, and production system that was more appropriate to the human situation. In my mind, direct marketing was a system of interactive transactions that would restore a measure of dialogue and human scale to the way we made, sold, and bought things.

The invitation to present these ideas to the business faculties of several great universities now seemed a wonderful opportunity. As I worked on my presentation, I could see more clearly the human values associated with direct marketing. Throughout most of history, people had made products to serve the special needs of individual people. This tradition of personal service was fundamental to our language. The existence of such names as Butcher, Baker, Potter, Shoemaker, Smith, Taylor, Hooper, Farmer, Carpenter, Plumber, Hunter, and Shepherd, and their equivalents in other languages, told us that we had, for centuries, been serving one another. The marketing of such services had always been person to person.

I began to understand that the Industrial Revolution was a relatively recent phenomenon, scarcely 150 years old. The systems of mass marketing, general advertising, and mass retailing reflected the marketing requirements of the standardized products with which mass-production factories now flooded the marketplace. These standardized products were a factory's inventory, goods produced without orders for customers unknown. Disposing of that inventory required mass distributors and retailers who would buy the finished products in bulk and then try to sell them. General advertising tried to persuade consumers to buy these mass products, and mass persuasion had soon replaced traditional, individualized service. Advertising would try to satisfy consumers' needs, even if the products it sold didn't.

As I thought about the history of production, selling, and advertising, I realized that mass production, mass retailing, mass media, and mass advertising constituted only a temporary historical phase. In time, consumers would once again demand the traditional services that producers had previously provided. Mass-production and mass-marketing systems, though they delivered goods cheaply, were too indirect and too indifferent to people's specific needs. While I didn't believe that we could or should reverse the benefits of the Industrial Revolution, we would have to modify them so that they once again served the consumer, especially now, when more highly individualized products were coming from abroad, from countries that had not committed themselves to mass production as heavily as we had. I felt sure that the best way to begin to restore personalized services was to put the producer back into direct contact with the consumer, to re-create their original dialogue, and the best way to do this was through the advertising, marketing, and distribution system that in 1961 I had named "direct marketing."

The title of the talk I gave at MIT on November 29, 1967, was "Direct Marketing—The New Revolution in Selling." I wanted to use the platform at MIT to proclaim that WRK was the world's first direct marketing advertising agency.

The chairman opened the meeting by introducing me as the leader of the direct mail advertising business, a common error then and now and one that I would use to my advantage. Direct mail is the part of direct marketing most people understand as being different from general advertising. Now I could explain that mail was only one of the media used by direct marketing to address individuals rather than masses.

I was apprehensive as I walked up to the platform. I had brought no visual aids—no props, nothing. The ideas themselves would have to create interest—if there were going to be any. I began by taking notice of where I was and who the audience was:

> I find it fitting today to be making this talk at MIT. . . . So many glamour industries have sprung from MIT research and the minds of its alumni that I wonder if anyone has really considered how all of

this has shattered the equanimity of the marketing community and the consuming public. To me, it has ushered in a new form of marketing, which I choose to call Direct Marketing. No matter what you choose to call it, I believe that it will take its place among the other glamour industries of our time. This new form of distribution used to be called mail-order selling.

No one squirmed or left as I had feared. I went on to explain that mail-order advertising was a way station, a stop along the path toward direct marketing:

What is the mail-order business, and where is it going? Mail-order and mail-order advertising are bigger, healthier and more vital today than ever before—even though much of it is no longer done by mail. . . . The very term itself has lost total validity, and it will be less applicable in the future. In a strict sense, mail-order means that the customer's order is sent by mail and that his merchandise is, in turn, delivered to him by mail. Already this is not true. Phones are easier, faster and more personal. But it will not stop there. More sophisticated and better methods of ordering and delivering will surely come, whether they be orders geared directly to computers, video phones, closed-circuit television, or some newer technology. What is true is that whatever the mechanics, we are dealing with a form of convenience marketing where the consumer is placed in direct contact with a warehouse, factory, or fulfillment center, which will deliver merchandise directly to his home. I believe the term Direct Marketing is more appropriate than mail-order selling. Mail-order will pass into history as an early, primitive phase of direct, in-home marketing.

I then tried to explain the need for direct marketing:

Why hasn't the awesome new power of convenience retailing killed old-fashioned, mail-order selling? Let's face it, convenience retailing has become very inconvenient. You need only watch women carrying babies through crowded aisles, pushing carts through in-store traffic jams, looking in vain for assistance when they need it, carrying heavy packages across vast parking lots where the only contact is between contending fenders, to realize what a misapplied semantic convenience retailing has become. Convenient for whom? The consumer is offered more and more self-service—a euphemism for no service at all.

The retailer, who historically provided a valuable link between manufacturer and consumer for which he was in a real sense paid by both is, by and large, a remittance man. He is a monument to the mass production and mass consumption era in our history which shows every sign of becoming obsolete.

I then suggested what I thought today's consumer wanted:

We are living in an age of repersonalization and individuation. People, products and services are all seeking an individual identity. Taste, desire, ambition and lifestyle have made shopping once again a form of personal expression.

The audience was paying attention, and I began to gain confidence. I pointed out how technology could be used to make the whole marketing process more human, describing what would come to be called the "Postindustrial Society."

A computer can know and remember as much marketing detail about 200,000,000 consumers as did the owner of a crossroads general store about his handful of customers. It can know and select such personal details as who prefers strong coffee, imported beer, new fashions, bright colors. Who just bought a home, freezer, camera, automobile. Who had a new baby, is overweight, got married, owns a pet, likes romantic novels, serious reading, listens to Bach or The Beatles. If we know all of these things, and we can, how could they be used in the ultimate marketing sense by a supermarket, discount house, or rack jobber? Neither can this knowledge be used for the limited advertising objectives of locating advertising targets. New marketing forms which will link these facts to advertising and selling must evolve—and this can be done in only one way—Direct Marketing, where the advertising and buying become a single action. Those marketers who ignore the implications of our new individualized information society will be left behind in what may well come to be known as the age of mass production and marketing ignorance.

Advertising is a branch of the education industry, entirely informational. And, as such . . . its job is increasingly to provide consumer satisfaction—instead of the product providing it. . . . Audience participation becomes absolutely indispensable in our kind of information environment. . . . One of the future aspects of advertising is the custom-made, the tailor-made. Instead of peddling mass-produced commodities, advertising is going to become a personal service of each individual.

Then came my argument for direct marketing advertising:

Direct Marketing sells while the thrust of selling energy is at its greatest force. . . . The ultimate participation in an advertisement is the fact that you can buy from it. There we have another definition of . . . Direct Marketing. It not only gets the order, but takes it as well. Advertising . . . must not only sell the consumer on the idea of trying the product, but it must cause him to continue buying it as well.

I had come a long way from the Max Sackheim school of mail-order advertising, and I hoped I had brought the audience along with me.

Why should consumers continuously shop for services, soap, soup, paper goods, cosmetics, etc., when these products can be personally delivered to their homes, according to their needs and tastes? They know what they want, their continued use of the product is measurable, and they should not have to waste valuable time in fetching and carrying.

I was now just one step away from the end of my presentation:

Advertising can be a personalized information service—if we realize that the bulk of our media today are addressed to a specific person or family. We know this to be true of direct mail. Direct mail must increasingly use its power to address specific individuals of known demography and characteristics, if it is to come to full flower. A television transmitter is blind, but a computer has a memory and selective vision. These, harnessed to the new printers which are being developed, can write tens of millions of personalized letters at low cost. A respondent to such a computerized letter recently wrote, "In this age of computers, it is refreshing to be treated once more as an individual." We are just a short step away from completely individualized, volume direct mail, which I believe will soon create personalized advertising opportunities we never dreamed of.

Suddenly, it was over. I was surprised at the long, enthusiastic applause. I later realized I had done more than make a successful speech; I had set an industry into motion and provided myself with a mission and a life's work.

A vision of a new form of marketing presented to the faculties of some of America's most influential universities was certain to get attention, and it did. The speech was reprinted in *The New York Times* and leading trade journals in the United States, England, France, and West Germany. It was entered into the *Congressional Record* under the heading DIRECT MARKETING by Senator Vance Hartke of Indiana, who said:

> Mr. President, recently Mr. Lester Wunderman gave what I consider a meaningful speech to the Boston chapter of the American Marketing Association at MIT in Cambridge, Mass.
>
> Mr. Wunderman describes the increasing employment of direct marketing techniques in the distribution of products and services. His remarks represent, in one of their aspects, a message of paramount importance to consumers. It shows how many of the large companies are meeting consumer demand for high quality products and services at lower prices than can be found in the traditional distribution network.

The speech established direct marketing as the modern successor to mail-order advertising, and in less than six months *The Reporter of Direct Mail* changed its name to *Direct Marketing* magazine.

WRK officially became a "direct marketing" advertising agency. I pressured our competitors and the industry associations to declare whether they would remain in direct mail and mail-order advertising or join the direct marketing revolution. They had little choice: they would have to join direct marketing or be left behind.

Large advertisers began to employ us. We received a few assignments from General Foods, which wanted us to help sell specialty foods, and from General Motors to popularize automobile leasing.

The 4A's also took notice of direct marketing. A direct marketing committee was formed within the association, and I was asked to be its first chairman. However, the bulk of WRK's growing business continued to come from traditional mail-order clients. Though we had now opened agencies in Montreal, London, Paris, and Munich, even there our main business came from large mail-order companies.

My goal of establishing direct marketing as a dominant new force was as yet unrealized. I felt like an explorer who had discovered a rich new land but had only begun to explore it as I waited for the great body of settlers to arrive.

In the spring of 1971, I came upon the third milestone on the road to direct marketing. This time it was not a speech but a major event. It was called "Direct Mail Day in New York," and it took place once a year. It was the largest, most publicized, and best-attended annual function of the industry in New York. The day was professionally managed by a committee of industry leaders. I had not participated in past years because I had wanted to keep myself and WRK at arm's length from the narrowly defined "direct mail" business.

Pete Hoke, the publisher of *Direct Marketing* magazine and an influential member of the committee, called me and said that he and Lee Epstein, a committee member and owner of a large direct mail production shop, wanted to see me. They came to my office and quickly told me what they wanted. The attendance at the last Direct Mail Day in 1970 had been disappointing. They were concerned that attendance at the 1971 event would be worse. We were in a recession, and it was harder to sell tickets to industry events. They asked if I would serve as chairman of Direct Mail Day 1971. I asked what I would have to do, and they told me I was to create the program for the day and appoint people to head its supporting committees. The Grand Ballroom of the Americana Hotel had already been booked, and it would be my job to attract 1,500 attendees.

My first instinct was to refuse, even though I was the first advertising agency president who had been invited to serve. WRK was not part of the direct mail industry. Less than 10 percent of our income came from direct mail. I told them I couldn't accept their invitation because they were asking me to be chairman of an event I didn't believe in. Direct mail was not my industry; direct marketing was. I would accept only if they changed the name to Direct Marketing Day. If they agreed, I would give them a day to be proud of. Otherwise, the answer was "No." Hoke and Epstein said they would have to consult the rest of their committee. A few days later, Pete Hoke called me and said that we would create the world's first Direct Marketing Day.

But I wanted to do more than rename the day, I wanted to start a new movement. To do it my way, I took over the program and publicity tasks as well as the chairmanship. The first speaker I chose was Peter Drucker, whose book *The Age of Discontinuity* had just been published to glowing reviews.

Drucker was an adviser to one of our clients, and we talked frequently. One day I asked him what he thought an ad should do to get attention. I've never forgotten his reply. He said, "A great ad makes each reader feel, this is for me and nobody else." Drucker agreed to be the keynote speaker of Direct Marketing Day, and his acceptance made it easy to recruit others.

Traditionally, Direct Mail Day had sold tickets by mail to previous attendees and to others in the direct mail industry who had never attended. But as the day approached, few people were buying tickets. I was disturbed and puzzled. Then I understood. The new audience for whom the program had been designed didn't know about it. We were selling tickets by direct mail, but the people we wanted were not on our mailing lists. I suggested that we use other media, such as telephone marketing. I wanted a toll-free number so that people could order tickets by phone right up to the last minute. I also wanted to announce the day with a full-page ad in *The New York Times*. The committee agreed—in part. They said they could do the phone and take care of the toll-free number, but a full-page ad in *The New York Times* would cost almost $10,000 and they didn't have that kind of budget.

I wasn't going to preside over a failure. It wasn't just another "day"—the idea of direct marketing itself was at stake. I had spent years arguing that direct marketing was a multimedia technique. In this case, we would have to use mail, phone, and *The New York Times*. I told the committee that WRK would create a full-page *Times* ad with a coupon and a phone number. I was absolutely certain it would more than pay for itself in tickets sold by reaching people who mail didn't reach. The committee resisted. Then I said that WRK would underwrite the ad. If it failed, the committee would pay nothing. If it worked, it would pay us for it. The committee agreed.

The ad appeared on the back page of *The New York Times* on Wednesday, March 17, under the headline ANNOUNCING DIRECT MARKETING DAY 1971. The subcaption promised "The inside story of a revolution which may change the nature of your business." The ad copy then said:

Direct Marketing is about: an oil company which found a new marketing guide by talking to its prospects by name; a food company which reduced its institutional business and found a fatted calf; an insurance company which sold 1,000,000 new policies without an agent or salesman; cosmetics companies which outsell the major brands without a single retail store outlet; magazines which need no advertisers; a book publisher which became the world's largest—without a bookstore; record companies which sell direct to

4,000,000 customers and know every one of them by name and taste; catalogues that talk on the telephone; manufacturers of photographic equipment who found a vast second market untouched by discount houses.

As soon as the ad broke, orders poured in by mail and phone. Direct Marketing Day 1971 broke every previous record for attendance. We sold out the house and attracted a whole new group, including the press, and WRK got its $10,000 back.

The next day, *The New York Times'* advertising column carried the following headline: 2,000 TURN OUT HERE FOR DIRECT MARKETING DAY. It added:

> A turnout big enough to amaze even its sponsors crowded the Americana yesterday for the first Direct Marketing Day in New York. Lester Wunderman, the Chairman, credits a good many of the approximately 2,000 people who attended to the fact that the committee practiced what it preached. It ran a full-page advertisement announcing the meeting in *The New York Times* complete with coupon and toll-free phone number. It got about 500 responses. Direct Marketing goes beyond direct mailing. It covers any form of selling that involves contact between seller and buyer, and almost every aspect of it was touched on during the day.

That day at the Americana Hotel I spoke about direct marketing— my way. I didn't repeat what I had said at MIT, because now I could say:

> There is a revolution beginning. Suddenly whole new forces have been unleashed which could rival the Industrial Revolution itself in the scope and nature of the changes they will make in our business and personal lives. . . . Nothing less than a revolution could have summoned up the vast new opportunities awaiting us in the decade of the Seventies.

I pointed out that while the country was in a recession, the 1960s had brought changes that most businesses had not yet digested:

> While our recent economic indicators have been becalmed, the change index has been blowing up a storm. . . . Observe the changing folkways and fashions of our time. Lay against these ideas, customs, traditions and businesses already dying of the future and the

new ones beginning to replace them, and one begins to perceive a dimension of change that suggests a crisis for some businessmen and an opportunity for others. . . .

Our society is in the throes of change, rebellion, crisis and opportunity. Forces at work to dehumanize and counterforces at work to develop a new humanism and new priorities. For in truth what we see in America as a major new marketing opportunity is the rebirth of individualism and human responsiveness, which may well portend the death of mass production, mass distribution and mass communication as we have known them.

Mass production techniques, which were the propellant of the Industrial Revolution, were based on two assumptions. The first was that there was a mass of people whose wants were, or could be made to be, so standardized that they would consume what the machine made and overlook the lack of customization because the price was right and the opportunity to have certain kinds of goods was unprecedented.

The second assumption was that even if the first assumption was wrong, advertising would persuade the consumer to want what the machine made, even if the product, price and quality were in themselves not wholly desirable. . . .

Demographics suggest that society is like a giant set of pigeon holes into which we can stuff the population of a country. . . . To the contrary, we are a population rebelling against every form of group definition. . . .

The point is that nobody is just like his neighbor or wants to be and, increasingly, people are striving for individual identification.

I then made a series of predictions for the 1970s:

Standard of living criteria are giving way to lifestyles. These new lifestyles are founded upon a deepening preoccupation with individuality. It will be more effective to sell goods and services that satisfy people's differences rather than their group similarities.

The possession of goods as a mark of social class is becoming less important than their contribution to a richer personal life. . . .

Advertising and marketing will no longer dictate public choice. . . .

To satisfy new needs, we will have to accept new standards. The first is that mass production must give way to volume, customized production. . . .

It is obvious that mass marketing and retailing cannot properly handle that vast number of product lines that our fragmented markets will require. . . .

Substituted for the standard of living will be the concept of the quality of life. . . .

There is as much new economic opportunity now in the satisfaction of individual needs and in the improvement of the quality of life as there was 50 years ago in the raising of the standard of living. . . .

Marketing and advertising must increasingly become a conduit for the increasing information dialogue between the producers of goods and the consumers. More and more, we in marketing must realize that we represent the common needs of both.

I was more than repaid for the work I had put into the Day. *The New York Times* published my speech in its Sunday Business Section, as did *Direct Marketing* magazine. A learned magazine in Paris, *Communication et Langages,* translated it word for word and headlined it on the front cover as LES OPINIONS NON-CONFORMISTES D'UN PUBLICITAIRE DE MADISON-AVENUE. Others also published it abroad. We heard good things about the Day from clients, employees, and the industry at large.

Direct Marketing magazine ended its report of the meeting by saying, "The first Direct Marketing Day in New York on March 31, 1971—the first to be held anywhere—was a day to be remembered as nearly 2,000 people stormed the Americana Hotel. Direct Marketing is 'where it's at' for the rest of the 70s and beyond."

I had raised the direct marketing flag. Direct Mail Days became Direct Marketing Days everywhere, and I was asked to be the keynote speaker at many of them. I accepted as many of these invitations as I could and therefore had the opportunity to introduce direct marketing to a global audience.

Other direct mail organizations also embraced direct marketing. The largest and most conservative of these was the Direct Mail Association of America. In 1974, it changed its name to the Direct Mail/Marketing Association, and in 1983 it became the Direct Marketing Association. In ten years, direct marketing had entered the worldwide vocabulary. But it still hadn't changed the way major companies did business.

By the 1970s, my life was better than I had ever hoped it would be. I was president and chief owner of the world's leading direct marketing advertising agency. We were successful in the United States and abroad. We had good clients, a talented staff, and little serious competition. We were getting favorable press and making substantial profits. I traveled the world for both business and pleasure. Despite our specialization, Wunderman, Ricotta & Kline became one of the thirty largest agencies in the world. I was invited to become secretary-treasurer of the 4A's and served with a distinguished board of directors that included most of the leaders of the largest agencies.

I had created a vision of the future for an industry. Perhaps I should have been satisfied. But I wasn't—and neither were others. I began to get calls from suitors, the heads of large general agencies who wanted us to merge with their companies.

I was not ready to sell, but the idea was now planted in my mind. My membership on the board of the 4A's was exposing me to intelligent, serious, able men who were devoted to serving their industry. But we had differences not just in management style but in business philosophy.

By 1972, I had strong beliefs about how to run and build a business—and I could do it my way. It was exciting to give WRK its special character, to create an organization and a climate in which others could work with satisfaction, security, and a sense of personal worth.

I made sure that the agency was run by creative people. In addition to serving key clients, my main task was to attract, train, and stimulate talented professionals. I frequently chose to forgo profits in order to get and keep superior talent. We operated more like a kinship group than a business. We had great loyalty to one another, encouraging one another's strengths but also mindful that everyone had periods of weakness and dependency.

I had strong management biases. I wouldn't hire MBAs or people with financial expertise, even though much of direct marketing depends on these skills. Our ads created measurable results and it was vital to understand these results, but I believed they could be better evaluated by people who could find patterns in the numbers. Our people were like astronomers. It took mathematical skills to plot the solar system—but imagination to grasp its meaning.

Many businessmen believed then, and more believe now, that their sole purpose is profit. This, I believe, is both a limited and limiting view. Vilfredo Pareto, the late-nineteenth- and early-twentieth-century

Italian economist, defined such managers as "rentiers," people who build nothing but just collect the rent.

But businesses that shave their costs too closely rarely produce new ideas. These cost-efficient, sanitized businesses without a mission become corporate zombies, the living dead of the business community. The real source of long-term profits is service to customers and the community—creating value, and not by cutting costs. I make no argument for inefficiency, but there is an irreducible limit to cost cutting and, conversely, no ceiling on the extra value to be achieved through imagination.

WRK earned excellent profits. We charged fair prices, which clients were willing to pay because of the contribution we made to their profits. We managed this by emphasizing creative output more than financial controls. We avoided the severe cost-cutting programs many advertising agencies attempt in lean years. I believe that any agency's results are the responsibility of management, which should reduce its own wages and bonuses before cutting staff. To fire employees because management has failed is to victimize the wrong people. WRK had some bad years, but during them only the managers suffered.

18

Discovering "Dialogue Marketing" and Life in Africa

WRK was growing and direct marketing was catching on, but in the late 1960s, I had lost the heady feeling of adventure. I was recently divorced and wanted to reconsider my needs and objectives. I decided to go to Africa.

Years earlier, in 1960, I had discovered the remarkable sculpture of the Dogon tribe of Mali and bought my first small piece. Over time, I assembled several hundred of the best examples of Dogon art.

In 1973, my collection toured thirteen major museums in the United States and became the subject of several books and television programs. Years later, it became part of the permanent collections of the Metropolitan Museum of Art in New York and the Dapper Foundation in Paris.

In 1972, I decided that, at last, I should visit the Dogon tribe in its remote and almost inaccessible region of Mali, just below the Sahara Desert, seventy-five miles from legendary Timbuktu. I had become as obsessed with the Dogon as I was with direct marketing—and for good reason, as it turned out.

Before I left, I decided to learn more about the life and beliefs of the Dogon. In Switzerland, I met with a psychiatrist, Dr. Fritz Morganthaler, who had done psychoanalytic work among the Dogon and had written a book with his colleagues, Dr. Paul Parren and Dr. Goldy Parren-Matthey, about his experiences there, *Les Blancs pensent trop* ("White People Think Too Much").

I met Dr. Morganthaler in his office in the old-town area of Zürich, after his last patient that day had left. His office and his practice were classically Freudian. He waved me to his patients' chair and offered me some good Swiss kirsch and a Havana cigar.

I asked him what he could tell me about the Dogon. Rather than answer directly, he asked a strange question: Could I accept powerlessness? Could I give the Dogon power and keep none for myself? If I couldn't, he said, I should stay home. I told him I gave up power to my clients every day. Dr. Morganthaler explained that if the Dogon thought I was too powerful, I would become like every other white man they had met during their long colonization by the French. They would resist me and entertain me as a mere tourist; they would lock me out of their lives and beliefs. He also told me that the Dogon had an extraordinary ability to use metaphors as explanations. If I wanted to understand them, I would have to master not only what they said but how they thought.

My good friend Eliot Elisofon, a *Life* photographer and Africanist, helped me assemble the proper camera equipment. He, too, warned that if I wanted to know the Dogon, my camera and I would have to become part of normal village life.

Henri Kamer, the French art dealer and adventurer from whom I had purchased a considerable part of my growing African art collection, offered to join me. Henri had been to the Dogon country a number of times and would be both companion and guide for my trip.

On the day I left New York, Dr. Pat Imperato, who had spent years working for the United States Health Service in Mali, accompanied me to Kennedy Airport. He told me he was going to equip me with a bit of magic. Using my small portable tape player, he recorded a speech in French for Ogobara Dolo, chief of the Dogon tribe. Dr. Imperato's tape introduced me as his friend and brother and asked Ogobara to accept me as such. And so I left for Africa.

I arrived in Abidjan in the Ivory Coast after stops in Senegal and Liberia, and checked into the Hôtel Ivoire. Kamer had not yet arrived. But at his suggestion, I called Monsieur Morel, the head of the French secret service in West Africa. He invited me to join him and a few friends for dinner at a nightclub. I agreed eagerly.

I asked M. Morel if there was anything I should know about the nightclub. He told me I would be safe if I did nothing without consulting him. The club, a large circular hut, was in a section of Abidjan beyond where the road and streetlights ended. Our small group was seated near the center, close to a worn wooden dance floor. The other patrons were all Africans, mostly men.

We were well into our dinner when a band began to play. As the rhythm picked up, I was aware only of the drums. Then a group of women dancers approached. Unlike in European or American dance, where the dancers follow the beat of the drums, in African dance the drums follow the rhythms of the dancers and their "language" contributes to the meaning of the dance.

When the dancers left, dinner was over. The band began to play again, and it was time for the audience to dance. I asked each of the women at our table, and all declined. Looking for someone to dance with, I noticed one of the show dancers, who was wearing a bright scarlet dress and red shoes and sitting at a table not far from ours. She was moving to the rhythm of the drums. I wanted to dance with her, and I said so to Morel. He replied sharply that I could not; if I tried, I would offend every African male in the club. He wouldn't be responsible for my safety if I left the table.

Just then, I had an idea. Despite Morel's warnings, I left the table, walked over to the young woman in the red shoes, and handed her my shoes. She looked up at me, startled. "What is this?" she asked in French. "My shoes," I said and returned to my seat. She held the shoes, looked at them, and suddenly laughed. She got up from her seat and began to walk around the nightclub, saying to everyone, "Look, he gave me his shoes." The men nodded and replied, "Look, he gave her his shoes." They weren't menacing, only curious. When she completed her circuit of the club, she asked me, "Why did you do this?" I didn't answer, but when she was seated I approached her again and said I wanted her to have them. "Why?" she asked. I told her my shoes wanted to dance, and since she was not permitted to dance with me, I would like her to dance with my shoes. With that I returned to our table, still shoeless. Once again she rose and circled the room. "He has given me his shoes because he wants me to dance with them. He has given me his shoes because he wants me to dance with them," she repeated again and again. The men laughed. Shoes were for dancing— they were sexually neutral.

I awaited her next move, which I hoped I had anticipated correctly. I didn't yet know Africa, but I did know about metaphor. The young dancer rose again, looked at me solemnly, reached down, took off her red shoes, came over to our table, and offered them to me. "What is this?" I asked. "My shoes," she answered. This time it was I who circled the room, holding up the shoes and saying, "She has given me her shoes." I looked for signs of hostility. There were none. The men laughed and repeated the line as they had with her. It had become a ritual conversation. When I returned to my seat, I was still holding her shoes. It was as if everyone now understood the will of the shoes. Finally, she put on my shoes, which were far too large. Everyone was watching; Morel was silent. I had begun something that now had its own momentum. I walked back to the girl and tried to put her shoes on. She laughed when she saw they wouldn't fit. Then, I asked, since our shoes wanted to dance, wouldn't it be all right if we stood in them while they did so? She circled the room again, saying, "Our shoes will dance if we stand in them." Everyone laughed. "Let the shoes dance," they said. And we did.

I had learned a lesson in how to use positive symbols to overcome prejudice and resistance. If I had simply asked the girl to dance, I would have violated deeply entrenched cultural taboos. Instead, I had begun a dialogue on new ground, one that began with a "Yes" instead of a "No."

But Africa was just beginning to teach me its rules. From Abidjan I traveled with the newly arrived Henri Kamer to Ouagadougou, the capital of Upper Volta (now Burkina Faso) and from there to Bobo-Dioulasso. In Bobo, I discovered the uniquely African process called "palaver," a seemingly endless ritual of reaching agreement.

Bobo-Dioulasso is one of the historic jewelry centers of Africa. The local artisans create gold filigree pieces of great beauty and delicacy. I wanted to buy a pair of earrings to take home. The negotiation for them took more than an hour even though I was in a hurry and didn't want to take the time to bargain over the price. But the ritual had to be observed. The seller first named his price. The buyer then had to present a counteroffer. Then the search for agreement began. Statements could be as subtle, elegant, and intellectually challenging as moves in a game of chess or as emotional as "May my mother and her whole family go blind if this object is not the most beautiful in the world." If you tried to escape the process by agreeing to the first demand, that price would suddenly be withdrawn. The ceremony had to reach its natural conclusion with a compromise agreeable to both parties. When a deal was struck and the tension of the negotiation was over, there would be a great show of pleasure and affection—embracing, handshaking, and flowery compliments. The purpose of the "palaver," I soon discovered, was not so much to arrive at a price but to create harmonious relationships.

Life in Africa seemed to be a series of "palavers." After Kamer and I hired a guide, a driver, and other helpers, we crossed the border into Mali, loaded with equipment including our personal effects, five rifles, and countless cameras. At the border, we were required to file customs forms listing every item we carried. It could have taken days, so we began to palaver and soon reached a satisfactory conclusion: with Allah's blessing, we would make gifts to the custom officials of seven bottles of beer, three bottles of wine, eight loaves of bread, and the equivalent of $56 in fees. It took only three hours. Years later, I would use this process to win business and call it "dialogue marketing."

And then Kamer and I were in Mali, on our way to the Dogon. But first we came to Ségou, a large village of the Bamana tribe, where we planned to spend the night. Kamer said we would have to stop at the local police headquarters first; there he asked the commandant for permission to camp in the area under his protection. That done, we visited the local tribal chief. Once again, we asked permission to stay and sought the chief's official protection. Because we acknowledged the superior power of the police and the tribal chief, we and our possessions were now safe. As Dr. Morganthaler had suggested in Zürich, we had gained power by giving it up.

A day later, we arrived in Bamako, the capital of Mali, where I had to apply for official permits to take photographs and motion-picture film. We received them and agreed to let a young military officer, Lieutenant Moussa Sidibe, accompany us. At first, Sidibe was hostile and wouldn't let us use our camera, and I saw that we would have to find a way to win him over. One morning, I told the others that we should prepare a ceremony. When Lieutenant Sidibe joined us that morning, I told him that we were a family traveling together and that, like many families, we shared a symbol of identification: we all wore watches. Only the lieutenant wore no watch. So, as head of the "family," I invited him to join our family by accepting our family emblem. I took one of the Timex watches I carried to use as gifts and offered it to him. He hesitated a moment and then smiled. Embracing me, he said, "Harmony is good." He put the watch on and embraced everyone in turn. From that moment on, we were "Moussa" and "Lester."

It was an early lesson in building relationships. What I didn't know at the time was that this and other lessons I would learn in Africa would soon change both my way of doing business and my life. Now we were ready to meet the Dogon people and their chief, Ogobara Dolo.

19
How to Be
a Chief

At five miles an hour, our truck bounced along the unyielding, rocky path to Sanga, the principal village of the Dogon. As we arrived, a crowd gathered. I clutched my tape recorder, which contained the message Pat Imperato had recorded in New York for Chief Ogobara. When we asked to see Ogobara, the crowd parted to make way for a slim, erect man who was clearly their leader.

Ogobara was of medium height and looked about my age. In his argyle socks and native sandals, he didn't look much like the African chiefs I had seen in the movies.

After Kamer's flowery introduction of me in French, I reached for Ogobara's hand, and we held hands while he completed a long ceremonial greeting. I then explained, in the best French I could manage (I had been taking lessons), that we had come because we wanted to know his people, photograph them, and experience the Dogon environment firsthand. We could do this only with his cooperation. Then I presented him with a "special gift": I pressed "play" on the tape recorder, and we heard the voice of Pat Imperato greeting Ogobara and other friends in the village. The effect was electric. I had brought the life force, the *nyama,* of the beloved and respected Dr. Imperato to the village. In time, I would become a "brother of the chief" and a "chief," but first I had much to learn.

Ogobara became my guide and teacher. We spent days visiting the village elders, whose language Ogobara translated for me. In time, our conversations became more intimate. I wanted to know what it meant to be a chief in the Mali of the 1970s. What were Ogobara's powers and responsibilities?

Years before, Charlie Perkins had shown me how to use power as head of one's own business, but Ogobara would teach me the uses of powerlessness. I knew that when I returned to New York, I was going to have to decide whether to merge WRK with a larger, more powerful company. I was worried by thoughts of what my role after such a merger would be. I feared becoming a *chef de paille*, or "straw chief"— a chief, in other words, like Ogobara. He had originally been appointed by the French and had remained one when Mali had become an independent republic, but he had no political, financial, or police power. So what kind of chief was he? I would soon find out.

One hot, sunny day, Ogobara and I walked to the top of a rocky hill that overlooked the Friday market in Sanga. People who had come in from the desert, the Mopti delta, and outlying villages were buying, selling, or bartering fish, onion balls, millet, cloth, spices, chickens, goats, milk, eggs, and so on. This was direct marketing, pure and simple—raw, efficient, and essential to the life of the region.

I asked Ogobara if he was chief of the market. He answered, "It doesn't matter." I pressed the point: Shouldn't a chief control the most important economic process in his village? "No," he replied. "The people know how to make the market—it doesn't need a chief." "What if somebody cheats?" I asked. "Nobody will," he replied. He then explained that the Dogon didn't need a chief to keep order—order was the natural state of things.

So why, I asked, did the Dogon need a chief at all? "Everyone needs a chief," he explained. That, too, was the natural way of things. Then he added that a chief also needed his people, because only together could they know who they were.

I still wanted to know what real power he had. "The power the people give me by their need for a chief," he replied. "A chief who cares for them, who wants everything to be right for them." That's what he did, and that was the power he had.

The Dogon were a family, a kinship group, surviving in a remote place with few resources and a difficult climate. Ogobara was the father of that family. He was steward and symbol of their culture and their lives—their past and future. I was beginning to understand the role and responsibilities of a chief.

Ogobara wanted to know what kind of chief I was in New York. I tried to explain business in America. I told him that my business family, the people I took care of, shared a special belief. I was afraid I would lose control of it, and them, if my "family" and I were taken over by a larger, more powerful group with a different belief. He told me that it wouldn't happen if my people continued to preserve and practice their own beliefs.

Soon after, Ogobara told the other chiefs and elders of the tribe that I was to become his brother and asked them to teach me what I had to know to become one of them. I learned that as animists they believed in a life force *(nyama)* that was the essence of every animate or inanimate thing. This life force had to be respected and protected. God was in everything, and there was a natural harmony to life and the universe that was not to be disturbed. The relationships of each person and thing to the others were part of this harmony, as were the family, the village, and the tribal group. I learned that to be a member of the group was to be loved and protected. I never really understood the meaning of love and relationships until the Dogon made me part of their kinship group. After they did, I left Sanga with another view of the world of the Dogon—and my own.

I returned home with an understanding of what it meant to belong to a kinship group. I had learned what a chief did, what powers he had to keep, and what he could give up. I was ready to consider a merger with a larger agency, and I knew I wouldn't become merely a "straw chief."

I did not return to Sanga or see the Dogon again until I visited there years later, early in 1976, on a honeymoon with my new wife. The Dogon married us in a three-day ceremony, according to their custom—and Ogobara was my best man. After all, I was a member of his "family." My tribal name was "Amma Sagou," which meant "Beloved of God"; my bride's, "Ya Domio," which meant "Beloved of the Beloved of God."

20

How to Merge with Another Tribe

In 1972, when I returned to New York after my first stay in Mali, I went back to work as head of WRK and chief spokesman for direct marketing. But my thinking had been profoundly affected by what I'd recently learned. Before my trip to Africa, I had been haunted by Dr. Morganthaler's question: "Can you accept powerlessness?" Now that question applied directly to my dilemma concerning a possible merger with a larger agency. I had been moved by Ogobara when he had told me the role of a chief was to take care of his people—to help them protect and practice the ideas, beliefs, and way of life that distinguished them from other tribes.

After much deliberation, I concluded that the best way of advancing the idea of direct marketing would be to merge WRK with a large and prestigious general agency. This would give us access to that agency's major clients, which would, in turn, add to the credibility of direct marketing. However, I still worried that by putting ourselves into someone else's hands, we would lose our uniqueness.

When I had told Ogobara that I was apprehensive, he had reassured me that I wouldn't lose control if our idea was strong enough and if we could continue to develop our ideas. This is what I wanted to accomplish, and now I would try to make it happen.

All this took place before "merger mania" struck the advertising community. While many agencies had gone public, they had not yet used their public stock to become massive communications conglomerates as they later would. I chose three agencies as merger candidates. Each of them was large, talented, and respected by the industry and held major accounts. Each had an individual, identifiable business culture. I now thought of them as business groups that had developed different tribal identities and belief systems, each headed by a chief with whom I had a personal relationship. The agencies were Doyle Dane Bernbach, Ogilvy & Mather, and Young & Rubicam. In 1973, they were all strong and growing.

Bill Bernbach, a friend for many years, was the soul of Doyle Dane Bernbach, nourishing a unique, creative culture. He protected the talented people who served under him and fought for the work they did. Bill was a moral force in the industry.

David Ogilvy was a showman and creative star, as well as a sound executive. Like Bernbach, he was the spiritual leader of his company. His people adopted his sayings, writings, and opinions as dogma. They also adopted his red suspenders, the company's tribal symbol. He taught, led, and was a father to his employees, becoming involved in their personal lives as well as their business decisions. David was a gifted leader and very much a chief.

Ed Ney, the most complex and interesting of the three, was the leading statesman of the advertising industry. Y&R's founder, Ray Rubicam, had left it a creative legacy that was summed up by his warning to "resist the usual." With its long tradition of innovation and creative leadership, Y&R had top clients and worked harder at the business of "excellence" than any of its competitors did. Ed Ney epitomized the character of Y&R: he was a brilliant strategist, a strong executive, and a humane, socially concerned leader. Y&R was a tough competitive team, and, like all winning teams, it trained hard and paid its dues. It worked as hard on unpaid public service campaigns as on campaigns for its largest clients. Ed Ney's Y&R was a tribe of winners with character.

My first discussions with Bill, David, Ed, and their associates quickly told me most of what I needed to know. I explained what I wanted, and I learned what they wanted.

- I wanted assurances that they were interested in direct marketing—interested enough to sell it to their largest clients. I was seeking not just a partner but a champion.

- I wanted to remain the head of my group, and I wanted my group to be separate from the parent company. I didn't want our people or our facilities integrated into the general agency. The culture of WRK would have to remain autonomous.

- I wanted employment contracts—legal assurances of power—to ensure the tenure of my key associates.

- I wanted a seat on the senior board of the parent company. That was the best way of having the larger parent company demonstrate its respect for WRK, direct marketing, and me. I wanted to be a chief among chiefs.

- I wanted an exchange of stock, not a purchase. It was not a question of taxes. I wanted the merged companies to have a key stake in each other's future.

- I would pledge allegiance to a new flag, but I wanted that flag to include WRK as one of its emblems. I also wanted help in strengthening and expanding our international companies.

- I wanted help not only in selling direct marketing to the general agency's clients but in selling it to the agency's managers and key employees.

It took only one discussion with Bill Bernbach to determine that, despite his genius, he didn't really understand direct marketing and had no passion for it. He was not the champion I was seeking.

David Ogilvy was another matter. David was fascinated by direct marketing and had been for years. He had admired the creative work of such mail-order copywriters as John Caples, Victor Schwab, and Max Sackheim and had often said so publicly. He was so enthusiastic about accurate, measurable results that he had once suggested that all his creative people be trained first in a direct marketing agency. As part of my merger discussions with David, I presented our work to a key group of his executives and he and his colleagues presented their work to us. David was the best presenter of advertising I had ever seen. I looked forward to the excitement of presenting a direct marketing campaign with David to O&M clients.

But despite David's charisma and his enthusiasm for direct marketing, I worried about merging WRK with Ogilvy & Mather, which had recently sold much of its stock to private and institutional investors (David and his key executives had become wealthy as a result). I didn't like the idea of public ownership of an advertising agency. The task of an advertising agency is to serve its clients, which means creating an environment and incentives that attract and keep talented employees. But no agency can serve two masters. The inevitable conflict between the client's need for services and the stockholders' need for profits is a real problem. I wasn't sure that even with David's enthusiastic support, Wall Street would permit Ogilvy & Mather to make the investments I thought a growing WRK needed.

In my notebook, I wrote, "I am comfortable with David and some of his colleagues. I am uncomfortable about the commitment to WRK by the next generation of O&M executives. I am totally uncomfortable about the presence of Wall Street."

At lunch with Ed Ney on June 18, 1973, I decided to merge with Y&R. Ed and I had served together on the board of directors of the American Association of Advertising Agencies. We had also played tennis together. We knew each other as executives who cared about our companies and our industry. We had also discovered that we both hated to lose—at anything.

That day, as we dined alone in my apartment, Ed told me that Y&R was still incomplete. Ed had become CEO in 1971, when the once-proud agency had been losing clients, personnel, profits, and momentum. Ed and a small group of colleagues had taken over, cleaned house, and turned the agency around. Under his leadership, it had once again become a benchmark agency. But Ed wasn't satisfied.

The world was changing, he said, and Y&R had to keep up. Advertisers no longer wanted separate agencies that did general advertising, public relations, direct marketing, or sales promotion. They wanted a single strategy, well executed in all disciplines. This was a new way of looking at the function of an advertising agency. Decades later, it would be known as "integrated advertising," and Ed was determined that Y&R lead this effort by agencies to satisfy all of their clients' needs.

I defined WRK and its future. I told Ed that I believed direct marketing was the future of advertising. So strong was my belief that I had left the best job in the mail-order advertising business in 1958 to start WRK on a shoestring. I had bet everything I had—money, career, reputation—on direct marketing because I believed it would one day become a giant business. I had spent thirty years mastering the art of making advertising measurable and profitable, and now I wanted to use what I had learned in a bigger arena. I then told the successful head of the best agency in the world why his current business might be facing a dead end.

I summarized for him the speech I had given years earlier at MIT. General advertising had gotten its start, I said, when machines had begun to produce tremendous quantities of standardized products for mass consumption; this had created the need for mass marketing, mass media, and mass advertising to move the goods. As a result, manufacturers had lost touch with the real consumers of their products. They didn't know who they were, where they lived, or what they really wanted. Mass marketing was a one-way street, and manufacturers were forced to advertise their products to regain whatever control and identity they could—and that, I told Ed Ney, was where his general agency came in. Mass advertising and mass media were the only link his clients had with the consumers who were buying and using their products.

He replied that I had just made the case for general advertising. Agencies such as Y&R influenced the distribution system and consumers' brand awareness. Correct, I told him, but that was not the end of the story. If it were, Y&R would continue to grow and WRK would shrink. But the opposite was more likely to happen as the mass market became less and less a mass, as was already happening. I told him that advertising would now have to focus on individual consumers' behavior. He looked skeptical. He asked if I really thought that direct mail was going to be more effective than all other media.

No, I told him, that was not what I meant. I believed that all mass media would eventually erode as they became so mass-oriented as to be irrelevant to everyone. Certainly, we used direct mail and telephone selling because they were the only "addressable" and interactive media then available. They were particularly effective when we had been able to learn something about the individuals we were writing to or calling. We also used magazines, newspapers, television, and radio to get potential customers to buy or "raise their hands." We knew who our customers or prospects were and where they lived, and we could "customize" our ongoing communications with our clients to make them more relevant. We could interact with the real-life needs of individual consumers, and we could measure the results and profits our advertising created. Someday soon, computers, electronics, and other forms of communication would provide interactive data-based media to bring shopping into the home by customizing advertising messages and the products they sold.

I ended by saying that direct marketing was the best way for manufacturers to communicate with and keep their customers. Direct marketing made possible a dialogue between buyers and sellers that could create long-term customer loyalty, rather than just onetime purchases.

Ney wasn't so sure. How could manufacturers keep track of tens of millions of consumers? he asked. Even if they could, how could they afford to? That, I assured him, was easy. The future key would be the computer, combined with television and telephone—a giant visual memory bank that would communicate with people one at a time about the things they wanted to buy, know, or enjoy.

What about retail outlets? he asked. Weren't larger stores being created to stock and move an increasing variety of products? How could they attract enough customers without mass advertising in mass media? This brought us to the crux of the problem. I explained that supermarkets, megamarkets, and shopping malls were a relatively recent mass-retailing phenomenon, but they were based on concepts of mass marketing that were already becoming obsolete. The theory that retailers, who didn't know what anyone in particular wanted, could stock all the products that everyone wanted couldn't survive. Some kind of home delivery system would eventually supply the specialized products individual consumers would increasingly want. A better, less time-consuming way of shopping would evolve, and the home would become the shopping center of the future.

He asked if things such as coffee, cars, airline tickets, or financial services could be sold directly. Could Colgate-Palmolive, General Foods, Gillette, Ford, and the airlines become direct marketers? I told him that they could if they chose to, but they would be forced to offer their customers the choice because consumers would demand it. I suggested that the influence of nationally advertised brands might, one day, decline.

He looked at me quizzically and wanted to know if what I was saying meant that what I called direct marketing would change not only how products are sold but what they would be. Yes, it did, I answered, except for one thing: it wouldn't be me or direct marketing that would change the way business was done. It would be the use of new technologies by consumers and the revolutionary force of history that would do it, whether we liked it or not. Young & Rubicam hadn't invented the Industrial Revolution, and WRK hadn't invented the Postindustrial Revolution. We had both been in the right place at the right time, providing the best services to advertisers who needed them. At that point the day's conversation ended. As he left, Ney said he thought we were onto something important. He asked if I would be willing to say it all again to his colleagues.

At a meeting at Y&R's offices, I found Ney's colleagues to be decent, intelligent men with the very special quality I had anticipated—character. Ed Ney and his agency gave the industry dignity. I knew they would provide direct marketing with a respected, powerful ally and make a critical difference with major advertisers.

Ney asked me to repeat some of our earlier conversation. I told the group why I thought direct marketing was going to grow and what I was looking for in a merger. I said I didn't want to sell WRK, which was a sound, growing business. We were succeeding very well on our own and could continue to do so, but I wanted a strong partner that would share my vision and commitment, a partner that would introduce us to America's largest corporations. I wasn't asking Y&R to acquire WRK; I wanted it to add direct marketing to its repertoire.

After several more discussions, we agreed to merge. Alex Kroll, then Y&R's creative director, said that Y&R didn't care if direct marketing grew larger than general advertising if that's what would best build its clients' businesses. It just wanted a division of Y&R to do it better than anyone else in the world. That was what I had been hoping to hear.

I called David Ogilvy and told him of my decision to merge with Y&R. "I was afraid of that," he said. He was gracious, though he vigorously and predictably disagreed with my choice.

As I had intended, we didn't sell WRK to Y&R but traded WRK shares for Y&R shares. The final price of the shares would be determined by the future profits of the combined company. I was appointed to the Y&R board of directors, the first direct marketer ever to be on the senior board of a major agency. That was good for me and good for direct marketing.

Ed Ney and I were both right. Direct marketing has become the world's fastest-growing advertising and marketing discipline—and "integrated advertising" is increasingly being used by many of the world's largest advertisers.

As for my fear of being forced to abandon our methods and beliefs—Ogobara was right. Y&R has not only respected our beliefs but helped to sell them to its major clients. Today, we share such accounts as Ford, Philip Morris, Du Pont, Swissair, Andersen Consulting, Xerox, AT&T, Clorox, Taco Bell, Viacom, Chevron, and Sears with our partners Young & Rubicam Advertising and Burson Marstel-ler, the world's leading public relations agency.

I needn't have worried about becoming a "straw chief." From the beginning, the people at Young & Rubicam showed great respect for us and what we did. Y&R has gone further than any other agency in encouraging us to be the best at what we do. Its belief in "best alone and better together" has created a partnership of equals in which we share our skills to help build our clients' businesses.

21

Creating a
New Direct
Marketing

F or years, I had been anticipating the day when direct marketing would come of age. Now that time had come, and I was expected to deliver the revolution I had promised. But how? In practice, the theoretical discipline I called "direct marketing" was still mainly mail-order advertising, and general advertisers had little they wanted to sell by mail.

Then we got our first break. Ed Ney called me just a few days after our merger and said he had arranged for the two of us to have lunch with James Ferguson, the chairman and CEO of General Foods, at its headquarters in White Plains. When we arrived, Ney introduced me to Ferguson, telling him that I was the "genius" who could bring direct marketing to General Foods.

After lunch with Ferguson and his executives, we talked about the mail-order business. They told me that they were investing millions of dollars in a "start-up" mail-order business called Creative Village, which had begun as three separate businesses, each offering craft and home sewing materials by catalog.

We were now the direct marketing agency for General Foods, then Y&R's largest client, but I had serious questions about the businesses we had been appointed to serve. General Foods' mail-order business was based on a shrinking consumer franchise with weaknesses that would, in time, prove fatal. The home sewing business, which in the 1950s and 1960s had seemed an attractive opportunity, was out of date in the 1970s, when both husbands and wives worked outside the home, stimulated partly by the women's movement and partly by the need for two household incomes in a sluggish economy.

Despite my reservations, I said we'd do our best, but when I looked at the three businesses closely, I saw that they were worse off than I had thought. The internal and outside consulting groups that had conceived and test-marketed the Creative Village businesses had tried to find a shortcut to success by selling subscriptions to the catalogs as if they were magazines. They asked customers to pay $5 a year for four regular and two sale catalogs. Without a renewal, the catalogs would stop coming. The idea was to market a "magalog," which was sold as a magazine but served as a catalog; the $5 subscription price would cover the cost of the catalog even if a customer didn't buy from it.

This may have seemed like a good idea to the consultants, but it hadn't worked. Many good catalog customers had turned out to be bad subscribers, while many good subscribers didn't buy from the catalog. The result was that good customers whose subscriptions lapsed were dropped from the mailing list, while nonbuyers who renewed remained on the list.

We corrected some of these and other major flaws in the marketing of the Creative Village businesses, but we couldn't reverse the declining market for home sewing and crafts. Nevertheless, General Foods respected our work. In time, we all agreed that Creative Village would never achieve the scale or profit that General Foods required, and the businesses were sold.

Over time, we continued to receive small assignments from General Foods while we searched for a direct marketing opportunity better suited to their basic business. It took ten years to find it, and when it finally came, it was such a surprise that it almost got away.

22

The King of Sweden's Coffee Comes to America— By Mail

I n the autumn of 1980, Young & Rubicam was asked to market, in the United States, products that General Foods made overseas. General Foods had recently acquired the largest coffee company in Sweden, the Victor Th. Engvall Company, founded in the 1850s, which marketed Gevalia Kaffe, Sweden's best-selling brand. The Swedes drank more coffee per capita than anyone else except the Finns, whose favorite coffee was also Gevalia. General Foods believed that it might make sense to market Gevalia in the United States.

Y&R already did the advertising for Sanka and General Foods International Coffees, as well as other major General Foods brands. A new assignment in the coffee category was a major opportunity for Y&R. Larry Shapiro, who supervised the General Foods account, offered what he called "a weird assignment" to Jerry Shereshewsky, a member of his group who was considered an unorthodox thinker.

Shapiro called the Gevalia assignment "weird" because Sweden was such an unlikely place to make a gourmet premium coffee. Colombia, Guatemala, Jamaica, and Kenya grew quality coffee beans, and coffee experts were normally represented in advertising as Latin Americans, French connoisseurs, or Italians, who made the world's best espresso. No one in America thought of Sweden as a source of good coffee. Y&R's research found that Americans actually liked the taste of Gevalia, but the Swedish connection left them cold.

Meanwhile, premium blends of coffee sold in gourmet and specialty food stores were attracting young, upscale consumers. Research had uncovered a growing U.S. market for a superpremium coffee, but no one could figure out how Gevalia could become a viable entry. Even if its Swedish origin could be made more attractive, it would cost at least three times as much as the popular supermarket brands.

The coffee's price ruled out supermarket distribution; if Gevalia were to be sold in the United States, it would have to be through gourmet and specialty shops. But when the Y&R team studied this market, the project seemed hopeless. General Foods had no experience with specialty-store marketing and the higher cost of its three-tier distribution system, which included a specialty wholesaler whose extra markups would raise Gevalia's price to $7 or $8 a pound at retail, about twice the price of other gourmet coffees.

To find a solution, General Foods turned the project over to the veteran General Foods marketer Bill MacClarence. MacClarence had run General Foods in Venezuela. He knew coffee, and he knew how to solve unusual problems. He and Jerry Shereshewsky made a good team. Shereshewsky was a lateral thinker, and MacClarence could get things done. They analyzed Gevalia's problems and opportunities.

Problems:
- Gevalia is a Swedish brand of coffee unknown in the States.
- Gevalia is not now packed in whole-bean form, which the gourmet market increasingly demands.
- Gevalia is not available decaffeinated, one of the fastest-growing U.S. premium market segments.
- Specialty-store selling is a three-tier distribution market that is difficult to reach and hard to support with national advertising and sales promotion.
- General Foods has no leveraged access to this market.
- There were no A. C. Nielsen data on specialty-store sales. General Foods would be marketing blind, without the market share data it is accustomed to.

Opportunities:
- There is a growing consumer demand for premium coffees.
- Gevalia Kaffe is a superior coffee made entirely of premium arabica beans. It contains no common, poorer-quality robusta beans.
- Gevalia is already packed in a variety of roasts from light to dark for the Swedish market.

- The Engvall Company has a long tradition of roasting quality coffees dating back to the 1850s. It is the official purveyor of coffee to the kings of Sweden, and every package of Gevalia Kaffe carries the royal warrant. Gevalia is literally "the coffee of kings."
- Americans who appreciate good coffee seem to like the flavor of Gevalia. The upscale segment of this group would probably buy Gevalia if a way could be found to distribute it.
- Gevalia is vacuum-packed by a special process within three minutes of roasting. The process requires no canning, and the vacuum preserves the rich, just-roasted flavor and aroma of the coffee without refrigeration or special handling. The flavor is literally "suspended in time."

Direct marketing came into the picture almost by accident. Y&R had organized one of its periodic "ad skills workshops," which introduce the special skills of the various Y&R companies to groups of managers and potential managers. I happened to be one of the lecturers at a workshop that Jerry Shereshewsky attended. We had never met before. I told the group how many products and services were already being sold by subscription: phone service; insurance; utilities such as gas, electricity, and water; daily and Sunday newspapers; magazines; and heating oil, to name only a few.

Then I described an experience I had had in the south of France, where my wife and I owned a second home. Because we used the house infrequently, we often arrived to find the fuel tank empty and the house cold. M. Lombard, who sold fuel oil, called *mazout* in France, was an independent dealer with a small tank truck. He delivered not only *mazout* but firewood and cooking gas. I asked him why he had let our fuel tank run dry. Because I hadn't ordered the *mazout,* he replied. I explained that I didn't live in the village full-time and couldn't tell when I was running out of fuel. I asked him how I could get *mazout* when I needed it. He told me that this would be difficult because I would have to ask him for a price. This seemed odd until he explained that when other village residents needed oil, they called not only M. Lombard but his competitors for bids on a tankful. They then bought from the lowest bidder.

I told M. Lombard that I couldn't do it that way because I couldn't keep an eye on the gauge. As much as I would enjoy receiving bids from him and the other sellers of *mazout,* I couldn't see a way of doing so. I offered him a deal: I would give him access to my house if he would promise to look at the fuel gauge regularly. I would authorize him to supply the *mazout* whenever the tank needed filling, and he would charge a fair market price. In other words, I would subscribe to Lombard's *mazout*. In return for my business, he would provide me not only with fuel but with an ongoing service. He asked if I would really do that, and I assured him I would, and so, over a glass of pastis, we concluded the deal. M. Lombard declared that if an *abonnement* (subscription) *pour mazout* was what I wanted, he would provide it. And he did. I never ran out of fuel again. M. Lombard found the idea of a subscription to heating oil so profitable that he began to call himself a specialist in *abonnement pour mazout,* and his business improved greatly. A subscription was a loyalty program, plus "automatic replenishment."

When Shereshewsky next met with the Engvall management in Sweden, he remembered my direct marketing lecture. He explained the process, and the Swedes seemed somewhat interested. He left promising to look into the possibilities and report again.

When he returned to New York, he showed up in my office with MacClarence and asked me to repeat "the French heating oil story." When I had finished, he asked if I thought we could sell coffee by subscription. I wasn't sure—I certainly hadn't thought about it before—but I laid out some ground rules. If we marketed Gevalia directly, there could be no retail distribution of any kind and no advertising but ours to launch the service. Packaged goods was the product category that had been most resistant to direct marketing, and we would have to break that resistance. If we did, we could then open the doors at other giant global consumer-goods companies: Procter & Gamble, Nabisco, Kraft, Colgate-Palmolive, Lever Bros., General Mills, Johnson & Johnson, and so on. I had merged with Y&R to expand direct marketing into just such companies, and so I became preoccupied with Gevalia Kaffe. If I could find a direct marketing solution, we could change the future of WRK and of direct marketing itself.

I created a special group to work on it. Shereshewsky transferred to WRK, and I gave MacClarence an office so that he could be a full-time working member of the team. When we needed anything from General Foods, Bill got it. More important, he was learning direct marketing on the job.

Because coffee wasn't a "collectible" or even a "replaceable," such as books and magazines, or a "useable," such as telephone service, I needed a new word to describe the process of selling something people regularly consumed. Remembering M. Lombard, I called the proposed Gevalia marketing process "automatic replenishment." And that's exactly what it was. If Gevalia were to compete with coffee sold in stores, we would have to offer General Foods and its potential consumers some unique advantages. "Automatic replenishment" could, in theory, let consumers subscribe to a constant supply of superior coffee. The subscription might be difficult to sell, but subscribers would be less likely to switch brands since they would never run out of Gevalia and therefore would never again have to go to the store for coffee— and possibly switch brands. With a good data system, sophisticated computers, and telephone hot lines, we could keep our subscribers regularly supplied with the amount of coffee they wanted. A great advantage of direct marketing was that it could produce what I called a "longer sale." Packaged-goods marketers measured the success of a product by its "brand share," its share of the total market for the category. They were interested in moving packages, not in loyal customers. But I was interested in the share of loyal customers we could attract to Gevalia. While the price of each package didn't allow for much of an advertising budget, a loyal customer could spend hundreds of dollars on coffee over time, even thousands in a lifetime, and this could be extremely profitable. I believed our subscribers would not behave like customers who had to shop for a product repeatedly at retail, and they would not be as likely to switch brands.

We called our direct marketing effort the "Gevalia Kaffe Import Service." A subscription would be a "loyalty" contract, and the increased sales per customer would provide substantial profit leverage. I was convinced that "automatic replenishment" would do for packaged goods what subscription selling had accomplished for magazines. More than 90 percent of most magazines were sold to subscribers, and I knew that more than 90 percent of the profit from packaged-goods brands came from repeat purchases.

I began by ordering Gevalia by the case from Sweden to use at home, and I liked its flavor and consistency. When I asked MacClarence about this remarkable consistency, he told me that Engvall's taster, Willy Pettersson, did for Gevalia what great wine tasters do for champagne or cognac: he kept the quality and taste of Gevalia uniform. Coffee beans are all different, even when they come from the same plantation, and their taste and quality change from day to day and season to season. No mix of beans, no chemical formula, and no technology can create a superior, uniform coffee. Only a great taster can blend and reblend coffee beans every day to make each batch the same. Willy tasted three hundred cups of coffee a day to make the necessary adjustments in blending and roasting. The unique Gevalia Kaffe taste existed permanently in his mind and memory.

I was now ready to sell General Foods on the idea of distributing Gevalia Kaffe through direct marketing alone, but this would take a lot of convincing. Our talk of direct marketing, databases, "automatic replenishment," telephone hot lines, attrition curves, and selling to the public on credit made their executives nervous. But Bill MacClarence was with us, and they trusted his judgment when he explained what we hoped to accomplish. As the months went by, more key people at General Foods supported us, but we knew that it was essential that the business show signs of promise if they were not to lose interest.

I had taken MacClarence and General Foods on a marketing journey into the unknown. They now trusted my judgment, but I would have to show them advertising they could believe in—and advertising was something they understood very well. They didn't like our first ads, and they were right. Our creative group had discovered how difficult it is to find fresh, descriptive language. "Rich," "strong," "aromatic," and "satisfying" had already entered the graveyard of coffee clichés, and here we were introducing a superpremium coffee and we couldn't explain why it was worth so much more than the usual price. To add to the difficulty, we also had to sell the idea of a coffee "subscription."

To help create an ad that would capture the unique quality of Gevalia coffee, I looked for a clue in the life and times of the company's founder.

Victor Theodor Engvall had been an ambitious young man living in the remote seaport town of Gävle, halfway up Sweden's long eastern coastline. One of the main cargoes arriving there from Central and South America and Africa was great sacks of unroasted coffee beans of every quality. At the time, coffee-bean roasting was done by small merchants rather than large companies. Engvall began his business by buying and roasting only top-quality beans, and he personally sold his fresh-roasted coffee door to door to the housewives of Gävle.

Over the years, he came to know the people in Gävle who really appreciated good coffee and built his business by sharing cups of coffee in the kitchens of his best customers. No matter how good people told him his coffee was, Engvall was never satisfied. He kept experimenting. He sold no coffee that he hadn't chosen, roasted, and tasted himself. Some people in Gävle said that Victor Engvall was "obsessed" with the idea of creating "the perfect coffee."

As his coffee became better known, he named it "Gevalia," the ancient Roman name for the town of Gävle. And as his business grew, he devoted himself more and more to selecting, blending, and roasting his coffee. But busy as he was, Engvall never stopped sharing cups of coffee with his best customers. He had learned that the more he visited them, the faster his business grew.

In time, new technology permitted Engvall management to vacuum-pack Gevalia within minutes after it emerged from the roasting ovens. It was still as fresh as the coffee Victor Engvall had roasted and delivered to his customers in Gävle every day. No written formula for the coffee ever existed. The special "Gevalia taste" had always depended on the skill, sensitivity, and obsession for perfection of the men who had blended, roasted, and tasted it.

Now I saw our advertising theme. It wasn't style, fashion, luxury or self-indulgence. It was Victor Engvall's "obsession" with "the perfect cup of coffee." Victor Theodor Engvall had been a direct marketer who shared his coffee and his vision directly with his customers. What we had to do was continue that tradition with our modern communication tools.

Jackie Stern, a talented WRK copywriter, and I soon came up with an ad that featured the "obsessed" master coffee roasters of Gevalia and the seaport town of Gävle. The headline read THE MASTER ROASTERS OF GEVALIA EARNESTLY BELIEVE THAT THEY MAKE THE FINEST COFFEE IN THE WORLD. The copy began, "On a narrow road in the small seaport town of Gävle, Sweden, in an old brick building, there are sixty-seven people who share a single obsession. They are dedicated to making Gevalia, the coffee they truly believe is the finest in the world."

General Foods told us to test the "automatic replenishment" program in a limited number of homes nationwide. We would use magazines to find people who would pay a premium price for what we believed to be the world's best-tasting coffee.

The research results encouraged us to take the theme of the Engvall "obsession" further. We did another ad that featured an old portrait of Victor Theodor Engvall himself. The final headline read THE MAGNIFI-CENT OBSESSION THAT PRODUCED THE COFFEE FAVORED BY KINGS. The copy for this new version began, "Over a century ago, in the small sea-port town of Gävle, Sweden, a man was seized by an obsession . . . to produce the perfect cup of coffee. His search began in 1853, when Vic-tor Theodor Engvall founded the company that still bears his name. He blended and roasted, tested and tasted with almost endless zeal. Al-though his fellow townsmen drank his coffee and found it superb, it never completely satisfied Victor Theodor Engvall. And when he handed the family business along to his sons, he also handed along the Engvall obsession." The ad went on to tell how King Gustav V of Swe-den, on a sailing excursion on the Baltic, had stopped briefly at Gävle, tasted Gevalia, and awarded it the royal warrant, appointing Gevalia the coffee purveyor to His Majesty and the Royal Court. The warrant has been renewed by every king of Sweden to this day.

The agency and General Foods believed we finally had an approach that would sell Gevalia Kaffe in the United States at a premium price. But good ads are only a part of a successful direct marketing business. There was still much to be done before we could launch a test.

The "automatic replenishment" system would have to keep pace with each customer's consumption and coffee preference. We also needed toll-free "hot lines" so that members could tell us to "speed up," "slow down," deliver quantities for special events, or stop ship-ments if they were going on a trip.

In Sweden, Gevalia was sold in regular and dark roast, but we felt that Americans would want a wider variety of choice, including whole bean and decaf. Gevalia began to produce both especially for the Amer-ican market.

Soon we had our package, our coffee varieties, and our advertising copy. Then we found the perfect premium, an airtight white porcelain canister that could keep an opened half-pound pack of Gevalia fresh. The canister was good-looking and useful and identified Gevalia as good enough to require special handling.

In January 1983, two years after General Foods had decided to bring Gevalia to the United States, we were finally ready for the test launch. But we needed to learn more from these tests than what the most ef-fective media were.

We used the final version of "The Magnificent Obsession" in both magazines and settled on the basic delivery plan. We would ask members to let us ship four half-pound packages, two pounds of coffee in all, every six weeks. We would enclose a bill with each shipment or charge the shipment to a credit card. The member could call or write us to skip shipments or to change the quantity or kind of coffee by roast, grind, decaf, whole bean, and so on.

The test ads were completed as planned, and we waited for results. We felt we had a winner, a business idea we could build on.

September 1984 was our major launch date. The "rollout" created the foundation of a good-sized business with substantial and growing sales. Gevalia became a regular General Foods brand of coffee—the only one sold by direct marketing.

That fall, my wife and I were invited to visit the Engvall Company in Gävle. I had made this journey in my mind a hundred times when I was searching for a persuasive advertising platform for Gevalia. I had "lived" with Victor Theodor Engvall, "visited" his customers' kitchens, "listened in" on their conversations. Now I could see where it had really happened.

We drove up to Gävle from Stockholm on a good road, mostly surrounded by forest. Gävle was larger and more modern than I had expected (my imaginary "visits" had taken place in 1853). It was a Saturday, and the Engvall management had opened the plant for us. That afternoon, there was a party in our honor. We toured the plant and saw the new roasting ovens devoted to U.S. sales and the packing lines where the Swedish and U.S. boxes of Gevalia were filled side by side. Then we were taken into Willy Pettersson's laboratory and tasting rooms. Willy blended some Gevalia coffee the way an artist mixes paints: undertones, highlights, subtleties—and then, all at once, we recognized the rich, familiar taste of the Gevalia dark roast we had been drinking since that day in 1982 when the red packages of Swedish coffee had begun to arrive at our home. I was watching the "Engvall obsession." Creating a "perfect cup of coffee" was not just a good advertising idea—it had remained as the core idea of the company's business.

General Foods was finally engaged in a regular dialogue with some of its ultimate consumers, a relationship that would in the future be enhanced by the new interactive media. Victor Theodor Engvall's "obsession" had inspired not only a great coffee but a new way of marketing. The Gevalia Kaffe Import Service would, I hoped, be the precursor of a new era of personal marketing and a new form of marketing dialogue. I had learned that direct marketing could transform a product into a service. In time, more packaged-goods companies will realize that the consumer is willing to buy and continue to buy the service a product provides, whether clean clothes, healthy teeth, good nutrition, or pet care. The product itself is always in competition, but the service needn't be if it is offered as an ongoing contract.

23

Time Flies

In July 1974, when *Time* magazine was selling 4,307,638 copies a week, of which 3,979,951 went to subscribers, I received a call for help from Kelso Sutton, vice president of the Corporate Circulation Department of Time Inc.'s magazines. Kelso told me that three recent postal increases would raise Time Inc.'s direct mail costs for subscriptions considerably. Only about 2 percent of the people who got those mailings responded, and now postage on the unanswered 98 percent had become unaffordably expensive. Even more serious was that all subscription copies were also subject to the higher rate. In the case of *Sports Illustrated,* the postal increases amounted to three times the magazine's annual profit. To make matters worse, old subscribers were resisting price increases, cancellations were rising, and new subscribers had become harder and more expensive to attract. Because readers weren't paying their share of the magazines' increased costs, advertisers were contributing 70 cents of every dollar of Time Inc.'s income. But advertising rates couldn't be increased significantly lest advertisers turn to other media. Unless Kelso could find a way to pay for the extra postage, three of Time Inc.'s major magazines would become unprofitable.

Sutton asked me to do something that Time Inc.'s Corporate Circulation Department had been unable to do for itself: he wanted me to find ways of increasing the price to readers by 300 to 500 percent and increasing circulation at the same time. I was to work with the circulation managers of *Time* and *Sports Illustrated*, but the ultimate responsibility would be his. He himself would be my client.

I accepted the assignment at once even though I had no idea what to do—assuming anything could be done at all. Time Inc.'s magazines were at a crossroad, and I relished the challenge—to say nothing of the potential income. My role was to change the way magazines acquired and charged for subscriptions, if I could.

Newsstand and supermarket sales are the most profitable way for a magazine to reach its readers. The distribution cost is less, and the magazine is sold at its cover price, not at a steep discount. Time Inc.'s *People* is one of the few magazines that circulate mainly through newsstands and supermarkets.

But *Time* sold only 9 percent of its copies on newsstands and *Sports Illustrated* only 4 percent. The rest were sold by subscription at deep discounts to new subscribers and somewhat higher rates for renewals. It wasn't that newsstand sales had been overlooked; *Time* magazine had been promoting them heavily on television. It was just that most consumers didn't buy magazines that way. Guaranteed mass circulation, the only kind advertisers invest in, had to be sold by subscription.

But there were other problems besides postage. As the magazines grew in size and number, it became harder to find mailing lists that didn't duplicate those already used. The pool of available names didn't grow fast enough, and as mailings were sent to the same lists more often, they became less productive. Even worse was that Time Inc. lacked a centralized database.

And because the company had favored circulation growth over higher subscription prices, the prices of the magazines had remained relatively static. Consequently, *Time,* which had sold for 10 cents an issue when it was launched in 1923, was now available to trial subscribers for as little as 20 cents a copy. Moreover, circulation increasingly depended on new subscriptions. By 1974, almost 50 percent of *Time*'s circulation consisted of subscriptions that had been acquired or renewed in the most recent six-month period.

I learned from the circulation managers of the three magazines that while their symptoms were not all exactly the same, they were suffering from the same disease. So I saw that the following would have to be done:

1. Ways of raising cover and subscription prices would have to be found. Since new subscribers resisted higher introductory prices, price increases might have to be disguised by offering shorter-

term trials. The price of the introductory offer would remain the same, but fewer magazines would be delivered over a shorter term.

2. Some improvements could be made in the company's direct mail strategy. But the fundamental challenge was to become less dependent on it. This meant that we would have to depend more on newspapers and television, which were not sensitive to postage costs.

3. The magazines would also have to achieve higher renewal rates, despite price increases. Circulation couldn't be maintained, much less increased, at renewal rates of less than 50 percent.

4. Each magazine was basically the same week after week, which meant that there was no reason to subscribe now rather than later. Something timely and startling would be needed. But what?

5. If subscription advertising were to be widely exposed in more visible media such as television, newspapers, and magazines, it would have to be of high quality. Typical hard-sell mail-order advertising wouldn't do.

Those were the fundamental problems, I believed, that would have to be solved. Others would undoubtedly surface along the way. The solutions would have to be flexible and imaginative. And I had always found serendipity the ally of aggressive problem solving.

Time Inc. was a large, smart, aggressive company, a major-league business that was, accustomed to winning. A "Time style" characterized everything it did. Now we had to change the way *Time* played the subscription game—for which, historically, it had made the rules.

I knew we would have to prove and reprove our merit constantly—not just to Kelso Sutton but to each of the magazine circulation groups and the senior corporate executives to whom they reported. Meanwhile, Young & Rubicam, Time Inc.'s traditional advertising agency, was in trouble. Y&R had assigned its most creative writers and designers to the account, but their work was unfailingly criticized.

Kelso had insisted that I remain personally involved. It was an unnecessary stipulation. Magazines fascinated me as major users of direct marketing techniques. A subscription essentially converted a single-product sale to an ongoing information or entertainment service. Such services could become a model for other kinds of products. Gevalia Kaffe had been a good example. Understanding magazines would help me learn more about how subscriptions worked.

Through the years, we had represented several special-interest magazines and had created some new ways for them to acquire circulation. The best example had been *Psychology Today,* a magazine that had gotten a lot of attention in the 1960s. But it had had a specialized readership, and because there were no productive mailing lists beyond its special area, it couldn't build a large circulation by direct mail. So we had created a series of compelling magazine ads to attract new subscribers and recommended that *Psychology Today* exchange ads with other magazines at a cost that was so low that *Psychology Today* could profitably place its ads before millions of potential subscribers. Years later, I helped Gloria Steinem and Patricia Carbine launch *Ms.* magazine by using other magazines as their circulation base. I treasure the first issue of *Ms.,* which was sent to me with a personal inscription on the cover. It read, "To Lester Wunderman, who helped as much as any man," signed "Gloria."

By the time we and our clients at Time Inc. had our teams organized and briefed, it was already late in the year. Remembering our success with *Psychology Today,* we created some "house ads" for each of the magazines to exchange with other Time Inc. magazines. This was our first opportunity to do creative work for each of the magazines, and we soon discovered just how hard our job was going to be. Not only did our proposed ads have to pass the Time Inc. "taste test," but research panels had to approve them before they could be tested. We were not accustomed to such rigid discipline. It wasn't the way WRK and I did our best work. We thought of ourselves as a commando group that achieved its objectives by any means necessary. But Time Inc. demanded structured strategies and executions, and this inhibited improvisation. If we were to succeed, one of us would have to change. Either way, success would require superior work, and creating it would be our main task.

For 1975, we proposed testing our new ads for *Time* in a variety of media from *Cosmopolitan* to *Esquire,* from *Business Week* and *The Wall Street Journal* to the *Saturday Review of Literature* and *The New York Times Book Review. Time* would exchange pages with these other magazines at cost, which meant that we could buy pages at 30 percent of the standard rate. We also proposed testing preprinted card-stock ads in newspapers.

On October 28, 1974, while we were hard at work for *Time,* Kelso Sutton appointed us the circulation agency for *Money* magazine. *Money* was his personal responsibility, and he was in a hurry to get started increasing its circulation. I knew this was going to be a problem the moment I reviewed the results of *Money*'s early direct mail efforts. Trial subscriptions were easy to sell, but the renewal rate was low. The editorial content of *Money* wasn't what readers wanted.

And then the external climate changed. Suddenly, we were in a recession. *The New York Times* reported that Americans were skimping on vacations, restaurants, meals, clothes, reading matter, and gifts. Among the categories hardest hit was reading, including magazine and newspaper subscriptions. This would create a problem for all of Time Inc.'s magazines—but it would turn out to benefit *Money.*

In November, we presented a preliminary marketing plan for *Money* for the first quarter of 1975. The introduction began with an assessment of the current economy and the opportunity it offered for *Money* and ended with a restatement of the problem for which we had been hired: "In view of the threatening increases in postal rates plus rising paper costs, we believe a direct marketing campaign in vehicles other than direct mail could not be better timed."

We proposed four test ads. The headlines were:

THE FIFTY BEST MONEY IDEAS OF THE YEAR

TEST YOUR MONEY SENSE HERE

$25,000 A YEAR AND GOING BROKE FAST

HE MAKES $20,000—SHE MAKES $8,000
TOGETHER THEY BARELY MAKE IT AT ALL

We tested the ads with focus-group panels. The winner was THE FIFTY BEST MONEY IDEAS OF THE YEAR—the only one making a positive promise to the reader. We weren't surprised. People will respond to offers of help. The circulation director of *Money* provided a budget of $600,000 for the initial tests. We forecast that the average advertising cost per subscription would be $6—less than the current cost of direct mail.

With *Money*, *Time*, and *Sports Illustrated* ready to test campaigns in January 1975, I was juggling three highly explosive bombs at once. By early January, it was too early for definitive results from our ads, but I went over to Time Inc. to walk the halls and get the feel of things. Over the years, I always found hall walking in clients' offices useful. That day, I found Bob Fisler, Time Inc.'s head of advertising, standing outside his office, looking unusually cheerful. I wondered why. Fisler invited me into his office and said he had tested six new direct mail pieces for *Time* magazine, and the early results seemed strong. He asked if I would like to guess which mailings had gotten the best results and if I could rank them accordingly. I studied the six mailing pieces and laid them out on his desk in the order in which I believed they had succeeded. I'll never forget the look on his face. I had pulled the trigger six times without flinching, and I was right on all six counts. He never proposed another game, but I decided that if he did, I wouldn't play. I couldn't be that lucky twice.

What got my attention was the winning mailing, which offered a free poster-sized lithograph called "Faces in the News." It showed fifty-two people who had made the cover of *Time* magazine. I asked Fisler for a copy. He said that it hadn't yet been printed in quantity and he had no extras, but it had seemed to lift results by as much as 35 percent. I had learned two potentially important things: *Time* magazine could offer premiums, and the right premium would significantly improve results.

Then it was time to analyze the results of our many January tests. The first information was that our television spots for *Sports Illustrated* were a home run. The acquisition costs per subscription ranged from $2 to $4, compared to the traditional $5 to $6 for a subscription garnered by direct mail.

Next came the results of our tests for *Time*. *The Wall Street Journal*, *Esquire*, and *The New York Times Book Review* hadn't worked, but *Cosmopolitan*, *TV Guide*, and newspaper preprints had.

The most disastrous result for us was that *Time*'s own ad featuring a cover photograph of the French-Canadian actress Geneviève Bujold did better than any of the four ads we had tested, which caused our *Time* clients to say that we were still just a "mail-order agency."

Then came the results for *Money* magazine. The successes were *Business Week*, *Newsweek*, *U.S. News & World Report*, *Playboy*, *Ms.*, and *Psychology Today*, all bought at a discount as exchanged space. The prices had been approximately 30 percent of the card rates, and once again we had acquired subscriptions for less than the price with direct mail.

As for our creative work, the winning ad was "The Fifty Best Money Ideas of the Year." The others were far behind. Our clients at *Money* liked our creative work, but, unhappily, they didn't tell that to their colleagues at *Time*.

Overall, I was encouraged by the results of our first efforts. We had tested television successfully. The exchange ads had worked. Newspaper preprints were promising. We had created successful ads for *Money* and *Sports Illustrated* but not for *Time*.

In late January, Kelso phoned to tell me he had decided to centralize all promotional magazine subscription activity at WRK and that he would notify the other agencies Time Inc. had been using for limited assignments. I also heard from another client, Joan Manley, the CEO of Time-Life Books, who said that since we were the agency for both the Magazine and Book Divisions, she would appoint us the master agency for all Time Inc. media contracts.

We were now ready to see if we could transfer our early success to *Time* magazine. The budget for September testing was $367,000. I decided to risk it all on what seemed to me the main chance for volume: preprints in newspapers from Maine to Hawaii.

But first, we had to find a way to beat *Time*'s Geneviève Bujold ad. We tested other personalities who had appeared on *Time* covers, such as Cher, Margaux Hemingway, and Princess Caroline of Monaco. But I didn't have much faith in the outcome. I felt better about our final two tests. One was to offer "Faces in the News" as a premium. Another was to try supporting the newspaper ads with 30-second television spots in six cities. Our experience with the Columbia LP Record Club and other clients indicated that, properly used, television support would more than justify its cost. I hoped this would work well enough to take the heat off the creative issue.

For *Money*, we proposed an expanded list of magazines for use in September. We also tested three new ads against "The Fifty Best Ideas," though I didn't believe any of them would do better.

At the same time, something disturbing was going on at *Money*. Because of our success in January with direct response television for *Sports Illustrated*, another agency had created a commercial for *Money* and been authorized to air it. Though this agency had no direct response television experience, its ad was producing subscriptions at an acceptable cost. I was surprised and chagrined.

I complained to Sutton, and he assured me that it was a mistake and that we would do all of *Money*'s television advertising for 1976. But my confidence in Time Inc.'s loyalty had been jolted—with good reason, as I was soon to discover.

I wanted to expand the success we had achieved on television for *Sports Illustrated* in January by making a better commercial and buying a heavier, more varied TV schedule. In January, we had paid an average of 20 percent of the regular rates for the time periods we had bought. Direct response television time operates like a commodity market, with bid and asked prices constantly changing. January is the most productive month of the year, because most general advertisers go off the air after Christmas. This creates surplus time, and in winter weather more viewers are at home watching television. It was, and still is, the best month to purchase the largest volume of good time at the lowest prices. Our time buyers would have made Cap Pinsker proud.

Chris Meigher, *Sports Illustrated*'s circulation director, liked the results he was getting from television but wondered if the television subscribers who responded by phone would pay their bills. He proposed testing a new commercial permitting orders only by mail. Meigher assumed that people who took the trouble to order by mail would pay better. He also suggested a test requiring viewers to pay $1 in advance by mail and another that required total payment in advance. There was no reason to believe that television responders would pay less well than those who ordered from direct mail—but Meigher insisted we be prepared for the worst.

For me, testing a 60-second commercial instead of a 120 was more important. A 60-second commercial would give us greater access to televised sports events, as 120-second commercials were often turned down by local television stations for fear they would slow down the action. We chose sixteen new television markets for testing. The September budget of $66,000 was budgeted to acquire 11,000 new subscribers.

We also recommended tests of print ads in such specialized magazines as *Football Digest* and the *Sporting News*. However, the print test with the greatest potential for expansion was a four-page card-stock insert in *TV Guide* for which we would buy a partial run of one million circulation. If it succeeded, we could roll it out to the whole circulation of twenty million.

Using the tools of direct marketing, we were rebuilding the circulation structure of Time Inc.'s Magazine Division. But as always, every change we proposed had to be tested individually, no matter how tedious and time-consuming. It was the only safe way of accurately identifying the key elements of success or failure. After the September tests were put to bed, we began to study the magazines' renewal techniques. We examined not only the content but the timing of their renewal mailings. We asked consumers why they subscribed, renewed, or canceled. We discovered that many current and past subscribers weren't certain whether they had or had not subscribed, renewed, or canceled. They continued to receive mailings from all the magazines, none of which clarified their status.

They were also confused about what the magazines cost—the "cover price" charged by newsdealers and the "subscription price" were different from those offered in space ads or television commercials. There were also "renewal prices," which differed from the "cover price" and the "trial offer price." Many people also felt that to subscribe was to be "hooked" for life. We recommended a comprehensible restructuring of the whole subscription pricing system.

The September results were good. The *Time* magazine newspaper preprints were profitable, and television support increased subscriptions by 30 percent. But the Bujold control ad was still 50 percent stronger than any of the alternatives. To my surprise, the weakest of the tests was the "Faces in the News" premium. The September results confirmed the successful January 1975 tests. Television support was clearly a strong plus. *Time* was ready for 1976.

The expanded television schedule for *Sports Illustrated* was also successful, as were the magazines we used, but the 60-second commercial had not worked as well as the 120. Ordering by mail had more than tripled the cost of subscriptions, and the all-cash offer had also produced subscriptions at an unacceptably high cost. But our basic offer continued to produce subscriptions at $3 to $4. *Sports Illustrated* was also ready for 1976.

Money magazine succeeded once again with its use of an expanded list of magazines bought at the exchange rate discount, and television also remained successful. *Money,* too, was ready for 1976.

But our clients were not ready. George Wiedemann, *Time*'s circulation director, agreed with Fisler that *Time* needed a second advertising agency to create better television commercials. Meigher discovered, as he had feared, that 37 percent of the subscribers we had attracted on television for *Sports Illustrated* weren't paying, and Sutton's assistant on *Money* wanted research done on the quality of *Money*'s television subscribers before she would accept any more.

Suddenly, nothing was ready for 1976. Wiedemann told me that he had changed his plans because Sutton had demanded an immediate price increase for *Time* in 1976. In 1975, the cover price of *Time* had been increased to 75 cents. Now it was to be raised to $1 for 1976. The "introductory subscription price" for 1976 would also be increased by 40 percent, from 25 cents a copy ($13 a year) to 35 cents ($18.20 a year). The "regular subscription price," $18 a year, would be increased to $22 per year. The higher prices would result in a heavy loss in renewals, and the new pricing system was no more understandable to subscribers than those that had preceded it.

Nevertheless, in 1976 *Time* was going to need substantially more than the 2.2 million new subscriptions we had planned for. To acquire them, we were going to have to go beyond our tests and make some leaps of faith.

My principal concern was how to raise prices and increase volume at the same time. Obviously, the new, larger targets required a new advertising "trigger," and I thought I knew what it was. To kick off 1976, *Time* had planned to publish a Bicentennial issue, an issue such as might have been published on July 4, 1776, with Thomas Jefferson on the cover. I wanted to offer it free.

We created a new newspaper preprint that replaced the Geneviève Bujold illustration with Thomas Jefferson and expanded the number of preprints to 30 million—28 million of which would feature the Bicentennial offer. To play it safe, we would retest the Bujold and Cher covers with the other 2 million.

We also created 30-second TV commercials to support the Bicentennial premium offer. We forecast that the Bicentennial premium offer would lift responses by 20 percent and that the price increase would reduce responses by the same amount. The budget was now $1,103,000. We budgeted for 95,000 subscriptions at a cost of $11.61 each.

We also created a 120-second direct response TV commercial featuring the Bicentennial premium to air in the middle of January and roll out each week thereafter if it succeeded. As a defense against "bad pay," the free Bicentennial issue would not be mailed until payment for the subscription had been received.

Wiedemann approved the plan even though the premium was untested. Fisler approved the creative but warned us again that another agency would also be creating a 120-second commercial to test against ours. I objected, but I couldn't dissuade him from making his "creative experiment." There was only one step left.

Wiedemann needed Sutton's approval, but on Friday afternoon he called to say that Sutton wouldn't approve a premium, even a special issue of *Time*. His rejection had been unequivocal.

Over the weekend, I called Sutton at home. He testily repeated all the negative arguments he had made to Wiedemann: He wasn't going to "downgrade" *Time*. Premiums were "a cheap fix" that, once begun, couldn't be stopped. I disagreed. I said that the offer of the Bicentennial issue was creative marketing and would enhance *Time*. It would bring more attention to our ads, commercials, and mailings. I told him he was being overly conservative. But Sutton had a quick temper, and I was afraid to set it off. I said, "All right, Kelso, it's your money," to which he replied, "Okay, but remember, it's your ass." With that the use of the premium had been approved, Sutton had changed the marketing history of *Time* magazine, and we finally beat Geneviève Bujold!

We awaited the results of the demographic study of television subscribers that *Money* had asked for, even though I knew what the results would be. The programs we had used attracted serious viewers who wouldn't subscribe to a magazine they didn't want and wouldn't pay for. Sutton was impatient for us to do more for *Money*, but we had to await the results of an unnecessary study.

The research revealed what we had expected. The subscribers gained from the TV ads were mainly middle managers, well educated and of higher-than-average income, *Money*'s target audience. We had every reason to use more television, and in late spring we went back on the air.

At *Sports Illustrated,* we finally convinced Meigher that even with the "bad pay," the low cost of acquiring subscriptions made television more profitable than direct mail, and I was certain that we could find ways to improve payment.

. . .

Nineteen seventy-six would be a year of decision for Time Inc.'s Magazine Division and WRK.

The Bicentennial premium offer for *Time* lifted results by more than 50 percent in newspapers, magazines, and direct response television despite the increased subscription price. TV support improved response by an additional 28 percent.

The ads and commercials for *Money* were powerful enough to support two price increases. A test of a premium late in the year created new possibilities for volume on television.

Sports Illustrated proved that higher-priced offers were not only more productive but improved payment. The only failure continued to be the 60-second commercials.

The 1976 campaigns set the magazines' ongoing subscription patterns. We had made print, television, and mail more profitable. Premiums helped us raise prices and correct "bad pay," because the premium was not sent until the bill had been paid. Higher prices provided higher order margins and higher "allowable" costs of acquisition. We had begun to change the way Time Inc. sold and priced its magazines.

Time Inc.'s *Annual Report* for 1976 described these successes in three headlines:

FIRST BILLION-DOLLAR YEAR

PROFITS SET NEW RECORD

STOCK IS SPLIT TWO FOR ONE

The text of the report included the following:

Equally significant was the 22% rise in circulation revenues. . . . The increase in revenues from readers of our magazines . . . raised the proportion of . . . earnings coming from circulation rather than advertising. . . .

In April 1976, Time adopted a basic US subscription price of 50 cents per issue ($26 per year), thus becoming the first major weekly to set such a high basic subscription price. The single-copy price was also raised last year to $1, which represented a doubling in less than two years. Despite these price increases, Time was able to maintain its advertising rate base of 4,250,000. . . . A Bicentennial issue recreating the events of 1789 was the second best selling issue in the magazine's 54 year history. . . .

Sports Illustrated's circulation revenues reached new peaks in 1976. Circulation revenues rose 11% aided by an increase in the magazine's cover price from 75 cents to $1. In line with Time Inc.'s corporate policy of increasingly looking to readers for direct support, SI's basic circulation price was raised from $16 to $20 in January 1977. . . .

Money continued to develop a loyal following of readers. In January a subscription went from $6.95 to $9.75. In November the newsstand price rose from $1 to $1.25. Subscription prices were upped again in January 1977, going to $11.95.

As reported by Time Inc.'s chairman and president, these victories seemed easily won. But for WRK, the war was not over. The commercial that Fisler had bought for *Time* magazine from another agency beat ours. It also looked better. Meanwhile, the effectiveness of our time buying for *Sports Illustrated* was being challenged by another direct marketing agency.

As the account grew, so did the competition. By 1977, Time Inc. was spending $13,850,000 with WRK—the Book Division $5,350,000 and the Magazine Division $8,500,000—and the magazine budget was growing fast. Our clients had changed. Kelso Sutton, who had hired us and became our champion, was promoted to vice president, Magazines. His replacement was Lawrence Crutcher. We had to sell ourselves all over again.

Direct response television had become a major medium for the magazines, providing an increasing share of subscriptions. It was also a growing part of our agency's business, and the visibility of the Time Inc. account led to other prospects. The trouble was that the techniques of direct response commercials had remained old-fashioned. One-hundred-twenty-second commercials produced at low cost and broadcast in bargain time had been fine for traditional direct response television clients, but that was beginning to change. Time Inc. increasingly compared the quality of our spots with those produced by general agencies for retail and brand support.

We could and did defend the efficiency with which we bought time. We produced a special report for Crutcher that analyzed all the time we had bought for Time Inc. in a given year. It contained station bills, rate cards, and an evaluation of every buy we had made. It showed that we had paid from 5 percent to 55 percent of the card rate, depending on the quality of the time periods bought. The total buy averaged 20 percent of card rates.

But it wasn't as easy to defend our creative work. Despite my claims for direct marketing, Time Inc. continued to criticize us as a "mail-order" agency. I knew it would take time for us to build better creative resources. But until we did, we would have to live by our wits. Every season after 1976 found us competing with commercials from well-known "creative agencies," as well as Fisler's internal group. With so much money at stake, our clients were surrounded by self-proclaimed direct response experts and other creative geniuses. We did better than I had hoped in the competitive shoot-outs. We won some and lost some, but we didn't lose them all and we never lost by enough to jeopardize the account. On the other hand, we didn't win by enough to eliminate the competition. The constant struggle sharpened our skills, and we began to make what I believed were more creative commercials. When we needed help, we borrowed creative directors from Y&R.

At the beginning of October 1977, we were asked to present a reel of all the commercials we had made for Time Inc. to Larry Crutcher and his circulation directors. He wrote to me on October 5, saying, "Many thanks for the 'perspective' show on Monday. As we all concluded, the pace at which you have developed in this field is truly startling. I think we were all embarrassed by elements of the early commercials and excited about how we could borrow some of the best ideas from one another as we continue to press for longer term and greater volume in the years ahead."

But we still couldn't make 60-second commercials pay. At a summer planning session for *Time* magazine, I proposed that we condense the commercial by not repeating the offer information more than once. The telephone operator who received the order could repeat it and even explain it in detail. The phone call would then become part of the sale, not just an answering service. By transferring questions about price and terms to the telephone, we were introducing a personal, interactive factor. The operator could not only ask how many issues the prospect wanted but could offer additional issues at the same price. The toll-free number call would reinforce the sale.

We tested this "operator upgrade" and found that "the average term has been increased 45% from 24 to 35 weeks. Assuming only a 70% payment rate on the $17.50 gross revenue, the allowable price we can pay per subscription has been increased from $8.50 to $12. With the higher allowable, television schedules can be expanded to include previously marginal stations and campaigns extended beyond the peak acquisition periods."

The additional value provided by the operator gave us a winning edge. What we had created for *Time* would also work for *Sports Illustrated* and *Money*. The successful 60-second commercial seemed to be at hand.

Then, suddenly, we almost lost the account. Time Inc. had become Y&R's eighth largest client, and other agencies were trying to acquire part or all of the business. Their persistence triggered a formal "review" of Y&R's work, including our part of it, by the magazines' publishers and circulation managers.

I was furious. WRK had done everything asked of us and more. We had raised prices, increased profits, and found new sources of circulation for all of the magazines. What was there to review? I created a presentation of our accomplishments. We had augmented direct mail with other media. We had helped raise subscription prices. We had invented the "upgrade," which had increased revenues for *Time* by 21 percent, *Sports Illustrated* by 10 percent, and *Money* by 16 percent. In 1976, we had created $10 million of additional profit from circulation for *Time* magazine and $2.5 million for *Sports Illustrated*. The results were there to be counted. I left the meeting in a visible rage.

The result of the review was that WRK and Y&R retained the *Time* magazine account, but Y&R lost *Sports Illustrated*. That eased the tension, and several years of good relations followed—until we got hit by a "bottle."

Once again, one of the country's leading "creative agencies" had been invited to do a commercial for *Time*. It was called "*Time* in a Bottle." It portrayed a castaway on a desert island, cut off from all civilization. A bottle came floating to the beach. It contained an issue of *Time* magazine, and the castaway was at once happily back in touch with the world. I thought the commercial was trivial, but it worked as well as ours—and on some stations even better. "*Time* in a Bottle" was used by Time Inc. as proof that creativity paid. It became the "control" commercial for *Time* magazine. We continued to buy the time, but we were now running second as *Time*'s creative agency. We tried repeatedly to beat "*Time* in a Bottle" but failed.

The following season, the "creative agency" overreached itself. It made one commercial in which copies of *Time* fell out of spaceships.

Even the people at *Time* knew it was ridiculous. The agency was asked to try again, and this time it produced a spot called "Wilderness" in which a man in an igloo was isolated during an Arctic blizzard. All at once, a Saint Bernard dog bounded into the igloo with a copy of *Time,* followed by other Saint Bernards each delivering another issue of the magazine. The isolated hero was once again in touch with civilization. Our friends at Time Inc. liked "Wilderness"—but it didn't work. *Time* was budgeting $15 per subscription—and "Wilderness" cost more than $42. It was a dead loss, and *Time* would fall short of its circulation guarantee if it used this commercial all season. It was time to put an end to the foolishness and to the other agency.

I asked our creative department to do a new commercial using the 60-second "Wilderness" footage as a centerpiece to which we would add a more persuasive offer. And so we created the "Judy wrap." "Judy" was supposed to be a *Time* magazine telephone operator. Wearing her headphone, she introduced the commercial by asking viewers to watch for a special offer. Then followed the 60 seconds of Saint Bernards. After that, Judy came back for 20 seconds and gave the toll-free number, repeating the offer of the premium and the introductory subscription price. In other words, we used the Saint Bernards to hold the viewers' attention for Judy's message. Our clients at *Time* were shocked when they saw that we had "wrapped" another agency's commercial with one of ours. It was unprecedented, but *Time* was in trouble and, despite the other agency's furious objections, it had no alternative but to test it. The results were hard to believe. The cost of selling subscriptions fell by 60 percent, from $42 to a break-even $17. We used the "Judy/Wilderness" commercial for an entire campaign. The season ended, but "Judy" lived on as a direct response television icon—imitated everywhere, even today.

Her secret was credibility. I felt that calling an unknown toll-free number was not as simple as it seemed. Viewers worried about who would answer the call and how difficult and expensive the transaction might become. "Judy" made it easy. She said, "Call this number and ask for me, Judy," and so on. It was like calling a friend. The real Judy was an actress named Ann Roberts who looked like the girl next door.

Because "Judy" had succeeded even with the Saint Bernards, we decided to give her a more important role the following season. For years I had been searching for the "missing link" between general advertising and direct marketing, and I suspected "Judy" was it.

Time had given Y&R a $10 million budget for what was called a "corporate benefit campaign." For this, Y&R had created a commercial called "*Time* Flies," using historic film footage to show the important events *Time* had covered. We and the creative team at Y&R then made a commercial using "*Time* Flies" footage seamlessly with "Judy" in a 120-second commercial. Judy did an 8-second introduction as she had before, identifying herself as a telephone operator at *Time* and promising to reveal a special benefit later in the commercial. The "*Time* Flies" footage followed, and an "announcer" made an offer. Judy returned with a 22-second close, inviting viewers to call her at *Time* to get an even better offer. The Y&R "*Time* Flies" footage was on film, but "Judy" was on videotape. Don Ross, "Judy's" creative director at WRK, wanted it to seem "as though a live camera had been turned on at *Time*'s response center."

"Time Flies/Judy" attracted new subscribers at $11 each, much more profitable than we had expected. During the months it was on air, so was the Y&R commercial, and they reinforced each other. In the following years, we did at least twenty versions of "Judy" for *Time* magazine and used "wraps" for *Sports Illustrated, Money,* and Time-Life Books. Not long after, we used the same technique to convert a Y&R commercial for Ford to direct response. We had found a successful method of linking brand-building advertising to direct marketing—but the next step would take time.

We also convinced subscribers to use their credit cards, making renewals easier and more efficient. Our early efforts had produced fewer than 10 percent credit card purchases. Today, *Sports Illustrated*'s Christmas offer attracts 85 percent credit card orders.

In 1974, Kelso Sutton had challenged me to find media other than direct mail and increase subscription prices by 300 to 500 percent. With persistence and imagination, we had succeeded and proved that direct marketing could work for a world-class client—and we had done so in competition with many of the world's most creative agencies. Now I was even more certain that direct marketing was ready to challenge general advertising.

24

Selling Ford Cars a "Chunk" at a Time

The Ford Motor Company is today our largest global account, but that wouldn't have happened if the behavioral psychologist B. F. Skinner hadn't taught pigeons to play the piano. In April 1979, Young & Rubicam became the agency for Lincoln-Mercury. The American automobile industry was about to be hit by economic problems and fuel shortages it had not foreseen. And the Japanese were about to launch a competitive attack for which Detroit was unprepared and from which it would never fully recover. It was at the beginning of this period that I began to think about how direct marketing could help sell cars. The American consumer was rejecting the design, engineering, and quality of the automobiles that Detroit was offering, and general advertising wasn't helping. American automakers were seriously out of touch with their customers.

Direct mail was not a new idea in Detroit, but I believed the automobile companies hadn't used it well. They thought it was a second-class medium and used it as part of their tactical sales promotion rather than as a strategy. Magazine ads and television commercials were taken seriously in Detroit, and decisions about which agency and which campaign to use were made at the highest management levels. But these same executives knew little, if anything, about the direct mail their companies did—nor did they care who provided it.

When cars were selling well, little direct mail was used. When sales fell off, mail and every other available sales and promotion tool—rebates, discounts, premiums—were employed to "move the sheet metal" out of dealers' stores. But the direct mail was poor, mainly reprints of magazine or newspaper ads stuffed into envelopes and mailed to lists of prospects supplied by dealers. These crude mailings were also sent to owners of competitive brands whose names were supplied by specialized list rental companies. The industry hadn't heard of data driven, knowledge based advertising. So when these primitive and irrelevant mailings failed to move cars immediately, the direct mail medium was blamed.

I didn't know much about the automobile industry, but I was certain that modern, information-based direct marketing techniques could help sell cars. I had to find a way to present our work and our strategic concepts to the right people at Ford.

I invited the managers of Y&R's Detroit office to attend a direct marketing training program, one we gave regularly to our employees. As a result, Y&R's Ford group saw the potential of direct marketing and agreed that we could help Ford sell more cars. They agreed to help us meet their clients, but it took more than a year to arrange a hearing for direct marketing at Ford's headquarters.

First, the Y&R executives in Detroit had to fill me in on the marketing situation at Ford. Like all American carmakers, Ford had been going through hard times. Chrysler had been saved from bankruptcy by a federal loan. Ford's new president, Philip Caldwell, had assured *The Wall Street Journal,* "We're not going down the drain." Ford's North American automotive operations were showing huge losses, which luckily were offset by their overseas earnings. Ford's share of the U.S. market had fallen to a dismal 21 percent, compared to General Motors' 46 percent. Against the backdrop of these gloomy events, I told my Y&R colleagues that I had some ideas for Ford. Ford was desperate for new ideas, and I felt that direct marketing should be one of them.

I was soon asked to take part in a major presentation by Y&R to Joe Cappy, Lincoln-Mercury's general marketing manager. Because direct marketing was a new concept to the automobile industry, my Y&R colleagues advised me to focus on the simpler issue of improving the company's direct mail.

I combined some of our most successful direct mail work into a tight twenty-minute presentation. Everyone agreed that my presentation was convincing, so I had no inkling of the disaster that would befall me the next morning, when we all went to the Ford conference room, one of the largest and most forbidding I had ever been in. The tables were arranged to form a long, narrow horseshoe. At its head sat Cappy and his staff. We were on one side, the more junior Ford people on the other. Each presenter had to walk from where he was seated to the open end of the horseshoe and then to the head of the table, a long and, as I was soon to find out, dangerous walk.

The reception of the Y&R presentations that preceded mine was polite but not gentle. Cappy and his executives were often harshly critical. As each presenter in turn made his case, he would receive a "thumbs-up" or "thumbs-down." The winners walked proudly back to their places. The losers would have been grateful to disappear.

Then it was my turn. I was introduced by Bill Power, the head of Y&R's Detroit office. I made the long walk to the open end of the horseshoe and up to the head of the table, carrying my presentation boards with me. It seemed to take forever to get the boards onto the easel facing Cappy. I kept telling myself that this was the big opportunity I had waited for: the beginning of direct marketing in Detroit.

When I was ready, Cappy asked what the subject of my presentation was to be. "Direct mail," I answered, following the instructions of my Y&R colleagues. His response was immediate and peremptory. He said that direct mail was a waste of money. He didn't like it and wasn't interested in knowing any more about it. It seemed wrong to argue. I picked up my presentation and walked back to my seat frustrated, embarrassed—and more determined than ever to sell direct marketing to Lincoln-Mercury.

After the meeting, the Y&R group evaluated the day's events, pleased that at least some of their proposals had been approved. Sensing my disappointment, they told me that with big clients like Ford you had to expect to win some and lose some. But I had lost everything, and I told my colleague Roby Harrington, who was in charge of the Lincoln-Mercury account at Y&R, that I wanted to try again as soon as possible. Who was Cappy's boss? I asked him. He told me it was Bob Rewey, the general sales manager. The next time, I resolved, I would follow my own instincts. I would not present direct mail but strategic direct marketing. The concept would be new to Ford, which meant I would have to sell it to a senior executive on a strategic level. If Bob Rewey was that person, he was the one I would have to convince. Rewey was said to be a tough, results-oriented manager. The tougher the better, I thought. Results were exactly what I could promise to deliver. I was also warned not to pursue the subject; it had become a sensitive issue at Ford.

The meeting at which I was to present to Bob Rewey began much the same as the one with Joe Cappy. Y&R presented a new marketing position and a new advertising campaign for the first small Mercury cars, whose success or failure would make or break the Ford Motor Company. Once again, I was scheduled to present late in the meeting. I didn't like being an anticlimax, but I had been told that there was no other way I could be included. As I entered the large conference room with its long U-shaped table for the second time, I was worried. Would anyone listen?

Rewey opened the meeting with a demand for proof that Y&R's advertising would be effective. He wanted to talk not just about advertising but about results. The meeting quickly turned into an argument. We felt that the campaign Y&R presented that day would eventually sell many Mercury cars, but how could we prove it in advance? As the argument continued, Rewey became increasingly annoyed. I tried to signal my Y&R colleagues to postpone my presentation, but they were too hotly engaged to notice.

Rewey had made his point, and now it was my turn. For the second time, I walked down the center of that long horseshoe table. If Rewey wanted accountability, I was ready to provide it. Accountability was one of the key advantages of direct marketing. But my Y&R colleagues had asked me to stay away from that issue, and after Rewey's performance, I knew why. Roby Harrington introduced me. Once more, I placed my presentation boards on the easel in front of the head table. The first board contained the title of the presentation. I had reversed it to its blank side, planning to reveal it after carefully setting the stage. But I was tense and turned the board over before I was ready. It read DIRECT MARKETING AND LINCOLN-MERCURY. Before I could say anything more, Bob Rewey, visibly annoyed, said that Ford didn't market directly; it sold its cars through franchised dealers. With that, he got up and left the room. I was left openmouthed in the middle of the horseshoe. For the second time, I had been turned down without a hearing.

For me, the struggle with Ford was more than a fight for another client; it was a battle for direct marketing. I had merged with Y&R because I wanted to work for clients like Ford, and I didn't accept failure.

I knew I couldn't go back to Cappy or Rewey. I would have to go to someone still higher, and that meant the head man, Gordon MacKenzie, general manager of the Lincoln-Mercury Division.

I tried to understand what had gone awry so far. I put myself into the place of the Ford executives and saw that I had tried to present direct mail as a new concept to Joe Cappy, but I knew it wasn't new and so did he. With Bob Rewey, my mistake had been to focus on my business, not his. He was committed to turning his company around. He needed help, not theory.

Ford represented an enormous opportunity for direct marketing, and Gordon MacKenzie was my last chance. As I thought about how to approach MacKenzie, I recalled an experiment in which psychologist B. F. Skinner had taught pigeons to peck certain notes on a piano in a specific sequence. As the pigeons had learned each note, they had been fed and their learning reinforced. Dr. Skinner had wanted to modify the pigeons' behavior and hadn't cared what their attitude about music was.

That experiment kept running through my mind. If pigeons could be "taught" to play the piano, if their behavior could really be modified, couldn't car buyers be "taught" to buy or consider buying a Lincoln or Mercury car? Automobile companies and their dealers offered prospective buyers incentives and rewards. But they were not structured to alter and reinforce behavior. Premiums, price incentives, financing advantages, and so on were offered to everyone at random. The rewards were bribes rather than parts of a learning strategy. Why not, I thought, stop advertising cars and begin "teaching" Lincoln-Mercury? If MacKenzie would listen, I could show him how to save the money he was now spending on tactical promotional rebates and discounts. One rebate program offering $300 to $500 on three Mercury models in 1980 was budgeted to cost the Lincoln-Mercury Division $43 million, an expenditure with no long-term value.

Skinner's experiment suggested a better way of selling cars. But before I could pursue this possibility, I needed to know more about how people actually learned. People, after all, were one thing and pigeons another. I called an old friend and fellow Dogon enthusiast, Dr. Hans Guggenheim, an anthropologist at MIT who was also an expert on learning theory, and asked him to help me learn about learning. For example, how did people go from learning simple arithmetic to understanding calculus? Easy, Dr. Guggenheim explained. The teaching of any subject was based on a planned "curriculum." The curriculum was designed by educators to teach an entire subject, one fact at a time. It was divided into what educators called "chunks," the amount of learning a person could absorb at one time. A curriculum was a planned learning program broken into "chunks" that were communicated, taught, and reinforced one at a time, like putting together a string of beads. Each bead was different, but when strung together they made a necklace.

Then I asked Dr. Guggenheim if he thought it possible to create a curriculum that could teach people to buy Ford cars. He didn't answer at once but asked a great many questions about the nature of the "classroom" I had in mind and the communication media that would be available. I explained how direct mail worked or could be made to work and how I intended to use it. Finally, he said he believed it could be done. We would have to create a "student body" of potential car buyers.

It felt like a big idea. I named it "curriculum marketing," and planned to sell it to Gordon MacKenzie with the help of Dr. Guggenheim, whom I hired as a consultant on the project.

What made it feel even more right was that we had a good product to sell. Ford's new Lincoln was better designed and better made than General Motors' Cadillac. When luxury-car owners were blindfolded and given rides in Lincolns and Cadillacs, they invariably said that the Lincoln was more comfortable. But when asked which car they were in, they invariably said "Cadillac." The Lincoln was a better car, but people thought Cadillac was superior, so much so that secondhand Cadillacs sold for 20 to 30 percent more than used Lincolns of the same age and condition.

Ford had closed the design, engineering, and manufacturing gaps to make Lincoln the better car, but we could help it close the perceptual gaps, which meant planning our teaching as effectively as Ford had engineered its luxury cars. I brought Dr. Guggenheim to New York, where he joined the small group working on Lincoln-Mercury at WRK. We were working secretly in our New York office. I wasn't ready to share our plans even with Y&R. Had I told Y&R that Dr. Guggenheim and I were going to try to sell a concept called "curriculum marketing" to its largest client, I might have run into opposition. This time I was going to do it alone.

When I introduced Dr. Guggenheim to his new colleagues at WRK, it was clear that they didn't know what to make of him. I knew Hans well, but even I found him a strange presence on Madison Avenue. He looked like an actor made up to play an absentminded professor trying to invent a secret advertisement to save the American automobile business. Dr. Guggenheim may have been a bizarre addition to our group, but he took to the task as if he had done it all of his life. He picked up my curriculum marketing project and instantly began to give it structure and creative substance. Hans believed that most advertising affected surface consciousness but created no deep commitment. He pointed out how, in most product categories, people made their choices based on trivial information.

We covered the walls of our conference room with questions people asked about buying a new car. The answers would become our new "curriculum." Consumers would "graduate" when they got the keys to a new Lincoln car. After the sale, owners would become "alumni." Their "postgraduate degree" would be the keys to their next Lincoln.

While we were preparing our presentation, conditions in the automotive industry continued to deteriorate. Research showed that loyalty to Ford cars had decreased from 49.6 percent in the fourth quarter of 1977 to 34.8 percent in 1980. That meant that just about two out of every three Ford owners were switching to a competitive brand. Loyalty to General Motors remained steady: 66.6 percent in 1977, 66 percent in 1980. But loyalty to imports increased from 49.6 percent in 1977 to 58.9 percent in 1980. The customers who left Ford would be the hardest to retrieve. They were not just disloyal; they were disillusioned and disaffected.

Henry Ford's mass-marketing tactics weren't working for Lincolns and Mercurys. The sales target for the entire division was 600,000 cars, of which only 100,000 were Lincolns. The more I studied the problem, the more I believed that targeted curriculum marketing was the right answer.

We then received a piece of very good news. Gordon MacKenzie had gone into the marketplace and talked to Lincoln and Cadillac owners face to face. He was listening to their problems and was making himself responsible for correcting the problems. We were sent a videotape of one of his person-to-person sessions. He was sensitive to the criticisms he heard and convincing about how Lincoln was solving its problems with its new Town Car, Mark VII, and Continental. He had committed the factory to producing a better product that was better engineered, better made, more fuel-efficient, and backed by a corporate commitment that went from the factory through the dealer to the customer. Listening to MacKenzie on tape, I was convinced that Ford was not just a faceless factory but a company run by dedicated, able executives committed to superior products and better service. I felt I knew Gordon MacKenzie even before I met him.

When we finished our work on the presentation of the "Lincoln Curriculum Program," I asked my Y&R colleagues for a meeting with Gordon MacKenzie. They were skeptical but willing to arrange it.

I realized I needed Dr. Guggenheim's help—but could I take him to Detroit? Lincoln-Mercury was Y&R's largest client. Did I dare take an outsider to a private meeting, particularly an eccentric professor with a heavy German accent? I had no choice; I needed Dr. Guggenheim's credibility.

Even so, I was cautious. I made certain that we arrived at the conference room early. I was seated, as before, with the presenters, but I put Dr. Guggenheim unobtrusively in the back of the room. I didn't want anyone asking questions, and I wanted to be able to exclude him from the presentation if curriculum marketing got the same treatment as my aborted presentations of direct mail and direct marketing.

MacKenzie entered the room and sat at the head table with Cappy and Rewey on either side. Y&R presented first, as usual, and then it was my turn. When I walked to the head table, I said "Hello" to Cappy and Rewey and shook hands with Gordon MacKenzie. I had decided that this time I wouldn't show my presentation until he and I had talked for a few minutes. But once again, I was asked the potentially deadly first question: What was I there to present?

I said I had come to present a radical new way of communicating the Lincoln quality story. It was not advertising but something much more persuasive. I told MacKenzie that he was already a master of the technique I was going to propose and that it was perhaps the only way of selling the new, superior Lincoln. He asked what I had in mind. I told him I knew he had been out in the marketplace. What I had in mind was a way for him to talk to many more than the few customers he happened to meet. He was interested.

I then briefly explained the theory of curriculum marketing. I pointed out that it was the way education itself worked, and I said I believed we could teach people to buy Lincolns again and again.

MacKenzie became involved in the presentation. His questions came at me faster and faster, and finally I decided it was time to reveal Dr. Hans Guggenheim, the world-famous authority on the science of teaching and learning. I asked Hans to come up and join me. I had made sure that he had not forgotten his glasses and his suit was pressed. He strode to the front of the room exuding dignity, authority, and charm. He had decided to play the role of the witty, confident, engaging scientist who was there to enlighten a group of laymen. He walked up to MacKenzie, held out his hand, and told him that he had the advantage of already knowing him. He had seen him on videotape and had recognized in him a born teacher who understood communication theory better than most professors.

The picture of that moment remains vivid in my mind. There stood Dr. Guggenheim, slight, thin, and just a few inches over five feet tall. He was holding Gordon MacKenzie's hand, as Ogobara Dolo had held mine. MacKenzie was at least a foot taller, brawny and strongly built. He should have towered over Hans, but somehow it was the other way around. They became "Gordon" and "Doctor" at once. The doctor encouraged Gordon to tell him his problems. MacKenzie began by saying that the Lincoln was now better made and better engineered than the Cadillac. It had better fuel efficiency and was more comfortable. But the public didn't believe it. Lincoln dealers were offering rebates of $5,000 to $6,000, but even these incentives were creating no significant retail traffic. His face flushed as he described his frustrations. He had a better product but didn't know how to make the public believe it except when he went out on the road and talked to people personally. Then he could persuade them to buy—but he couldn't personally talk to everyone.

Hans seized the cue. He answered, "Yes, Gordon, you can, you can talk to them all. You can teach them to buy your car because Lincoln is now better than Cadillac." Like an orchestra conductor bringing another instrument into play, Hans then turned to me. It was time for my formal presentation.

I told MacKenzie that direct marketing techniques could be used for teaching. I explained that I had consulted with Dr. Guggenheim to assure myself that the idea of curriculum marketing was psychologically valid. The program we had developed used the scientific techniques developed by educators. We were going to teach Lincoln owners and ex-owners that the new Lincolns were better than Cadillacs. We were going to listen to their questions, problems, and doubts and answer them specifically. We would do the same with Cadillac owners. We would teach them, too, enough about the new Lincolns so that they would begin to feel comfortable and familiar with them—and with the idea of owning one. Then I made a full presentation, boards and all, to MacKenzie, Rewey, and Cappy. They listened to every word.

I told them that curriculum marketing was a new concept best used when:

- The target audience was highly identifiable.
- The product being sold required a major purchase decision.
- There was a high threshold of resistance, ignorance, or inertia.

I then explained how the curriculum would use a series of contacts:

- The message in each contact was built on the previous message.
- By the end of the series, the entire sales story would be delivered.
- Each contact invited some form of response from the prospect.
- Subsequent contacts would be personalized to react to previous responses from the consumer.
- The cumulative effect of the series would be to establish an ongoing personal dialogue with each consumer.
- The ultimate goal was to maximize the impact of the advertising message through "customization" and "scheduled reinforcement."

Though a curriculum marketing program could be adapted to generate immediate sales, it was best suited to changing behavior over time. The object of curriculum marketing, I stressed, was to move the consumer toward purchase, one step at a time. Existing consumer attitudes toward Lincolns ranged from very negative to very positive. I described them:

- *Most negative, unwilling to consider:* "I had one and didn't like it"; "I drive the competing brand."
- *Negative:* "I am unfamiliar with the brand."
- *Least negative:* "I don't know very much about it"; "I just never thought about having one."

- *Neutral attitude:* "Show me."
- *Positive attitude:* "It sounds good."
- *Passive consideration:* "I'll think about it when I'm ready."
- *Active interest:* "Tell me more about it. Where can I see one?"
- *Purchase/usage:* "I already own one."

The curriculum program objectives were:

- To persuade current owners to remain loyal to Lincoln
- To persuade potential customers to communicate with Lincoln
- To persuade potential customers to visit a dealership
- To persuade potential customers to take a test drive
- To persuade potential customers to purchase a new Lincoln
- To continue to communicate in a loyalty cycle

The section of our charts that explained how the curriculum program would function included the following elements:

A Program Overview

- Send enrollment letter to customer with a census (questionnaire) determining:
    - a. Areas of greatest interest in car purchase and maintenance
    - b. Time frame for buying new car
- Analyze responses.
- Correlate fast- and slow-track buyers with their preferred areas of interest.
- Send out customized "curriculum" in a four-"lesson" plan.
- Continue dialogue by constantly providing the opportunity for the prospect to respond to each mailing.
- Provide reinforcements and action incentives in each mailing. These reinforcements and incentives would be cumulative.
- Create a dramatic "graduation" event leading to final sale.

When my presentation was over, there were many questions. MacKenzie wanted to know who would sponsor the program, the factory or the dealers. I told him that he himself should sign the letters and the questionnaires as if he were having one of his face-to-face consumer sessions.

I wanted special phones installed in his office that would be answered "Gordon MacKenzie's office." We would train the operators. I wanted Lincoln to be interested in its customers both before and after they bought a car.

Research consistently revealed that the car-buying public was suspicious of car dealers. However, they trusted the factory and wanted more direct communication with it. They wanted the manufacturer to care about them and the cars they bought. Lincoln-Mercury did not sell directly, but it had to behave as if it did.

The meeting was a triumph. We were asked to do a curriculum marketing program for Lincoln. Gordon MacKenzie agreed to sign every letter. Joe Cappy later told Bill Power that it was one of the most interesting presentations he had seen and asked whether we had hired Dr. Guggenheim from "central casting."

Finally, we had an active client. The concept of curriculum marketing converted us from being just another supplier of tactical direct mail to a unique strategic marketing and communications resource for Ford. Curriculum marketing became a buzzword at Ford. Executives from the president on down were now saying that our technique could give Ford a strategic communications advantage over its competitors—and these were the same men who had earlier rejected "direct mail" and "direct marketing"! This time we had packaged ourselves and our work better.

But would the plan work? It would take months to create and mail the entire first series of communications, and the results could not be analyzed until the public had had a chance to react.

Once the results were in, we formed an internal research group and hired the best outside consultants we could find to analyze them. The first indications were positive. Almost one third of the people who received the questionnaire completed and returned it. Their responses triggered the next letter in the series. Five hundred thousand people were included in the initial test groups. They were divided into separate cells, each of which received a variation of the program.

Before we received any hard numbers, I heard from Gordon, who told me that the special phones installed in his office for the program were ringing off the hook. The car-buying public was thrilled to discover that the top executive at Lincoln wanted to know how it felt about the company and its cars.

We discovered a strong correlation between the number of mail contacts made and the subsequent buy rates of Lincoln and Ford cars. Those who received the entire series—the questionnaire and three additional mailings—bought almost twice as many Lincoln-Mercury and

Ford cars as a control group that had received no mailings. Luxury cars—our "target"—accounted for 48.1 percent of the sales. Other Lincoln-Mercury models accounted for 17.29 percent and the lower-priced Ford cars for 34.7 percent. Best of all, 23 percent of those who bought Lincolns were currently Cadillac owners. We had succeeded in "teaching" Cadillac owners to buy Lincolns.

Because the program began with a questionnaire, we collected much information about which cars a family owned and why, what their buying intentions were, and when they intended to buy another car. Those who received all four mailings were 75 percent more likely to buy a Ford product in the next seven months than those who received no mailing. The results of each "curriculum" mailing, unlike those of ordinary direct mail programs, were additive. As we had predicted, the more mail people received and read, the more learning took place. And the more learning, the more buying. The curriculum marketing program of testing, teaching, and reinforcing was a success.

The answers to the questionnaires also provided information that made it possible for us to identify and isolate the three key ingredients of consumer satisfaction. They were "value," "quality," and "no major problems." These three factors could accurately predict overall consumer satisfaction 72.5 percent of the time.

The questionnaire also disclosed the one key condition that most often led to a sale: the intention to buy a car within the next three months. These people were six times as likely to buy as the average car owner was. The questionnaire helped us identify these prospects.

The entire program cost $794,783. The total purchases of Ford cars made by the test group amounted to $9,608,817. The profit from those purchases was $1,752,000.

The Lincoln Curriculum Program became a regular part of Ford's advertising. The incremental profits from the program have been as much as 240 percent of the advertising investment. I believe that the curriculum theory of data-based target marketing has a far greater potential than any other form of advertising. Advertising is a form of teaching that leads to selling, and the best way to teach is with a programmed strategy. Curriculum marketing converts "suspects" to "prospects," prospects to customers, and customers to repeat buyers. It is relevant and instructive at each phase of a car buyer's purchase history.

As a result of our first success, we were asked to create a curriculum marketing program that would create better understanding and awareness of the product design and quality changes taking place at Ford in the company's most difficult market, California, where the perceptions of the company were poor and sales and owner loyalty low. Owning a Ford in California in those days was tantamount to declaring yourself "out."

The California curriculum consisted of three mailings. The first, a report on vehicle quality, was titled "Quality: The Highest Priority"; the second, a design report, was "The New Direction"; and the third, a report on new products and features, was "The Driving Experience."

The mailings were sent to owners of Ford cars, owners of competitive cars, readers of car-buff magazines, and "influentials" such as doctors, lawyers, dentists, CPAs, aerospace engineers and other high-technology specialists, business leaders, and university professors. The letters were to be signed by Harold Poling, then executive vice president of Ford North American Operations. We had moved up the ladder almost to the very top of the company.

Research would be conducted in three waves of in-depth telephone interviews: the first to precede the mailings, the second to follow approximately a month after all the mailings had been sent, the third three months later. Curriculum marketing had been given a strategic task normally reserved for general advertising. Those at the top of the power pyramid at Ford would personally audit the program, a great accolade for direct marketing.

The results were impressive. Ford reported that one month after the final mailing was sent, the Ford Motor Company scored dramatic gains among recipients of the mailings, in terms of both buying intentions and overall attitudes toward the company and its products.

A follow-up report was issued on the results of the final wave of the research. It stated, "The major conclusion . . . is that the initial gains were well sustained three months after the mailings. . . . Claimed recall of receiving and reading the brochures remained as high as they were after one month."

Once we had persuaded the Lincoln-Mercury division of Ford that we could create unusual solutions to difficult problems, other interesting assignments followed, including one from the Ford division. It was to devise a program to sell more Ford cars to women.

Women were buying 40 percent of all cars sold in the United States, but no one had yet figured out the best way of creating advertising specifically targeted at them that was neither patronizing nor sexist. Ford executives had found that advertising that addressed women overtly resulted in a negative reaction. Women felt that they were being "talked down to" or "hustled." There was also the risk of a reaction from men if they were excluded from programs in which only women could participate. A recommendation had been made to establish a separate administrative entity at Ford to service the unique car-buying problems of women. As a group, they were experiencing special difficulties in purchasing cars.

We suggested that a curriculum marketing program could be created that would establish a dialogue with women car owners and prospects. It would encourage them to reveal their needs and problems. Based on the results of the dialogue, we could help Ford develop effective special services and offers. Direct mail would be used to announce these services and to generate showroom traffic and sales. The objective of our program would be to dramatically increase the retention of current owners and accelerate the acquisition of new buyers.

We created a program designed to prove to women that the Ford Motor Company and its dealers recognized and cared about their special needs. The test markets we were assigned were San Diego and Dallas.

The Women's Curriculum Program we created began with a mailing that featured a questionnaire. The letter was sent and signed by a high-ranking woman executive at Ford, who encouraged recipients to talk about the car-buying problems that troubled them most. It also asked about their future intentions with regard to buying a Ford. The first mailing was sent to 160,000 women in San Diego and Dallas. A control group of 80,000 women in the same markets would receive no mailings. The initial results were encouraging. Thirty-two percent of the women who already owned Ford cars responded to the questionnaire, as did 17 percent of the owners of competitive makes. Most respondents said that they strongly disliked the way they had been treated by the sales and service personnel at their Ford dealers. They felt that the salesmen had ignored or patronized them and that the mechanics in the service bays had been uncooperative and some even sexually aggressive.

As a result, Ford created a special training program for dealers in San Diego and Dallas. While that was a major step forward, I didn't think it would overcome the negative psychological relationship that existed between the women and the dealers. Women felt powerless and fearful at the dealership. To overcome these feelings of inequality, we created a psychological "power" device for the women in our test program.

The second mailing in our curriculum series, which was sent two months after the questionnaire, thanked the participants for their candor and advised them of the dealer training program and other steps that Ford had taken. The women were asked to visit their Ford dealer again, but this time they would be equipped with a new psychological weapon. We asked them to help Ford evaluate the results of its training program. If they visited a dealer and were well treated, they could help reward the sales or service people who had been helpful and supportive. They could also penalize those who weren't. We provided special rating forms and certificates each worth $25. They could, at their discretion, award a $25 certificate, payable by Ford, to a sales or service person who was helpful. Or they could withhold it and file a negative evaluation report with Ford. As a result, it would be the women who would control the relationship. As an added incentive, Ford provided a $25 gift certificate from a local department store to those women who visited a dealership and took a test-drive. While Ford provided the "test-drive" gift certificate to the women in the test group, Ford dealers had to validate the fact that recipients had actually test-driven a Ford. Thus, the women and the dealer could reward each other. It was a way of motivating and rewarding interactivity and relationship building. Among the reasons the program succeeded was that neither the dealer nor his sales or service personnel had any way of knowing which of the women who entered his dealership was carrying the $25 certificates and the rating form. To be safe, they treated all women as if they did, and research verified the improved behavior.

The third mailing in the program was a "graduation event." An invitation was sent to all of the respondents to the mailings. It invited them to a fashion show that would be held in their local dealer's showroom on just one special evening. The dealership would stay open that night, and his showroom would be decorated for the occasion. All of the invitations were personalized, and the women were encouraged to bring their friends. Wine and cheese would be served, and the evening would include a special service seminar. There would also be information on how best to finance the purchase of a new Ford. Attendees would also receive a gift 14-karat gold bracelet just for being there.

The program was more successful than we had forecast. Fifteen hundred women visited just one dealership in San Diego, many for the first time. Each invitee brought an average of 1.5 guests. So many women showed up that the police had to be called in to help direct the traffic. No dealer in San Diego had ever before had 1,500 prospects in his showroom on one evening—much less 1,500 women.

We audited the results of the program after the first six months. Sixteen hundred incremental sales were identified in the two test markets as a direct result of the program. The sales rate of Ford cars to the women in the test program was two and a half times greater than the control group that had received none of the material.

The Women's Curriculum Program was so successful that it became a national event that moved from city to city for several years.

Dr. Guggenheim's promise to MacKenzie that such programs would go "deeper into the brain" than general advertising had come true. "Curriculum marketing" was just one of the direct marketing ideas we created for Ford. The company was to become a laboratory for many of our most advanced new direct marketing concepts. And we continue to make surprising discoveries together. We also made powerful new friends.

One of the most enthusiastic was MacKenzie himself. His success with the Lincoln-Mercury Division—particularly in establishing the Lincoln Town Car as America's favorite large luxury car—led to his transfer to Ford Europe's headquarters in the United Kingdom, where he became responsible for all Ford marketing in Europe. Ford had no direct marketing agency in Europe, and I wanted the job.

One night at dinner with MacKenzie and two members of his staff in London, I reminded him of the success we had had with curriculum marketing in the United States. As I reviewed the case studies of our U.S. successes, his two aides became more and more interested. I explained the theory and practice of scientific direct marketing. Ford and WRK, I said, had used direct marketing to support automobile sales in the United States. No European company had yet done anything like it. With this advantage, it would take years for the competition to catch up.

By dessert, I knew it was time to put the question to MacKenzie. I reminded him of the quick, positive decision he had made when I had introduced him to Dr. Guggenheim in Detroit. Now I wanted his support to make WRK his European direct marketing agency. He smiled when I reminded him of Hans. He said that he was all for it if his aides agreed. They did, and Ford Europe became WRK's first and largest pan-European account.

The account was not only large, prestigious, and profitable, it served to bind our network together. All our European offices shared the account. It was a challenge we could solve together. We did and made direct marketing history on the way.

Computer and research skills were creating consumer databases in the United States and Europe from which an advertiser could select audiences whose common characteristics identified them as most likely to buy his product. This discovery of relevant buyers created a whole new dimension and opportunity for direct marketing. To take advantage of these new possibilities, our agency created an advertising system I called "targeted relationship marketing," or "TRM," "Targeted" meant that we could identify media that gave us just the audience we wanted. "Relationship marketing" recognized that advertising could not only inform and persuade but build ongoing interactive relationships between buyer and seller. We began to explore ways of reaching people who were not only in a position to buy our clients' products but might want to.

We quickly put these new insights into the role and function of advertising and direct marketing to the test. Ford Germany developed the Scorpio, a fast, maneuverable, comfortable, sports sedan that had been named the European Car of the Year.

Y&R, Ford's agency in Germany, had launched the Scorpio there, and WRK Germany had been involved in the introductory campaign. The campaign was so successful that Lincoln-Mercury U.S.A. believed the Scorpio could be sold in the United States as a German-built luxury sports sedan at a lower price than a BMW or Mercedes-Benz. We knew the car wouldn't sell itself just by sitting in dealers' showrooms. We would have to locate and target a special group of consumers who were new to Ford and tell them enough about the Scorpio to make them switch.

Y&R recommended that the Scorpio be launched with an eight-page advertisement in magazines that reached the appropriate buyers. These magazines had a combined circulation of 25 million. I asked Y&R to design the ad so that we could include a detailed response device. The final ad included a coupon that offered more information about the Scorpio and also asked a few questions. The respondents would become our database.

We then created a series of direct mail pieces for the car. After we did our best to presell it, we hoped, respondents would visit their local dealers to test-drive this largely unknown vehicle. We also targeted a group of 200,000 owners of competitive imported German luxury cars who would receive mailings similar to those that were sent to the respondents of the ad. In all, 206,000 people responded to the print ads and received the direct mail information program we had prepared. We created two test groups: responders to the ad and those on rented lists of luxury car owners. I called the responders "prospects" and those on the rented lists "suspects." The 206,000 prospects bought 288 Scorpios. The 266,000 suspects bought only 45.

The behavior of the two groups pointed to a serious weakness in data-based marketing, a weakness that explained the woefully small percentage of responses to most direct marketing efforts based on rented lists. Speakers at direct marketing industry meetings like to boast of results as high as 2 percent to 3 percent, but it would be more accurate to say that only 97 percent hadn't responded, whereas previously 98 percent hadn't. What had happened to the advertising that brought no response, what I called "the price of silence"? Mailings are expensive; a good one is a terrible thing to waste. I decided to find out why people didn't respond.

Traditionally, advertising messages had flowed "downstream" from advertisers to consumers. Consumers had always been the audience no matter what the media, including data-based advertising. Though advertisers could now choose their audiences more carefully and air their messages more accurately, the direction was the same: "downstream," from seller to buyer.

But consumers were now beginning to move "upstream"; they were ready to express their needs and intentions to a manufacturer. Customers could now use toll-free phone numbers to call advertisers to get information about their products, and many companies were including these numbers in their ads and on their packages. Prodigy, the first on-line service for computer owners, connected consumers to many data-bases, as the Internet would soon do far more widely. In France, the government telephone service was providing Minitel computer termi-nals to consumers free of charge. With a Minitel, a consumer could re-ceive information from thousands of services. The new direction was "upstream." Consumers could now reverse the historic flow of infor-mation. The difference in the behavior of the "prospects" who had moved "upstream" and the prospects who had been sent mailings "downstream" led me to think about a new dimension of advertising for Ford. I called it "consumer-initiated advertising" as it reflected the consumer's wishes expressed "upstream" to the advertiser.

Though the Lincoln Town Car was now America's favorite limousine, Lincoln had strong competition in the two-door and four-door per-sonal luxury-sedan category from Mercedes-Benz and BMW, and later from Toyota, Nissan, and Honda. How could Ford carry over its suc-cess with the Lincoln Town Car to the Lincoln Continental? The Con-tinental had been totally redesigned with custom features, and the fit and finish were superior to those of any car Ford had ever made. The new Lincoln Continental was truly a world-class car, but to succeed it would have to overcome years of inappropriate design, poor technol-ogy, and sloppy manufacturing. Y&R and WRK were given the job of relaunching the new Continental.

The campaign was in three parts:

- Prospects who had been sent a questionnaire were asked to express their interest in the Continental. In all, 15,229 of them did so. They were the first group to be sent information about the car.

- The second group consisted of people who had responded to a se-ries of four black-and-white teaser ads in upscale magazines on four consecutive right-hand pages. The response device in the ads was a toll-free phone number that prospects could call for more in-formation.

- The third and largest group consisted of people who responded to a six-page insert in 27 million copies of upmarket magazines. The insert contained a business reply card like the one we had used for the Scorpio.

We knew that consumers thought seriously before they made a phone call. Therefore, we were not surprised when only 4,455 people, a mere .04 percent, responded to the "teaser ads" that listed only the toll-free number. But these callers were serious prospects. Almost half (45 percent) said they would be in the market to buy a car within three months; 17 percent owned Cadillacs; 19 percent drove European luxury cars. We had reached our target market with precision.

As we expected, most of the responses and sales came from the six-page insert, which used both a business reply card and a toll-free number. The ad was answered by 151,934 people, of whom 84 percent used the business reply card and 16 percent the toll-free number. *Newsweek, Business Week, Forbes,* and *Fortune* pulled responses from almost 1 percent of their circulation. Automobile magazines pulled nearly 3 percent, an extraordinary response.

The Lincoln Continental relaunch campaign sold 2,670 Lincolns—1,353 Continentals, 931 Town Cars, and 386 Mark VIIs. We attributed a sale to advertising only when we could identify the purchaser as having responded to our ads. We also sold 4,778 other Ford cars to our responders; this doesn't include those who didn't respond but who went directly to a showroom. Those who had responded to the toll-free number in the teaser ads provided the highest buy rate, 6.14 percent. I was now absolutely certain that consumer-initiated advertising, or CIA, was going to work in the future as more interactive media became available.

We continued to test interactive teaching programs. The "graduates" of a subsequent Lincoln Curriculum Program bought cars at a 3.95 percent rate. Of that group, 9.5 percent had filled out the questionnaire. We also tested the effect of a "curriculum series" of letters versus a "one-shot" mailing. The recipients of the "one-shot" bought at a rate of 1.17 percent. Those who received the four-letter "curriculum series" bought at a rate of 4.36 percent, an improvement of almost 300 percent.

The results of our advertising would, of course, be evaluated against the cost and importance of what was being sold. Consumers were being asked to make one of the most expensive purchase decisions of their lives, second only to the purchase of a home.

Our experience in the United States helped us in Europe. Our data-based direct marketing in the United Kingdom led to the creation of advanced information and database centers at Woking and Byfleet, twenty-two miles from London, where a central database for marketing was housed. It is integrated with Ford Europe's manufacturing center to ensure the ongoing integrity of the data. It is also integrated with other Ford systems, such as Ford Credit and Ford Customer Service, to maximize its value.

The Ford campaign is, in principle, similar to the one we created for Columbia Records and its dealers in 1955. No record dealer then and no automobile dealer now could afford the technology and marketing investment required for a state-of-the-art information and data-based consumer direct marketing system.*

Direct marketing is making many contributions to Ford Britain and its dealers. It helps retain customers: loyalty to the Ford brand is 67 percent, the highest in the U.K. automotive industry. It also adds to customer satisfaction: in the esteem of its customers, Ford is second only to the premium Japanese products. In addition, direct marketing helps Ford win customers from other brands: in 1994, approximately 400,000 phone calls from owners of other car brands were stimulated and processed. Sixty percent of these were sales-related inquiries; of these, 50 percent were converted to sales within three months of the

---

*At Woking and Byfleet, Ford Britain has invested in the most modern computer, laser printing, and telephone marketing technology. The plant, its equipment, and its data are owned by Ford, but it is managed and staffed by more than three hundred Wunderman employees, who capture data and create communications for the 1,100 Ford dealers in the United Kingdom. We store and use the stationery of each individual Ford dealership and its sales manager to create relevant communications that will encourage loyalty and further sales on the part of the 4 million Ford owners in the United Kingdom, as well as the best sales prospects of competitive brands.

We also serve Ford Britain's Merchandising programs, Parts & Services operations, Ford Credit, Ford Contract Motoring, Ford Dealer Advertising Association, Ford Motability, Ford Fleet, and Jaguar.

All reminders, results, warranty notices, surveys, updates, loyalty mailings, and new car promotions are designed, printed, processed, and mailed by us. The centers also receive, respond to, and process the 100,000 phone calls a year that result from Ford advertising in the United Kingdom. These "leads on line" are instantly sent appropriate mailings and directed to their local Ford dealer.

The heart of the Ford Britain direct marketing and data system is called CUPID, an acronym for Ford Britain's Customer & Prospect Information Database. CUPID is Ford's only marketing database in the United Kingdom, therefore all mailings are sent to prospects with total relevance and without expensive and irritating duplication. Ford customers and prospects receive promotional material and dealer promotions when they are most likely to be in the market for a new car.

original call. Direct marketing helps Ford manage, measure, and reward or penalize its dealers through marketing management of the data. Data-based direct marketing helps Ford's field sales force personnel by providing them with information their dealers want and need. And, most important, Ford's direct marketing program provides Ford's management with the information it needs for planning and evaluating programs. The effectiveness of the database and the advanced use of direct marketing techniques have made Ford Britain a paradigm within the Ford Motor Company.

Our experience with Ford has proven that direct marketing is a powerful competitive weapon in today's global marketing wars. It will become even more so. To win, a company has to have the best products and the most scientific marketing tools. Advertising that pays will be chief among them.

25

American
Express Cards
Welcome Here

Anne Rosenzweig, the chef of the restaurant Arcadia on East Sixty-second Street just off Madison Avenue, greeted my wife and me and told us that we were the first of our party to arrive. It was a typical blustery March evening in New York, and the restaurant was not yet crowded. We chose a quiet booth in back.

As we awaited the arrival of our guests, my thoughts wandered back through the years to 535 Madison at the corner of Fifty-fifth Street, where I had learned my trade with Max Sackheim; to the summer day in 1958 when I had quit and gone off on my own; to 575 Madison, just two blocks north of 535 Madison, to which the fledgling WRK had moved in 1962. There, the agency had grown from a small specialist shop occupying a tower suite to a respected global business overflowing three floors of the building. I realized I had been preparing for tonight's dinner for all of those years.

We were expecting Aldo Papone, president of the Travel Related Services Division of American Express, and his wife, Sandra. We were going to celebrate the appointment of WRK to be part of the riskiest marketing action American Express had taken since it had launched the American Express Card in 1958.

The company had moved its headquarters to a larger, more modern space in New York's World Financial Center. It reported that it had tripled its cards in force to 23.8 million. Charge volume has increased to an annual $636 billion, and the card was now available in twenty-nine currencies. The card was now accepted by 1.7 million service establishments. Despite the company's published reports of good news

Louis V. Gerstner, Jr., its president, and James D. Robinson III, its CEO, would soon be gone. The fast track the company was on had become treacherous.

So it was no surprise when in the summer of 1986, Y&R received a visit from Jerry Welsh, executive vice president of American Express, who was responsible for selecting and maintaining relationships with the company's advertising agencies.

Welsh insisted that his visit was routine, but we knew that when someone like Welsh visits an outside agency, something is up. Welsh was careful not to use such phrases as "agency review," "the need for another point of view," or "new brand positioning." We suspected that someone higher up at American Express had sent Welsh shopping, but we didn't know what he was looking for or why.

In fact, Y&R and American Express were taking the first steps of a bureaucratic mating dance, which is never performed without ceremony and a great deal of backing-and-forthing. Welsh's visit was followed by a series of meetings between a team from Y&R, including me, and various American Express executives, including Aldo Papone; Ed Cooperman, president, Consumer Card Group, USA; Jon Linen, president, Direct Marketing Group; Phillip Riese, vice president, Business Development; and others who attended our meetings less frequently.

The American Express group was guarded and secretive, and we were sworn to the strictest confidence. Publicity would instantly end the discussions. American Express mentioned no specific subject or assignment, and none was promised. Yet the composition of the group and the extensive meetings suggested that something big was afoot.

What added to the mystery was that American Express had chosen to go outside its two regular agencies. American Express was loyal to its incumbent agencies. David Ogilvy had nurtured his agency's relationship with American Express, and when he had retired, he had shifted this special responsibility to his successors. From where we sat, the relationship looked solid.

McCann-Erickson was American Express's second agency, but its efforts had been limited to global advertising for the Gold Card. The assignment was recent and the advertising not well known, but the relationship was reputed to be stable.

Clearly, we were being tested, and we felt that if we passed, the discussions would become more specific. American Express had long been on Y&R's "most wanted" list of prospects. It was a famous brand, and brand positioning and brand awareness were Y&R's basic business. In a world of mass-produced goods and services, Y&R believed the public wanted brands with "personalities." I wanted to get to the point faster, but Y&R was eager to demonstrate its theories and capabilities.

I wanted to explain WRK's approach to direct marketing and how it could help American Express, but first I had to awaken the American Express group. I said that as a charter cardmember, I had been receiving American Express mailings since 1958. I had found them creative and elegant but largely wasted. American Express was sending almost 500 million letters a year to its cardmembers and an equal number to prospects, much of it thrown away unopened because of a strategic flaw, one that would continue to weaken American Express. And I said I suspected the erosion had already begun.

The problem, I said, was that the company was exploiting its cardmember base tactically for short-term profits, instead of building a long-term relationship with its customers. Customers were being offered luggage, hi-fis, television sets, exercise equipment, home decorations, and other stuff they didn't want. The cardmembers were probably irritated by these mailings. Their silence was not neutral; it reflected an attitude toward American Express on the part of its customers.

Cardmembers, I said, would eventually feel free to discard the company's mail unopened, except for bills. American Express was not only wasting the better part of what it spent on direct mail but jeopardizing its cardmembers' loyalty. I looked at Papone and Welsh. I had their attention.

American Express, I told them, would have to upgrade its direct marketing approach. The competitive bank cards were mass marketers, sending mail indiscriminately to the entire marketplace and reaching and selling to many of American Express's primary targets. The bank cards had not only successfully invaded American Express's market, they were invading its cardmembers' wallets. American Express had lost its exclusive hold on its cardmembers.

I said that to compete successfully, American Express must market more relevantly and more efficiently than its bank card competitors, which charged high interest rates and could afford inefficient mass mailings. The bank cards had the advantage of size, but they spoke with

four thousand uncoordinated voices. American Express, with its uni-
fied data-based information system, could target cardmembers and
prospects with messages relevant to their individual needs. It could
offer specific services rather than just plastic cards. The tool used to accomplish this could be WRK's targeted relationship marketing, or
TRM, which targeted messages to individuals to build the relationship
between a marketer and selected customers or prospects. I described
our work for Ford, Time Inc., Kodak, IBM, Gevalia, and the Columbia LP Record Club, but by then my time was up.

Papone and Welsh were adamant about the strength of the American Express brand image. Despite its shrinking share of the market,
they continued to believe that American Express was the only card that
actually had an image. Bank cards, they felt, did not have brand images,
and therefore American Express was not in competition with them.
American Express had always been the leader in growth and profitability and still was. The bank cards, they said, were not winning.

Evidently, American Express had come to Y&R not to change its
current advertising but with something else in mind that Welsh and Papone had so far not disclosed. They seemed more receptive to my presentation than to Y&R's, and Papone, in particular, found our concept
of customized persuasion intriguing. The meeting ended only with an
agreement that the discussions should continue.

Summer became fall, fall became winter, and we continued to meet.
The dialogue began to focus more on WRK than on Y&R. Direct marketing and TRM seemed to be a hot button, and I became the favored
member of the Y&R group. As a result, I began a series of informal
meetings with several American Express executives. Murray Miller, an
adviser to Aldo Papone and the American Express global trou-
bleshooter on new-cardmember acquisition, was an old friend. He
agreed with me that American Express was defeating its purpose by sat-
urating its cardmembers with mail. He also introduced me to some of
the problems American Express was having in acquiring new members
in such key markets as Germany, the United Kingdom, and Japan. I was
certain that Miller supported our becoming an American Express
agency, but it was not his decision; it was Papone's.

Papone and I began our own talks. He wanted more detailed answers to the questions he had raised at our presentations. I felt that
while he was interested in WRK, he was also reluctant to add another

agency to the American Express roster. He might accept WRK, but Y&R would be too competitive with his current agencies.

In September, Jon Linen and I began to discuss the possibility of WRK doing some work for the Direct Marketing Group's new financial services, for which no agency had as yet been appointed.

By developing my personal network, I was learning how to work with American Express. The main thing was simply to be there. I was given an ID card for access to the American Express Tower, and I literally walked the halls there as I had years before, when I had looked for new business by visiting offices and offering our services to anyone who would listen. The people at American Express saw me so often they soon believed that I belonged there. And in my rounds I learned that American Express was secretly planning to launch a revolving credit card. Plans were not complete, nor had management given the go-ahead, but there was an internal debate about how to get into the business. I heard that Papone was running the project, and I assumed that our discussions had to do with the new credit card. That Papone had not yet discussed this new card with me suggested that the company was still reluctant to deal with a new agency and that it had not yet completed its internal preparations. American Express seemed to want to do business with us, but it was a political decision.

A revolving credit card to compete with the banks' would be revolutionary for American Express. American Express needed the banks to sell its travelers cheques, and a competing card might anger them. It was like the Columbia Record Club and Columbia's retailers. The outcome would be noticed on the highest level. The same was true of the decision to select a new agency. Ogilvy & Mather had senior management's ear. To launch a new card, Ogilvy would move mountains and chairmen. Much was at stake, and the careful deliberations reflected how serious the issue had become.

Our seventh presentation to the American Express executive group would take place on November 10. An internal Y&R memo summed up the situation:

> We have made a half-dozen presentations in the last four months to different members of the American Express group, and through our discussions, we have learned that American Express has several problems with the green card marketing program.

(1) The (premium) bank cards have been growing at the expense of the green card, forcing American Express into a narrower and narrower segment of upscale customers. . . .

(2) In both the US and Europe, American Express has been unable to continue to build its green cardmember base at historic growth rates. . . .

American Express has indicated that they are considering the introduction of a "companion revolving credit card" to the green card to blunt the bank cards' efforts. It will be made available only to current Cardmembers.

As a result of the plan to market a "companion card" to current members, . . . American Express is considering hiring WRK . . . our best opportunity to date at American Express lies in the Direct Marketing area . . . unseating Ogilvy & Mather Direct may become a real political issue.

And then the long months of making presentations and building relationships began to pay off. On October 30, we were visited by two of Jon Linen's chief lieutenants. They had asked for the meeting because they had to make some quick decisions about agency assignments for the Direct Marketing Group. The next day, Linen asked me to visit him. I arrived at his office to find him relaxed and in an expansive mood. He told me he had decided to break the rules by hiring WRK as the agency for a new financial service to be marketed by his group. His staff had recommended WRK, and he agreed. He knew that the incumbent agencies would protest to their highly placed friends at American Express, but since no agency had as yet been assigned to his group he had the authority to make and defend the decision. We shook hands, he saluted with his ever-present cigar, and it was done. We had finally become an American Express agency.

The pace quickened. I could feel the difference on November 10, when I again presented to the entire group. We were now part of the family and no longer outsiders looking in. I was certain that we were presenting for the assignment of launching the company's new revolving credit card, and I explained how targeted relationship marketing was relevant to those needs.

I explained that TRM was a way of building a dynamic relationship between a marketer and individual customers and prospects by dealing with their individual differences rather than their similarities. TRM recognized that, as a rule, 20 percent of customers account for 80 percent of sales. TRM could identify those potential buyers and convert them to loyal customers. TRM's target was a customer's lifetime value rather than a onetime sale. I then showed TRM mailing systems that had created surprising response rates of 25 percent or more and built consumer loyalty and larger market share.

The meeting ended, and no further presentations were proposed: a good sign. We were told that we would hear from the company again in the next few days. But as usual, I was worried when the meeting ended. Was there something we had overlooked? Had I been convincing enough?

A few days later, the answer arrived. Phillip Riese, who had been appointed manager of the project, sent me a twenty-three-page "Briefing Document" dated November 17, 1986, which confirmed the rumors that American Express was about to market a new revolving credit card. "Our objective," it said, "is to introduce a card product that helps cement our relationship with our Cardmember base. Specifically, it will be a new revolving credit card." It added, "Your objective within the next two weeks is to develop: Communications Strategy, Launch Program, Initial Creative." For the first time, WRK was being invited to compete with the other American Express agencies for a major assignment.

The Companion Card (a temporary code name) was to be offered only to American Express cardmembers. It seemed to me that how and to whom the new card was initially offered wasn't very important. The critical point was that American Express was being forced into the revolving credit card business to protect its current membership from switching to bank cards. But I didn't believe the process would stop there. To really compete with the bank cards, American Express would have to do more than protect its cardmember base: it would have to attack the competition. A business committed to growth can't be simply defensive.

I didn't know much about revolving credit cards, and I was sure the competing agencies did. We had two weeks to catch up. In 1958, when I had worked on the launch of the American Express charge card, business executives had said they needed something more flexible than the American Express Travelers Cheque. They wanted a card that would be honored worldwide and provide a responsible, convenient record of tax-deductible expenses. The card's original customers hadn't wanted revolving credit—and they probably still didn't.

American Express was still best equipped to provide such services to businesspeople. Its experience and power in the travel and lodging industries, combined with its international acceptance and strength in global financial services, had provided the utility and prestige that business executives wanted in a charge card. The American Express Card had quickly overwhelmed the competition. The slogan "Don't Leave Home Without It" was more than a brilliant advertising line; it was a perfect statement of a successful corporate strategy.

However, times had changed. The American Express Card was still growing profitably in the 1980s because it offered prestige and recognition, but its lack of revolving credit, as well as its lack of acceptance by many retailers had created a marketing gap that the bank cards were exploiting.

As I studied the bank cards, I was amazed at their growth and profitability. They were already a $100 billion business and gaining speed and power. The card launched as the "blue-collar" InterBank Card in 1966 had in 1981 become the more upscale MasterCard. Now owned by an association of 25,500 banks, it claimed a membership of 100 million members worldwide. VISA, also launched in 1966, as Bank Ameri-Card, a credit resource for the nonaffluent, was now owned by an association of 17,000 banks issuing 124 million cards a year. It, too, had moved upmarket. As many as 4,000 member banks were aggressively marketing these cards both locally and nationally, not simply in the communities or states in which they did their normal business.

By the end of 1985, it was estimated that 100 million Americans were carrying 700 million credit, charge, debit, or retail cards, an average of seven cards each. American Express cardmembers were no exception. The American Express Companion Card was intended to recover, as well as protect, American Express's share of its own cardmembers' spending.

American Express cardmembers were still the heaviest individual users of cards. In 1985, the company's 21.7 million cardmembers had charged more than $47 billion. The card was available in twenty-nine currencies, and while it was accepted in more than a million locations, the company had never focused on retail establishments.

During the same period, $70 billion was charged by the 124 million

VISA cardholders and $45.5 billion by the 100 million users of MasterCard. These cards' base was retail sales, and they were accepted at more than 3 million locations. The prime competitive target of these bank cards was the American Express cardmember base and its large travel and entertainment spending.

And the fight was heating up. VISA had issued 3 million Premier Cards and MasterCard 2.5 million Preferred customer cards to compete with the prestige of the American Express cards. The bank cards were going after a dominant share of the total $331 billion retail charge market. American Express was planning to launch the Companion Card only to defend its membership base. This strategy seemed too cautious to me.

Consumers were saturated with offers of cards. As a result, direct mailings, which had traditionally pulled better than 4 percent, were now producing less than half that figure. And in 1984, VISA's television campaign highlighted its greater number of service establishments with the line "And they don't take American Express." VISA was shifting its emphasis from quality of service to quantity of establishments.

As I studied bank cards further, I was astonished by their extraordinary profitability. An article in *The American Economic Review* by Lawrence Ausubel of the Kellogg Graduate School of Management at Northwestern University gave me my first inkling that bank cards were an effective consumer booby trap. Ausubel concluded that "the ordinary (pre tax) return on equity on banking is on the order of 20% per year. Credit card businesses earned annual returns of 60–100% or more. . . . 3–5 times the ordinary rate of return in the banking industry."

A court decision in 1978 and the repeal of state ceilings on interest rates had effectively deregulated the market by 1982. Consumers, however, seemed not to care that there was no effective limit on interest rates. Despite high interest rates, most banks had bad debts of less than 3 percent.

"VISA and MasterCard volume was created by some 4,000 competing banks, which owned their cardholder accounts and determined interest rates, annual fees, grace periods, credit limits, and other terms. Thus, the market for MasterCard and VISA is relatively unconcentrated. The top ten firms control only two-fifths of the market, and the next ten firms control only one-tenth of the market."

The article also suggested that "consumers [were making] credit card choices without taking account of the very high probability that they will pay interest on their outstanding balances."

The article found

> Evidence of Consumer Irrationality . . . consumers who do not in-tend to borrow . . . continuously do so. . . . Despite interest rates ex-ceeding 18% per year, typically three-quarters of active credit card accounts at major banks are incurring these high financial charges (on balances averaging over $1,000) at any moment. . . . [Many] consumers who borrow on credit cards are unaware of how fre-quently they do it or, more likely, deny (to themselves and others) that they do it. . . . [T]hey do not intend to borrow but . . . contin-uously do so. . . . The experience of credit card marketers is that con-sumers are much more sensitive to increases in the annual fee than to commensurate increases in the interest rate. . . . This behavior . . . is again consistent with the existence of consumers who do not intend to borrow but do so anyway.

Bank cards were and are enormously seductive and highly profitable. Even today, 70 percent of bank card users pay high interest rates on their revolving balances. The cards were particularly well suited to the needs and personality of "yuppies" and to the optimism of the 1980s that everything would continue to go up. It was on this slippery, high-stakes chessboard that American Express was about to risk its king of prestige. It was going into direct competition with VISA and Master-Card and the 4,000 banks that issued them.

The American Express brief for the Companion Card referred to "an enormous struggle for market share . . . not just [among] existing cards, but also [because of] the threat of several new entrants." The market, the brief reported, was "extremely profitable. Financial institu-tions see it as a way of developing a relationship with a client to sell other products [and] there is a great deal of confusion in the market, creating tremendous opportunity."

American Express believed that the prestige and services offered by its existing cards, all of which would apply to the Companion Card, plus a competitively lower revolving interest rate, would ensure the new card's success. The brief also recognized that the bank cards had been able to charge the merchants a much lower percentage fee on transactions because the banks earned so much from their high interest rates. It said that because "bank card merchant acceptance is at least twice that of American Express, the Companion Card, cannot, therefore, replace a bank card." This would, unfortunately, prove to be accurate. What American Express didn't recognize until it was almost too late was that while the Companion Card would not replace a bank card, a bank card could replace the American Express Card. But that battle wouldn't be joined until another ten years had passed.

Despite these limitations, I believed the credit card would, in time, become the basis for American Express's effort to expand its business in the United States and abroad. We had no time for consumer research. We would have to rely on our own sense of the market to create a winning proposal. The solution, I suspected, would come from a better understanding of consumers' self-delusion about revolving credit. We had to know how and why they fell into the "booby trap" of revolving credit when the ideas of "debt" and being a "debtor" were culturally so abhorrent.

George Gallup, the pollster who had examined attitudes toward credit for many years, said that in the last ten years the percentage of Americans who believed it was "not okay or never okay to buy on credit" had never dropped below 60 percent and more recently had fluctuated at around 70 percent. However, during that period installment debt had grown by almost 400 percent.

To Gallup's question as to whether "credit . . . should be used to let people live the kind of life they want or something to use as little as possible," 70 percent answered "As little as possible." Only 27 percent admitted that "It was valuable." When asked to choose "the one important thing that the phrase 'financial fitness' meant," 39 percent said "being free of debt."

The cause of this massive contradiction was the "unloanlike" nature of the credit card transaction. The buyer used the card to make a purchase and pay for it to the seller's satisfaction. The consumer didn't have to apply for credit or even decide to use it at the time of purchase. His only decision was whether to pay the bill in full or in part when it arrived. His "line of credit" would satisfy the seller. That was the "booby trap" in action.

I felt our presentation should be built on a strategy I had first encountered when selling lavender plants for Charlie Perkins. We hired as a consultant Marshall Blonsky, who taught semiotics—the science of language and symbols—at a local university and who had also edited an authoritative book on the subject. Just as Dr. Guggenheim of MIT had helped persuade the Ford Motor Company that curriculum marketing would answer its problems of market share and consumer loyalty, Blonsky would now leverage the credit card contradiction for American Express.

When I discussed the problem with Blonsky, he understood at once. He explained how words such as "debt," "credit," "loan," "revolving credit," "borrowing," "debtor," and so on had totally different meanings to different segments of the population. There was, he said, one major system of meaning for the masses and another for the elite. Using the appropriate elite words and symbols for American Express could spell the difference between success and failure for the company's new card. I realized our advertising would have to change the "irrational" act of unacknowledged borrowing into an action that was an overt, acceptable use of power and control. The privilege of revolving credit could be used to distinguish the Companion Card from the bank cards and support the prestige position of American Express.

Our presentation proposed to change the way American Express cardmembers understood and used their potential financial power. Eighty percent of American Express cardmembers already carried at least one bank card, so we would have to offset our disadvantage in retail coverage by making a psychological distinction between the use of the American Express Companion Card and its bank card competitors. We would tell American Express cardmembers that they lived in an "elite system," and we would use certain code words to reinforce that position. Blonsky helped select these words and redefine their meaning. In this way, we could position the new card as a unique privilege for those qualified to use it.

We devoted a section of our presentation to what we described as "The Key Words Within a Credit Signification System." Some examples were:

	BANK CARD MASS SYSTEM	AMERICAN EXPRESS ELITE SYSTEM
Credit	Know you need it, fear it.	A tool for leverage.
Revolving credit	Not really well understood; socially coded as low.	Taken for granted.
Debt	Fear word; the door to the poorhouse; embarrassing.	Viewed in productive relation to wealth/or business needs.
Loan	Will I qualify? Something feared; the result of uncontrollable circumstances.	A flexible instrument to better manage one's financial universe.
Debtor	Frightening, almost archaic in its significance; (Dickens).	Does not exist "for us," only "for them."
Liability	Personal risk; a weakness.	A necessary counterpoint on my balance sheet.
Cash flow	Don't understand it.	Central construct of money management.
NET-NET	CREDIT CREATES LIABILITY Credit is a weakness, an embarrassment to be denied	CREDIT CREATES ASSETABILITY Credit can be power, a vital part of asset management

In other words, we decoded the meaning of "revolving credit." Revolving credit made the bank cards and their users part of the mass culture and its lower status. It "undressed" the self one showed to the world.

Our positioning was that the American Express Companion Card would let cardmembers expand their asset base when they chose to do so. American Express would offer this privilege to a limited group of cardmembers by special invitation. Our implicit message would be "If you are one of the select people for whom borrowing is an act of personal leverage, leave VISA and MasterCard and move up to the Companion Card." We would position the new card as "The Natural Complement to the World's Most Respected Card."

The new card had no prestige of its own, and there would be no advertising to introduce it other than direct mail. So we borrowed the prestige of the American Express Card already in cardmembers' wallets to compete with the bank cards that most American Express cardmembers were already using. The Companion Card might not replace or displace those cards, but I hoped we could apply sufficient symbolic chloroform to make them inactive.

American Express had already determined that the annual fee for the Companion Card would be $15 and the interest rate would be considerably lower than what major bank cards charged, the exact rate to be determined just before the actual launch. The new card would be offered only to those members whose tenure was longer than one year and whose assets and payment history made them creditworthy, a launch universe of only 4.3 million eligible names, a relatively small group but one we hoped would provide sufficient members that the card would be honored by service establishments we were not now reaching. Our mailings would have to attract many more responses than American Express had been getting so far, which meant we would have to change the way American Express thought about direct mail.

What we feared most was apathy—that the mailings, however attractive, would be put aside or ignored as just another ho-hum offer from American Express. A mailing that isn't read can't persuade, no matter what it offers. So our principal creative task was to ensure that cardmembers who got the mail would read it. Normally, we would support such a new product launch with radio, television, and newspaper advertising, but that was also precluded by the brief. We listed the formidable obstacles to success:

- We would have to launch a new product using only one medium, direct mail. And that to a limited universe.
- We would have to introduce a new behavior from American Express, i.e., revolving credit.
- We would have to sell a service that, in the main, was already being bought from others. That meant competing head-on with the bank cards for the revolving credit purchases made by our cardmembers.
- We would have to successfully sell the new card to those cardmembers who had the greatest net present value. To do so, we would have to overcome the clutter created by American Express's own overmailing to its best customers.

Given these problems, I felt we should create several series of interactive mailings expressly for each segment of the American Express list:

Green, Gold, and Platinum—mailings that would create ongoing service relationships instead of focusing on immediate sales.

I was certain that our direct mail program was persuasive enough to sell the new card. But I was uneasy. We still had to find a way of getting American Express cardmembers to read the mailings announcing the Companion Card.

I found the solution as I was making a chart of the persuasion sequence. The series would have to begin with an announcement of the new card . . . or would it? Why couldn't the first letter simply announce the announcement? What if it was simply a first-class "personal" letter from the president of the Travel Related Services Division of American Express? It wouldn't try to sell anything; it would only ask cardmembers to watch their mail for something of special importance that would arrive in the next several days. And so we created a short note from Aldo Papone on his own stationery and mailed it first class. It would become known as the "Aldo letter."

The mailing sequence we would propose was:

1. The "Aldo" preannouncement
2. The announcement offer
3. A resolicitation with a survey questionnaire
4. A group of alternative "dialogues":
   a. A customized follow-up to survey responders
   b. Telephone follow-up to survey responders
   c. Noncustomized follow-up to nonresponders
5. Continued follow-ups to survey responders
6. Continued follow-ups to nonresponders

We created the following two charts, which compared our proposed series to the traditional American Express use of direct mail:

CHART 1

TRADITIONAL AMEX MAILING PARADIGM	EVALUATION VIS-À-VIS COMPANION CARD
No preannouncement of mailing.	
Direct solicitation requesting immediate response; only other possible outcome is nonresponse	May not be read; assumes prospects are "ready to buy" when AMEX is ready to promote; no special impact
No integrated system of follow-up	Does not position the new card as the most important new product from AMEX in recent years
No attitudinal screening via survey	
No attempt to build dialogue in resolicitation	

CHART 2
WRK Persuasion Sequence Strategy

CHARACTERISTICS	EVALUATION
Preannouncement: First-class letter from Aldo Papone previews and highlights soon-to-arrive solicitation mailing. Highly personal in tone and design.	Sets new card mailing in context of specialness: will enhance opening and readership of subsequent mailing.
Initial solicitation: Each cardmember segment (Green, Gold, Platinum) receives discrete package with preapproved maximum line of credit. Cardmembers are invited to select the level of credit they desire within established limits. Design and tone of mailings leverage the perceptual equity of each card and cardmember segment.	Packages support the AMEX brand image in a way that is differentiated from traditional mailings. Each customer segment is provided with relevant information.
Resolicitation with survey: Each cardmember segment receives a resolicitation mailing several weeks after the initial effort. The mailings are designed to reinforce the offer and stimulate response. The survey encourages nonacceptors to respond and provides personal data attributes to drive future follow-ups.	Packages support prestige imagery and reflect AMEX's effort to gain feedback/opinions and "reasons why." The intent is to create a dialogue-and-persuasion sequence.
Integrated follow-up series: Instead of start-and-stop recontact as usual AMEX approach, an integrated series of follow-up efforts to nonresponders/nonacceptors is recommended.	AMEX behaves like a company that "markets with a memory." Profile data from survey responders can enhance the relevance of subsequent messages.
Data Analyzed: To identify best subgroups and message "fit" to overcome objections among initial nonacceptors.	Nonresponders to receive generic follow-up.

The two weeks passed, and suddenly it was time for our presentation. I was sure that defining revolving credit in a way that reinforced the American Express prestige position was right for the new card. I believed we would get high marks for strategic thinking and that our direct mail strategy would be effective and different. American Express needed an unusually high response rate from a limited base of eligible cardmembers, and the use of a relevant, interactive direct mail campaign was the only way I knew of to achieve the budgeted percentage of response.

But while I felt good about our work, I worried about the social dynamics of the presentation. While the core of a new-business presentation is always the quality of the strategic and creative work an agency presents, there is also an element of theater. The audience has to like the actors as well as the play. I felt we were at a disadvantage because the presenters from the incumbent agencies had a long-standing camaraderie with the clients.

The American Express people had already assembled: Papone, Cooperman, Riese, and Anne Busquet, a senior American Express marketing executive, all of whom I had presented to before. I was with people I knew, in a place that was familiar, and all at once I felt at ease.

I got right to the point. I explained why and how we had arrived at a vocabulary to position the new card and why we believed that American Express would have to employ targeted relationship marketing to accomplish the extraordinary percentage of response it was seeking.

There are two kinds of audiences for new-business presentations. One is cool and restrained, afraid to give positive signals prematurely. The other realizes that it and the agency have to be partners if the campaign is to succeed. The character of the group most often reflects the personality of the client's representative. Aldo was intelligent, witty, open, and supportive, and he put his own stamp on everything we presented.

When I finished my opening remarks, it was time for Joel Tucciarone to present our strategy in detail. He turned to Papone and, to everyone's surprise, began to recite the opening lines of Dante's *Inferno* in Italian:

> *Nel mezzo del cammin di nostra vita*
> *mi ritrovai per una selva oscura*
> *ché la diritta via era smarrita.*

Papone joined in, and the rest of us held our breath. It was an unforgettable moment. Tucciarone's choice of the opening lines of the *Inferno* was inspired. It was as if Dante had prophesied American Express's problems in his opening verse:

> Midway in our life's journey, I went astray
> from the straight road and woke to find myself
> alone in a dark wood. . . .

The following verses describe how Dante is filled with hope, seeing the Hill of Joy illuminated by the sun. His journey toward the hill is blocked by evil until he finds Virgil, who will lead him from error.

And so, with the help of Blonsky, Dante, Tucciarone, and Papone, and with a sound strategy, a better theory of direct mail, and some inspired creative work, we were awarded the account.

I was remembering all that as the Papones arrived at Arcadia for an evening of celebration. That week, American Express had officially announced its intention to launch the Optima Card, a revolving credit card. Papone proposed a toast to our joint effort. He raised his glass and declared, "The good news is that you have the Optima account—the bad news is that you can't fail." As always, he underscored the critical nature of the outcome for his company, his career, and our relationship.

Happily, we didn't let him or his company down. We launched in May. The initial objective had been 543,000 cardmembers out of a final eligible universe of 6,442,772. I thought the target was conservative given the low membership fee of $15 and the interest rate of only 13.5 percent, but American Express was accustomed to low response rates. WRK and American Express made a pool for the best guess of the actual results. I won the Gold Card pool with an optimistic estimate of 20 percent. The actual response rate was 22 percent. The total mailings produced an extraordinary 1,093,025 responses, almost double the budgeted number.

And the members spent more than had been estimated. The forecast had been for an average of $249 per cardmember per month. The spending in July averaged $260.46, in August $336.98, and in September $345.63. American Express had launched Optima to compete with the bank cards for more retail-store business, and within six months Optima became one of the top ten issuers of revolving credit cards. We were off to a quick start, but for me the U.S. launch of Optima was just the first step. I wanted the entire global account.

That wasn't going to be easy. We had won the U.S. launch of the Optima account in competition with Ogilvy & Mather, but this was only the start of a worldwide competition. We changed the name of our agency to Wunderman Worldwide, and I did some politicking. In November, I asked Ed Cooperman, president of American Express Travel Related Services in the United States, to arrange a lunch with his counterpart who would make the international decisions, G. Richard Thoman. Cooperman recommended us for the global account.

Conversations with Thoman turned out to be harder than I expected. He was willing to consider and even encourage our role as an additional international agency resource for American Express. Ogilvy & Mather, he said, was the global agency for the American Express brand and McCann-Erickson served the Gold Card, but there was no agency of record for the largest part of the business, which consisted of communications with cardmembers and service establishments. But first we would have to prove that our network was strong enough to do the job. I was certain we could do this. I would also be expected to be as involved in the international account as I was with the U.S. business. I agreed. The third condition would be more difficult and costlier to satisfy, and it was beyond my control. He demanded that we and our parent, Y&R, divest ourselves of competitive credit card accounts everywhere in the world. He wanted us to be as available and committed to American Express as Ogilvy & Mather was. When I looked into the number of conflicts within the Y&R system, I was dismayed. We were advertising VISA Premier Cards for Crédit Lyonnais in France and the Gold MasterCard for the Royal Trust in Canada. Y&R was advertising the Access Card (MasterCard) for six banks in the United Kingdom, the EuroCard (MasterCard) for Commerzbank in Germany, and the ANZ Card for ANZ Bank in Australia, the largest client of Y&R's Melbourne office.

I put the question to Y&R's two top executives, Alex Kroll and Peter Georgescu, and to my surprise they were willing to clear the Y&R conflicts in the United Kingdom and Germany. The only account they wouldn't resign was that of the ANZ Card in Australia. I arranged for them to meet with Thoman. The major problems were quickly resolved. We all agreed to take Australia and the ANZ Card "off the table" for the time being. With the way cleared, Thoman formally invited us to present our international qualifications for the launch of Optima in five international markets.

On December 14, we were to compete against Ogilvy & Mather and McCann-Erickson at American Express headquarters in New York. As always, I was worried. O&M had built its business on global clients; we hadn't. I wasn't very concerned about McCann-Erickson, since its strength was in Japan, where it had a joint venture with Hukuhodo, Japan's second largest advertising agency. We were strangers with whom the clients had no previous experience. The American Express international managers had been lobbied hard by the O&M people they regularly worked with.

I told Aldo Papone my concerns and asked him to open our presentation by introducing us to Thoman's group. I knew he would make no recommendation, and I didn't ask for one. I wanted only an official blessing of our agency as an approved global resource for American Express. Papone agreed. He didn't recommend us, but he did say that our Optima work in the United States had been outstanding and that he believed that with minor modifications it would be effective anywhere in the world. When our presentation ended, Thoman asked me to meet privately with him and his aide, Paul Applegarth. He told me he liked our work and was optimistic about our chances of winning the account. He suggested that Applegarth and I talk further. We did. No decision was made in December or the first weeks of January. I used the time to visit the presidents of the American Express offices in Toronto, London, Paris, Frankfurt, and Tokyo. They all seemed to know that we had the blessing of Papone and Thoman, but they wouldn't agree to work with us until they received the official word.

On January 22, 1988, I got it. Applegarth called me in Tokyo and said we had won the international Optima account and that he would send the details by fax to the Hotel Okura, where I was staying. That night I received the confirming fax from him.

He awarded us the Optima account in Canada and the United Kingdom. He also suggested that we continue discussions with local American Express management in France and Japan. He said the decision had been made in our favor because of the high-quality work we had done for the Optima launch in the United States and the quality of our presentations for the international business. He reminded me of the promises we and Y&R had made to shed our competitive accounts by the end of the year. He wanted us to have no conflicts of interest anywhere in the world. He also reminded me of the assurances I had given that I would remain personally involved in the creation and review of our agency's work on the Optima account in every country. He asked me to personally confirm their understanding—which I did. Best of all, he said that American Express looked forward to a long and growing relationship with me and my colleagues.

And so our agency and I had finally become a global resource for the world's largest, most successful direct marketer. I knew that my life and our business would change, and it began to do so the very next day.

Stephen Friedman, president of American Express for Japan and Asia, called me and said that the peripatetic Papone had arrived in Japan with Tommaso Zanzotto, the head of American Express Travel Management Services. He asked if I would like to join them all for dinner. I said "Yes" before he had finished the sentence. He gave me the address of the restaurant Papone had selected. I thought that this was getting to be fun, but it turned out to be even more exotic than I had imagined.

The restaurant, which my driver finally located after the usual difficulty of finding any address in Tokyo, turned out to be an ancient palace, built by an emperor's son for his mistress. The main floor was now divided into two sections, one a public restaurant, the other a private room, formerly the son's salon with its original furniture, decoration, and art. In the center of this enormous room was a table where our group was to dine in the traditional fashion of Japanese nobility. We were a group of five: Papone, Zanzotto, Friedman, Alan Moore (a Wunderman Worldwide executive in the region who would be responsible for the American Express account in Japan), and me.

The others were already seated when I arrived. Behind each of them, in traditional costume, was a geisha, including one to attend me. That was the first surprise of the evening. The geishas poured warm saki into our beautiful small porcelain cups, and Papone raised his cup for the first toast. Each of us followed. It was my welcome into the American Express international family. The meal then began with what seemed to be a never-ending series of exquisite, if unrecognizable, dishes. The saki flowed freely, as did our conversation. I was instantly impressed by Friedman and Zanzotto and was just beginning to sense that in American Express I had found not just a new client but a family of intelligent, sophisticated, and powerful men. Then there was a rustle of silk, and a group of musicians in traditional costume entered the room and took their places on a small, slightly raised platform. The food, the drinks, the geishas, the company, the music, and the beauty of the room were unforgettable, an evening to be treasured—a kind of balancing of the books for some of the grim years I had spent on my path to this place and this group.

When the dinner ended and the geishas withdrew, the talk turned to business. Papone was once again effusive on the subject of our successful launch of Optima and the new techniques and talents we had brought to American Express. He said he wanted Friedman and Zanzotto to work with us. I knew they were getting the message.

As we prepared to leave, Papone turned to me and asked when I was going back to New York. I told him I was scheduled to leave the next day. He asked if I wanted a lift. I thought he was referring to the long drive to Tokyo's Narita Airport. "No, no," he said, "to New York. I have the company plane—and it will be just the two of us."

And that's the way it was. The following day Aldo Papone, the CEO of the American Express Travel Related Services Division, and I reclined comfortably across the aisle from each other in an American Express Gulfstream for the fourteen-hour flight from Tokyo to New York.

Papone, as always, was good company. We discussed the main problems he felt the company faced and the strategies that were being employed to solve them. The discussion became an insider's executive tour of American Express that would otherwise have taken me years to make. What I remember most was a discussion provoked by the text of a talk Papone had given to an audience of concierges of the world's leading hotels. Papone's point had been that the concierges and American Express were in the service business. They were judged by the same criteria and held to the same standards. Their function was to satisfy their customers. Papone's point had been that if they did their work well, the reaction of their customers should be "I didn't think you could do that!"

It was a point well taken, but I didn't feel it went far enough. I told Papone that in the domain of technology the statement was appropriate, but in the world of service it was not. Service, I felt, was measured not only by what was accomplished but by what was intended. I suggested changing the word "could" to "would" so a customer would express satisfaction by saying, "I didn't know you *would* do that!"

I asked Papone what he wanted American Express to become. How did he plan to move the company forward? He said that American Express had three major strengths he wanted to build on. First was prestige: he wanted the American Express Card to serve the needs of special people and to identify them as such, a form of recognition and reward. Second, he felt the Corporate Card could become a major tool for the management of travel and entertainment facilities and expenses. American Express was as dominant in the executive travel and entertainment market as the bank cards were at retail, and the Corporate Card could be a major source of growth and profit. Third, he felt the company's financial services could be greatly expanded. Revolving credit was just the first step. Banking, insurance, and investing would just as surely become growth opportunities. He forecast this growth globally. The world was getting smaller, he said, and Europe, Asia, and the developing nations would all require the services provided by American Express.

The normally tedious flight to New York from Tokyo seemed too short. At Westchester, we said good-bye at the airport. As my car headed for Manhattan, I went to reset my watch, but we had arrived in New York at the same clock time it had been when we had left Tokyo. Our flight had been an interlude, suspended in time and space. I looked at my notes and realized that this trip with Papone could become one of the defining moments of my career.

American Express was to be my first opportunity to test the universality of direct marketing. Was what I had learned from Charlie Perkins, the Columbia LP Record Club, or Acousticon Hearing Aids applicable to Jim Li, who headed American Express in Hong Kong, Hector Cuellar, its president in France, Steve Goldstein in London, or Jürgen Aumüller, president of American Express Europe? I was determined to find out. It was time for me to plan my own agenda.

Then a metaphor came to mind. For an advertising agency, American Express was like a vast oil field. Wherever one drilled, there was potential revenue. I knew that Ogilvy & Mather would fight us for every assignment. But the more places I attacked, the less force it could bring to bear for defense. The greater the element of surprise, the less prepared it would be. By attacking as many points as possible, I would not disclose my main objectives. And I had decided what those were.

Papone had outlined the three main areas of growth for American Express: the brand, lending, and travel. I was mainly interested in the latter two. While the major current business of American Express was in the Green, Gold, and Platinum Cards, I felt that those would not be the high-growth areas of the future. Optima, on the other hand, was the beginning of lending, off-site banking, and the use of electronic digitized money. Travel would also grow exponentially. Business was becoming increasingly global, and business expenses (travel and entertainment) would expand faster than consumer spending, thereby requiring more corporate oversight.

As my next target, I chose the Corporate Card. Launched in 1970, it had descended directly from the executive service card I had recommended to the company in 1958. I myself still carried a Corporate Card in the name of Lester Wunderman at Wunderman et al. I was a "charter member." The Corporate Card was part of the Travel Management Services Division of American Express, headed by Tommaso Zanzotto.

When I had met Zanzotto in Tokyo, I decided I would like to know him better. As I did, I found that, like Papone, Zanzotto was a brilliant, imaginative marketer. He didn't overanalyze ideas. His gut reactions quickly computed their pros and cons. And I found that he had ambitious plans for the Corporate Card.

The agency of record for the Travel Management Services Division was Ogilvy & Mather. But almost no advertising was being done for the Corporate Card, and I felt that the O&M sentries protecting the account were probably asleep at their post. I was certain that there was much room for improvement. American Express had a virtual monopoly on business travel and entertainment. MasterCard had not launched its Business Card until 1985. VISA had not yet entered the market, and Diners Club was fading fast. There was literally no competition except from American Express itself. Many executives of large companies and owners of small companies were American Express Gold or Platinum cardmembers. The Corporate Card offered less prestige and no additional or special business benefits for corporate executives. But it was the most profitable card in the American Express portfolio because the business executives who used it spent more than personal or Gold cardmembers did. In 1987, the Corporate Card had provided 50 percent of the growth of charges of all American Express cards. At the time, there were two kinds of Corporate Cards, one for large businesses and one for small businesses that was called the Company Card internally (this distinction was later abandoned). In the United States, the annual pretax profit from each Corporate Card was $70.23, as compared to the Company Card at $57.24 and the Green, Gold, and Platinum Cards at $36.09 each.

The Corporate Card represented 29 percent of all American Express cardmember spending, and the growth potential was huge. American Express had only four million Corporate cardmembers, equally divided between large and small companies. The Corporate and Company Cards were the Sleeping Beauties of American Express, and I wanted to be the prince whose kiss would wake them up.

After years of high growth, it had recently become harder to acquire new Corporate cardmembers. To get new members, we would have to offer more value and better benefits of specific interest to the owners and managers of both small and large businesses. The cards also needed their own identity, which meant separating them from the Green, Gold, and Platinum Cards. The Company Card for small businesses had a potential market of thirteen million small companies, which could be reached only by advertising. So far, the advertising had been limited to direct mail. I asked Steve Alesio, the marketing director of Travel Management Services, whether we could try a mailing for the troubled Company Card, and he agreed.

Our mailing contained a number of improvements. The return address on the envelope was changed from "American Express" to "Small Business Services" to signify that it wasn't just another American Express mailing. The mailing featured the one business advantage the card then offered, quarterly management reports, which identified and summarized how, where, and by whom the cards had been used. The copy identified the Corporate Card as a badge of pride and entrepreneurship. Our mailing improved results by 18 percent. We had promised to create better advertising for the Corporate Card, and I knew that the next step was for our agency to be accepted as a "partner" by the Corporate Card marketing group. I attended every meeting of our agency and the Travel Management Services marketing group. I also continued to build my relationship with Zanzotto. As I had hoped, the Ogilvy & Mather sentries remained asleep while we quietly infiltrated our objective. We became the de facto agency for the Corporate Card for small business. Then, suddenly, there was no more time for stealth.

In February, at Zanzotto's request, Alesio and his team created a "High Growth Business Plan—Small Company Market—1988–90." The fifty-two-page plan opened with the statement, "The small business marketplace holds substantial opportunity for American Express. However, after a promising start, Corporate Card growth in this market has slowed recently." The document described the large profits the cards were already contributing and said the market potential was twelve to fourteen million small companies, which were responsible for 50 to 70 percent of U.S. employment and most of the creation of new jobs in the United States. These companies spent more than $70 billion annually on travel and entertainment. They also spent heavily on insurance, office supplies, and business services. American Express's current share of the small-business market of thirteen million companies was only a million accounts using two million cards.

The plan reported on a 1987 study that showed that fewer than one third of small-business owners understood the difference between personal cards and Corporate Cards. The group was determined to create and own the product category. To do this, they proposed adding new product features relevant to the priorities of small businesses and to create a new positioning of the card by creating a dramatic image of small-business success. They wanted their communications to "shout about the category so that the marketplace would know that the Corporate Card existed and that it was important." To achieve all this, they requested an advertising budget for 1988–89 of $20 million.

The report was also critical of the design of the Corporate Card, which was similar to that of the personal card except that the member's company name was included. As a result of this similarity of appearance, only 28 percent of the companies researched had said that "the Corporate Card is for companies like mine." The case for a distinctive and more prestigious design was reinforced by the fact that 30 percent of those canceling their Corporate Card had elected to move up to the Gold or Platinum Card.

While the report had originally been requested by Zanzotto, it had become a major subject of corporate interest. Copies were sent to Papone and Gerstner, which worried me. I had quietly gained a foothold on the Corporate Card account, but could I keep it?

I hoped to improve our position by getting an early start. The Corporate Card category would soon become much more competitive. MasterCard had entered the business, and VISA would be launching its own Business Card on April 1, 1988. On April 18, *Advertising Age* reported that "VISA isn't targeting MasterCard in its advertising. Like MasterCard, it will go after the American Express Company." A VISA spokesman said, "It's taken us a while to figure out how to beat the pants off American Express."

The plan to relaunch the Corporate Card was approved, and I worked at getting the assignment. I decided to act like the incumbent agency and assume the appropriate responsibilities. O&M, now fully awake to both the danger from us and the size of the opportunity, mounted a full-scale attack. As a result, the clients couldn't tell who the real incumbent was. While individuals took sides, it was to the group's advantage to encourage competition. I felt we were ahead of the game. O&M was the fat-cat agency of the past, which had awakened to the opportunity only when the advertising budget was increased. We were the hungry new agency, which had volunteered to help at the start, and we had also created the most recent and most successful direct mail advertising.

We quickly created a detailed advertising plan consistent with the American Express document. Our title was "Ideas That Will Make a Difference: American Express, the Corporate Card 1988/89." We proposed surrounding the prospects with advertising at home, at work, and en route, and we would make it easy for our prospects to respond. Because 20 percent of new small businesses were owned by women, our campaign had to recognize their growing role. Because small-business people tended to work hard and late, we needed to persuade them that the Corporate Card worked as hard as they did.

We were asked to submit our final media plans and creative work by mid-April. The media budget for the relaunch of the Corporate Card was the recommended $20 million, of which $9 million was allocated for the first four months. To reach the target audience of thirteen million small companies, we proposed that half the initial budget be spent on 30-second commercials to be run on network television. The rest would be for one-page magazine ads with bound-in response cards, two-page ads in national newspapers, and 60-second "image" commercials on radio to stimulate calls to an 800 number. Additional 120-second direct response television commercials would be used in key markets. They would be timed to support the arrival of the direct mail. The media plan was designed for total impact.

Now we needed a big idea to get the attention and agreement of those entrepreneurs who had the courage and vision to succeed in small business. We knew they were a special elite who deserved respect, support, recognition, and, most of all, useful services from American Express. For years, they had been relatively apathetic about the Corporate Card. We would have to find a way to change that, and we had less than a month to do it.

Mike Becker, our creative director, took his camera and his tape recorder and went out to do what he called "ethnographic interviews" with local businessmen. He talked to a doctor, a building contractor, a metal fabricator, and a man who built burial vaults. He photographed them at work and at home. Then Mike assembled his creative teams and showed them the research and his own interviews. He knew from his "listening" that our "big idea" would have to be about pride, recognition, and special services.

The deadline was imminent, so we turned to Becker's team for clues. Several ideas seemed promising, but Judy Walsh, a copywriter, had written three words we knew at once were the answer. They were: "To Your Success."

"To Your Success" became our "big idea," and Mike's interviews convinced us that the advertising should feel like a documentary. People who ran their own small businesses would be interested in others who were doing the same. So we created a series of short documentary salutes to people who were building small businesses and showed how the Corporate Card was helping them.

Some of the print headlines were YOU TAKE THE RISKS, YOU GET THE REWARDS; YOU'RE NOT A COMPANY MAN, YOU'RE THE COMPANY; YOU WOULDN'T WORK A 14-HOUR DAY FOR ANYONE BUT YOU; YOUR ONLY REGRET SINCE GOING INTO BUSINESS—NOT DOING IT SOONER. Each ad was illustrated with a photograph of small-business owners at work. The television commercial featured the same small-business people at work and highlighted the special benefits offered by the Corporate Card: automatic disability insurance; discounts on business supplies; special rates for car rentals, hotels, and travel; and the quarterly management reports. The print ads and the commercial signed off with the phrase "To Your Success" and carried a toll-free phone number. When Becker found that a small college in New York owned the phone number 1-800-SUCCESS, he arranged to buy it if the campaign were accepted.

To keep production costs low, we created ads only in black and white and used black-and-white footage borrowed from other commercials. We used still photographs of the businesspeople we showed in the commercials—since those were all we had.

The May deadline came all too quickly, but we were ready—barely—to present "To Your Success." On a sunny spring day, our group went down to the American Express Tower.

Mike Becker set up his own portable lectern and began his presentation by describing his "ethnographic interviews." He showed the photographs he had taken and described the lives and needs of his subjects so well that they almost seemed to be in the room with us. Then Mike unveiled the creative work: first the print ads, with their challenging headlines and documentary photographs, and then the radio and television commercials. I never took my eyes off Alesio and his number two, Barbara Barsa. I saw them relax as Mike presented the campaign. They had some "minor problems," which, they said, they would put aside for the moment. The next thing to do was to take the campaign into research and, if the results were good, present it to Zanzotto.

In our focus-group interviews with small-business owners in various locations, the panelists were not told the subject of the research in advance. After asking some general questions to put them at ease, the interviewer asked, "What are the first things that come to mind when I mention the American Express Corporate Card?" The answers were "I never heard of it." "What does it do?" "Why do I need it?" "It's for large corporations." The panelists' feelings, if any, were passive or negative. They either didn't know about the card or didn't think they needed it.

The interviewer showed the group our print ads and then played the commercial. The response was enthusiastic. Comments ranged from "They really talk about the small-business person," "It's not just for larger corporations," "It's about us," "A great product," "What's the phone number? I'd like to apply now." We couldn't have asked for more. The advertising instantly changed the attitudes of all the people in the research groups—and many of them expressed an interest in acquiring the card.

We edited the tape of the focus groups to show first some typical, negative opinions about the card before we presented the advertising. Then we showed the advertising, and finally, we showed the groups' positive reactions. We were now ready to show the tape to Zanzotto. We made our presentation brief, showed the research, and then offered to present our proposal in greater detail. We never got to do it. Zanzotto stopped us and said, "Let's put the commercial on the air, as is, and right away." We tried to explain that we couldn't because we didn't own the footage and we had no releases from the people Becker had photographed. Zanzotto wouldn't listen. He picked up the phone and asked Papone if he could spare us a moment. We walked to Papone's office at the other corner of the fortieth floor. Zanzotto asked us to play the research reel again. We played the tape, and Papone, too, said, "Put it on the air." Once again, we had to explain the problems of footage and releases, but both remained adamant about running the commercial the research groups had seen. They recognized it as a winner and wouldn't give it up. Finally, we had won the largest piece of the American Express account we had yet competed for: an assignment that would use all media—globally. Best of all, it fit my expanded vision of direct marketing.

We had never created print ads or radio or television commercials for American Express. Even though more than 70 percent of our agency's work was creating and placing print ads and commercials, we were thought of as an agency that specialized in direct mail, and this misperception was especially true of our larger clients. I was certain that the Corporate Card advertising would prove to American Express that direct marketing techniques could provide brand values (attitude and recall) and behavior (requests for Corporate Card membership). But we were going to have to prove it.

We didn't have money or time to take a camera crew on the road in search of subjects, so Becker took another shortcut. He wrote to ten photographers in various parts of the country and told each of them what he wanted. The campaign objective was to "salute small-business owners as the driving force in American business," to "capture the spirit and pride of accomplishment." "Pride is the most important element in this campaign, and the public should be able to read it in the faces of those photographed." He wanted real people who owned and ran their own businesses. When the photographs came in, we would choose only the best.

After the first few arrived, we knew we were going to get what we needed. The subjects were as interesting as their photographs: Dick Cargill, a farrier from Minneapolis; Smokey Davis, a rodeo promoter in Houston; Jane Heinz, a pet tender from Denver; Ray Villasana of Tony's Tortilla Factory in Houston; Arthur E. Martin, a boat builder in New Hampshire; Giovanna D'Agostino of Mamma D's restaurant in Minneapolis; Todd Goldenberg, a luthier in New Hampshire; and others like them. They were as varied as America, and all shared the pride of enterprise and the excitement of doing it their way.

But all at once, our clients changed their minds. They asked us to execute the commercials and the magazine ads in color, and though we had only stills, they wanted action in the commercials. What they wanted was for us to follow the American Express style of glossy production values. That was their "minor objection" to our presentation. We tried to do it their way, but when we sent our first rough cut of the commercial to Papone for approval, his comment was "I hate it a lot." This helped us persuade the Corporate Card marketing group to let us return to black and white and the documentary grainy look. We redid the ads and commercials, and finally everything was approved. On September 6, "To Your Success" was launched.

We received our first comprehensive review of the results in a copy of a memo dated October 10, 1988, by Barbara Barsa addressed to Zanzotto. It said:

1) 2,700 calls are being received each week over the 1-800-SUC-CESS telephone number. . . . This is resulting in 1,000 incremental Cards per week.

2) "Take-one" application volume has increased 40–50% since the start of the advertising.

3) Incoming direct mail Card applications are at record levels since the September 15th start of the Fall campaign.

4) Outbound telemarketing for the sale of supplementary Cards . . . will represent 33,000 new Cards in 1988 and 60,000 in 1989.

5) New services greatly strengthen anti-attrition efforts recently launched with the Save-A-Cardmember unit. 34% of Cardmembers who call in to cancel their membership subsequently decide to maintain their membership status.

6) The Small Business Services . . . signature in direct mail appears to be effective. . . .

7) Early results show new services have increased response to follow-up acquisition mailings when the following small business features were highlighted:

Travel Plan +39%
Disability Insurance +33%
Automobile Leasing +21%

There is no question that the new advertising and services are effective. . . . "To Your Success" advertising definitely looks like a big success.

The campaign delivered on all the promises I had made for it and fulfilled my vision of direct marketing as a discipline that used all media to modify the behavior of the prospect audience and, at the same time, enhance brand awareness and the brand image—a breakthrough that could one day change the way advertising was done.

We continued the campaign into winter and spring 1989 with continued success, and our budget was increased. American Express was enthusiastic. We had successfully launched Optima, and now we had saved the Corporate Card. It was time for us to go global.

We had launched Optima in the United Kingdom, Canada, and Japan and relaunched the Corporate Card for small businesses in Hong Kong, Japan, the United Kingdom, France, and Germany. Our commercials, print ads, and direct mail worked in Chinese, English, French, and Japanese. I discovered that good advertising was global. The substance remained the same; only the nuances changed. In Japan, for example, where the culture suppressed the notion of individual achievement, the commercial became a salute to "People Who Did Good Work." Soon, the global business of American Express occupied almost all my time. I should have known that it couldn't last. New problems had arisen that I should have anticipated—but I had been too euphoric.

The first was that our global network, when put to the test, was not as strong as that of Ogilvy & Mather, which had built a strong direct marketing network to serve American Express. Had I sold more than we could deliver? O&M didn't give up after we had won the Corporate Card account for small businesses. They retained the account of the Corporate Card for large businesses, which did almost no advertising except for an occasional ad in *The Wall Street Journal*. But as we approached 1989, American Express, as planned, was preparing to launch a new design for the Corporate Card. Since the card redesign would apply to both large and small businesses, Ogilvy & Mather demanded the right to present advertising for the relaunch and changed the rules so that the winner could take all. Thus we had to compete again for the whole account. I may have been the hare, but O&M was the tortoise that wouldn't stop or go away. While O&M had little to lose on the Corporate Card, we had everything to lose if we lost the small-business account, including the hope of servicing it globally.

The ads announcing the new Corporate Card design were scheduled to run January 2, and the competition went right down to the wire— Christmas. Both agencies had presented the week before, and the Corporate Card marketing group couldn't, or wouldn't, choose. They sent both agencies' presentations to Papone at his home in Connecticut, where he would decide. We received the decision on December 26. It had been a working Christmas, but it was a Happy New Year for Wunderman Worldwide. We won the entire account, and our advertising continued to work. Soon, there were more than half as many Corporate Cards as Green Cards, and Corporate was gaining fast. By 1994, there were seven million Corporate Cards in force in the United States, almost double the number in 1989. Seventy percent of the *Fortune* 500 companies and 84 percent of the *Fortune* 100, as well as millions of small businesses, had joined the Corporate Card program. We had hit a gusher.

We were awarded the Corporate Card advertising for Australia, Mexico, Puerto Rico, Brazil, Argentina, Chile, Venezuela, Singapore, Thailand, Australia, and Taiwan. But the American Express Company of the 1990s was not the same confident company it had been in the 1960s, 1970s, and 1980s, when its growth and profits had been unprecedented. Increasingly, the company was assumed to have become arrogant and isolated from the market by success. When the credit card market abruptly became more value-oriented, VISA and MasterCard were in a better position to cope.

American Express had built its brand on a charge card that offered prestige and service, and the card had been accepted by those service establishments that served such cardmembers. It had been positioned as the card of the rich, famous, and powerful and those who aspired to be. American Express had become a symbol of an economic aristocracy, a symbol that became increasingly controversial as public attitudes came to appreciate value more than image. Suddenly, utility and empowerment were more appealing than prestige. Universal coverage meant more than elite service and selectivity. MasterCard cobranded its cards with AT&T, General Motors, and other large companies. American Airlines offered frequent-flier rewards to Citibank VISA cardholders, while rates as high as 19.5 percent enriched the banks that provided VISA and MasterCards. American Express thought of itself as a service provider, but for the banks, credit cards were a way of making millions of small loans at high interest rates.

The American Express brand and the services the company provided to its core group of select cardmembers held the business together, but by the 1990s, both profits and membership were falling fast. The American Express charge card was, as I had suspected, no longer a platform for growth. As the company changed its ways, our assignments changed accordingly. To expand its distribution system, American Express decided to cobrand its card with other strong brand names such as Hilton Hotels and Delta Air Lines, and we were asked to make those partnerships productive. The Optima Card became a platform for new lending products, and we were chosen as the agency for a new Optima True Grace Card. The company began to seek segmented markets such as seniors and college students, and we were assigned those new products, too. In its 1995 *Annual Report,* American Express reported that its "United States consumer lending portfolio had increased by 23% to $10 billion." Travel Related Services was merged with its fraternal financial services company, IDS (Investors Diversified Services), and we were assigned the task of helping to create a new "virtual bank" as the company entered the digitized electronic age. We were asked to test debit cards, charge/credit cards, and other variations of card products in Europe. We are doing work for the company's sites on the World Wide Web.

Advertising for the Corporate Card finally supplied further proof that direct marketing could affect not only attitude and behavior but brand awareness. In 1995, one of our commercials called "Heart and Soul" was proven to affect both consumer behavior and attitude. Like many of its predecessors, it featured the unique benefits of the Corporate Card and brought in applications at a lower cost than direct mail did. Meanwhile, Ogilvy & Mather, the agency in charge of the American Express brand image, created a commercial to enhance the Corporate Card brand. Its commercial, which did not ask for a response, was tested against ours, and research was conducted on the effect of both commercials. "Heart and Soul" produced a record number of applications for the card, and it had a more positive effect on the brand.

Today we are the largest provider of direct marketing advertising to American Express. We have become part of the company's future and it has become part of ours.

For me, working on the American Express account has been like taking a postgraduate degree in learning how to make advertising pay.

26
Which Way to the Future?

Direct marketing has come of age. A report commissioned in 1992 by the Direct Marketing Association and updated by WEFA (Wharton Economic Forecasting Associates) in 1996 showed that U.S. sales revenue attributed to direct marketing was estimated to be $1.1 trillion annually. Twenty million workers were employed as a result of direct marketing activities, and 58.3 percent of all advertising in all media was devoted to direct marketing efforts. Direct marketing draws record crowds everywhere. Ten thousand six hundred people attended the 1995 Annual Convention of the Direct Marketing Association. Twenty thousand attended Semaine Internationale du Marketing Direct in Paris.

It has become a subject worth studying. Newspapers, magazines, and newsletters on direct marketing are now published regularly. More than fifty books have been published on the subject, and universities give undergraduate and graduate degrees in direct marketing. Every major advertising agency now practices it, mainly with special direct marketing subsidiaries. And I have had the benefit of learning about successful direct marketing from the wide variety of client companies both here and abroad that my agency and I have served over the last thirty-eight years. Wunderman, Ricotta & Kline, now Wunderman Cato Johnson (WCJ), is the nineteenth largest advertising agency in the world. It has 2,300 professionals in 65 offices in 36 countries and billings in 1995 of $1.688 billion. It does direct marketing for companies such as ABN Amro Bank, Air France, American Express, Andersen Consulting, Apple Computer, AT&T, Blockbuster Video, Chevron,

Colgate-Palmolive, Danone, Du Pont, Ford, Jaguar, Kraft General Foods, Nintendo, Novell, Philip Morris, Robert Bosch, Sears, Roebuck and Company, Sony, Time Warner, the U.S. Army, the U.S. Postal Service, Viacom, Xerox, and many others around the world. In 1995, WCJ, with a growth rate of 27.6 percent, was the fastest-growing of the top twenty-five global agencies, the only one to grow at a rate of more than 25 percent. At the rate it is growing, WCJ will become one of the world's top ten advertising agencies by the year 2000.

Much remains to be done. Direct marketing advertising must become a strategic rather than a tactical tool. Direct marketing must learn to intercept and affect the behavior of consumers no matter how and where they shop; it must create dialogues between buyers and sellers, and build these dialogues into enduring relationships. Direct marketing must be based on information exchanged, retained, and used collaboratively by consumers and producers of products and services. It must eliminate layers of intermediaries in the channels of distribution and communication. It must make the home the new marketplace and the consumer and his or her unique needs the center of marketing. It must be increasingly personal, relevant, interactive, measurable, and profitable. Leadership requires constant innovation.

Futurists like to propose names for the society that lies ahead. I prefer to be more practical and deal with what I call the "post-present." The post-present already contains vehicles of change, some of which are already in motion. The post-present is accountable here and now. The future is not.

As the Information Age develops, megaretailers have seen their volume and profits erode, as have the shopping malls. Giant, unattended, self-service, noninformational retail warehouses no longer provide the values customers or manufacturers increasingly want. Price is only one aspect of service and can be reduced only so much by marketing intermediaries. The way of creating effective combinations of price and service is by creating knowledge-based direct channels between manufacturers and consumers in which the media become the marketplace. The Industrial Revolution created the practice of branding, but in the Information Age, brand images increasingly provide only a thin shield against competition.

Advertisers and marketers have long believed that the product and the brand are the center of the marketing universe: "the product as hero" or the focus on "brand equity." Brand images and brand personalities are key icons of the Industrial Revolution, a totally attitudinal construct that assumes that attitude is the primary determinant of consumer behavior. In the hands of such masters as Ray Rubicam, David Ogilvy, Bill Bernbach, and Leo Burnett, the concept worked. The Hathaway Man with his eye patch meant adventurous shirting; the Jolly Green Giant was a gentle creator of perfect produce; and the Volkswagen really proved that less was more. These ideas were simple, relevant, and memorable. But can they work as well in today's fiercer, more complex, and more information-packed society? I doubt it. Today, advertising is increasingly measured by harsher criteria. Many of the world's largest advertisers have demanded that their advertising be more directly accountable for sales. What consumers think of a product or service hardly matters unless it affects what they actually do— and do again. My own psychological preference is behaviorism, which relates directly to experience. I believe, as did B. F. Skinner and other behaviorists, that experience provides meaning, which then modifies behavior, and it is behavior that creates deeply felt attitudes. It is the modification of ongoing consumer behavior that advertising and marketing are all about. At Wunderman Cato Johnson, our aim is to impact behavior. The consumer is our hero.

I believe that the successor to the brand image in the post-present will be the "brand experience." The "brand experience" goes beyond the attributes of a product. It is a gestalt that includes the advertising, the package, where and how the product is sold, the price, the consumer's satisfaction from using the product, the service provided, the continuous renewal of the product's uniqueness, and the development of an interactive relationship that bonds the buyer and seller after the sale is made.

Many successful companies already understand this. General Motors, Chrysler, and Ford have cobranded credit cards so that they can satisfy their customers and provide them with discounts on future purchases. British Airways offers three tiers of Executive Club services: Blue, Silver, and Gold, depending on how much a member uses British Airways. IBM is planning a Gold Service for its best customers that will provide them with special access to the company through the Internet. Ford is using a sophisticated database to serve its best customers better. Air France guarantees its best and most prestigious customers a seat on the plane on which they wish to fly through membership in Club 2000. Hertz provides a special Platinum Service to a limited number of its very best customers. AT&T has many ways of recognizing and rewarding its best customers. The "brand experience" goes beyond the attributes of the product itself.

Traditional advertising flowed "downstream" from advertisers to consumers and never the other way round; it was a statement from one to many. In the post-present, much of that will be reversed. Consumers will go "upstream" to access each advertiser as a database for the product information they want. Federal Express has provided Internet access so that customers can see where their packages are at any time. And virtual communities will be created by consumers who want to go "sidestream" to chat with their global neighbors. The largest volume of use of on-line services such as America Online, CompuServe, and the French Minitel is by members who communicate with one another. Business-to-business direct marketing will account for $543 billion in sales in 1996. The seventy-five million businesses in the world with fewer than one hundred employees will also want to exchange information as they buy from and sell to their peers. Large businesses will also want to use communications to sell to businesses whose purchases are too small to justify an in-person sales visit. They will also increase their advertising for the generation of leads for their salesmen. Business-to-business advertising is the fastest growing form of direct marketing advertising. It is predicted to grow 10.2 percent annually for the next five years. And the best is yet to come.

A stronger, expanded direct marketing discipline will result from digitized communications transmitted at the speed of light, communications that are instantly global; from vast quantities of information stored on minichips, intelligent machines, and electronic agents; from informed transactions and empowered consumers. The result will be that buyers and sellers will be able to communicate and serve each other relevantly in a global marketplace. Transactions will be expedited instantly. Consumers will know what and where the companies are that offer products and services of their choice. Manufacturers will know and be able to satisfy the needs and style and color preferences of each of their customers through computer-driven robotic manufacturing. Electronic agents will know what we want to see, hear, know, and buy, and they will help locate the best sources. These, plus a more efficient use of today's fastest-growing interactive media, direct mail, telephone, and on-line communications, will characterize the direct marketing of the coming millennium. They will also change the nature of work, the location of jobs, the function and process of production, the directional flow of communications, the process of persuasion, the function and form of retailing, and how, what, and where goods and services are sold.

Corporations will manage customers and how they behave rather than products and what they represent. The brand manager will be replaced by the customer manager, who will be responsible for satisfying consumers' needs. A "share of loyal customers" and a consumer-centered strategy will build profits better than old-fashioned concepts such as "share of voice," "share of mind," and "share of market." A "brand" must become not just a cluster of a product's values but also a fulfillment of consumers' needs. New technologies of mass customization, robotic manufacturing, and computer memory banks; new uses of information in marketing; the growth of service and software industries; the development of new media; and the incredible improvements in our ability to communicate are the raw materials of the post-present.

What changes will these new empowerments and technologies make possible? How will they stimulate the shift from products to services? In the post-present, a new kind of value bundle will be introduced that I call a "prodice." It looks like a product but acts like a service. I believe that people will increasingly want to buy what things *do* rather than what they *are,* just as many drivers would rather not own a car that can break down, rust, age, lose value, or become technologically obsolete. Leasing has become the fastest-growing segment of automobile sales as drivers increasingly want to own the service of transportation and not the physical car. General Motors is already exploring the sale of miles rather than cars. Eventually, consumers will be able to buy a continuing service to provide clean clothes rather than laundry products. They will prefer a service that supplies cooked meals rather than a microwave oven. Some people won't even want money. They will prefer "smart" credit cards that are replaced if lost, can be used in any country, and earn air miles, hotel upgrades, and other rewards. These will not only transfer money but provide information that will guide buyers and sellers to a more relevant sales dialogue. Buckminster Fuller described money as "information in motion." Money has been digitized for a long time: banks send money to one another electronically, and people use digitized money to buy things by phone. The postpresent will contain a cornucopia of new digitized financial products, services, and transactional modes.

If I could, I would contract with a soap company to supply all the products that wash my clothes—the washing machine, the detergent, and anything else I need—for a monthly fee. All I want is clean clothes. As long as the service is good, why should I change brands? The Gevalia Kaffe Import Service is a model of what can be done.

I would like to sign a long-term contract with Colgate-Palmolive for toothbrushes, toothpaste, dental insurance, and whatever else good oral health requires.

I'd turn my pet's nourishment and health over to a provider of food, health insurance, and veterinary care. Why shouldn't there be health maintenance organizations for pets? I don't want to buy tasty pet food, I want a happy, healthy dog or cat. So why switch brands?

I want to buy the service, not the stuff. If a manufacturer continues to own a product, it has to make the product work. It has to replace it before it becomes obsolete, and it has to service it because it's the manufacturer's and because I am a valuable customer it can't afford to lose. When manufacturers own the products and sell only the services, they will design products differently and build them more durably, and they will keep in touch with their customers.

As always, consumers will choose the form of shopping that provides the most value and greatest convenience. At the moment, this is the promise of the megaretailers, the ultimate nondirect marketers. But in time the megaretailers may die of a disease to which their own strength has made them vulnerable. As intermediaries between the manufacturer and the consumer, they provide the value of distribution, but they, as all retailers, also add cost to the products they sell.

The megaretailers have reversed the rules of retailing. Instead of "location, location, location," they sell "price, price, price." They deliberately build their outlets in low-rent locations away from high-traffic centers, and the technology they exploit is the automobile. Instead of paying for traffic, they create it by featuring price. Megaretailers are called "category killers" because their buying power lets them sell at retail for less than a small retailer pays at wholesale. In Iowa, where Wal-Mart is particularly strong, half of the stores selling men's and boy's clothes have gone out of business in the last ten years. So have a third of the hardware and grocery stores.

I have witnessed this effect in the two villages in which I have homes: one in the south of France, the other in a small town on Long Island, New York. My French village is now without a baker, a butcher, a grocer, or a hardware store. I now have to shop at megastores called Champion, Casino, or Carrefour that are miles away. My ex-butcher, Francis Gaglio, now drives one of the village's two taxicabs. On Long Island, Fran DePetris closed the small market his father had opened more than sixty years earlier. There Fran had learned how to buy the best produce from the local farmers. Fran's son, who became the store's butcher, knew exactly the cuts of meat my family preferred. And the DePetrises delivered. But now there is a megastore located in a large mall on the outskirts of town. It is open twenty-four hours a day, seven days a week. Fran, like the rest of us, needed his sleep, his days off, and his markup to survive—so he closed his store. I miss the personal service that Francis and Fran used to provide.

As the weekly market in the village square gave way to the personal retailer, who gave way to the supermarket and then to the megamarket, the geography, personality, function, and technology of retailing have changed from transactions in which buyer and seller influence each other reciprocally to transactions with no dialogue at all. Retailers no longer care what or why consumers buy, as long as they buy from them. It's up to marketers and advertisers to influence consumer behavior wherever their products are sold. Because 70 percent of consumer purchasing decisions are made on site, the shelves of megaretailers are now an advertising medium, and shelf space is now sold to manufacturers just like newspaper space and television time. These retailers have become the gatekeepers of distribution and charge accordingly. But in the post-present, manufacturers won't want to pay these heavy tolls, and neither will consumers.

The real income of most Americans has been declining since 1973. "Downsizing" and "reengineering" have become the rationale for mass layoffs even in those companies that have traditionally supported their workforce in good times and bad. When the unemployed find new jobs, they frequently earn less than before. To maintain their standard of living, more family members have gone to work, some seek second jobs, and many have gone into debt. In Europe, not one net new job has been created in twenty-three years.

Only the upper 20 percent of American wage earners continue to prosper. The result has been pressure on the costs and pricing of the value chain of distribution. The megaretailers have succeeded in part because the majority of their customers have been willing to trade service and convenience for lower prices. The next reduction will have to be in the costs of such marketing. Procter & Gamble intends to reduce its marketing costs by 25 percent to 20 percent, which means that advertising and media will have to become more effective and more accountable. The company has begun to stop distributing coupons to be able to reduce the everyday prices of their products.

The megaretailer, with its "cash-and-carry" strategy, saves the consumer money, but a rent-free virtual store will be even more efficient. The megastores' overpopulated shelves have become a cemetery of brands, tombstones on the shelf that say of each inert packaged product, "Here lies . . ." Megaretailers are already in decline. Kmart has been doing poorly, Caldor and Bradlees have declared bankruptcy, and, as I write, the profits of Wal-Mart and other chains have begun to decline. In preparation for the future, Wal-Mart has announced Wal-Mart On Line, a joint venture with Microsoft to sell merchandise on the Internet. I believe that this will be the last decade of the dominance of on-site retailing as we know it. Consumer decisions will continue to be made on site, but the site will move into the home as shopping services open on line.

Video on demand, home shopping, on-line games, and directory services will become increasingly convenient and less costly. They will stimulate new, as-yet-unthought-of services conceived to exploit the information superhighway's unique attributes. Some Web sites are already claiming several hundred thousand "clicks" or "contacts" each day. Video rentals, at $12 billion, are already greater than ticket sales at movie theaters. Home shopping television channels already sell more than $2.5 billion worth of products a year, and catalog sales are worth $69.9 billion a year. Add to these E-mail, off-site education, teleconferencing, and government information services, and we can see the beginning of a revolutionary new communication, information, and entertainment shopping system. The information superhighway will most likely be some combination of telephone, broadcast and cable TV, and local-area computer networks. It is not clear who will pay for what, but the consumer will be empowered as never before. The call of the Industrial Revolution, "This is what I make, won't you please buy it?" will give way to that of the Consumer Revolution, which will declare, "This is what I need, can't you please make it?"

Large general advertisers such as Procter & Gamble, Sprint, and Motorola have recently demanded that their advertising become accountable for sales, which means that advertising that affects only consumer attitudes, rather than a decision to buy, is likely to be too costly compared to infomercials, entertainment commercials, interactive commercials, games, contests, and other forms of interactive advertising and publishing.

"Contact strategies" will replace media strategies. Relationships will count far more than exposure. Video on demand, advertising on demand, and shopping on demand will change the way consumers watch television. TV will no longer provide mass audiences for advertising because masses of viewers will no longer choose to see the same program at the same time, except for important live events. As audiences continue to fragment, so will advertising that seeks to deliver relevant sales messages to consumers shopping for entertainment, products, and services of their choice. Manufacturers will use these new communications media to learn and supply the products individual customers want through the new techniques of mass customization. Factories will become smaller, more versatile, and more accessible, either on line or on foot. The next step won't be the megaretailer but the retail factory or the factory that retails through media. Already, optical stores such as Pearle Vision, LensCrafters, and others are providing eye examinations, prescribing and making lenses, and fitting them to frames while you wait. Film stores are developing and printing pictures on site.

So what does the post-present imply for information-based advertising that affects both behavior and attitudes and creates measurable profits? Research has proven that loyal customers produce 90 percent of a brand's profit—that onetime sales create a loss. In 1995, 291.9 billion discount coupons for products were distributed; of these, fewer than 2 percent were redeemed. The average discount offered was 68 cents, a total of $4 billion. What a waste when a "onetime" sale or "product trial" doesn't even cover its cost, when it's a pure expense and not an accountable investment. The marketing mathematics are persuasive. It costs six to ten times as much to get a new customer as it does to retain an old one. But the consumer's loyalty is not for sale. Loyalty is possible only if the consumer continues to be *totally* satisfied with a product or service. Customers who are only *partially* satisfied are the most likely to attrite or switch brands. Loyalization must be continuous. Effective direct marketing attracts customers with the intent to loyalize and loyalizes with the intent to bond. The purpose of marketing and advertising has always been to sell products. Hereafter it will be to sell products through long-term relationships. Marketing investments will be made against a consumer's lifetime value.

There is a word I learned from my Dogon tribal brothers in Mali. Every Friday was market day, and since there were no stores, pedlars, or any other way of locally buying or selling, people walked for miles and days to get to the market. Each sale was a ritual accompanied by much palaver—arguing, bargaining, and talk. When buyer and seller finally agreed that the transaction had met the needs and expectations of both, they would clasp hands and simultaneously say *"Habama,"* which literally means "We have done well together."

Direct marketing is *Habama*!

Acknowledgments

This book, and my career, would have been unmanageable without the help of loyal friends and talented colleagues. Many will have found themselves in the preceding pages, but there are some who merit special attention.

There was the first generation of direct marketers at Wunderman, Ricotta & Kline, who helped create a new industry. My brother, Irving, whose support and unique ability to write copy that moves people to act are part of the emotional and creative foundation of my life. There were also the other founders of Wunderman, Ricotta & Kline, without whom it wouldn't have happened: Ed Ricotta, a talented art director, who knew how to design response advertising and Harry Kline, the best business-to-business writer I ever met. Harry left early for reasons of health, Ed took retirement just prior to our merger with Young & Rubicam, and Irving left soon after the merger to do his own thing. There was also Peter Rabar, with whom I shared clients; Peter continues to do brilliant marketing and advertising for Columbia House. There were Lew Smith, our first creative director; Tom Knowlton, whom I kidnapped from the Book-of-the-Month Club; and Peter Rosenwald, who set up our first international offices in Montreal, London, Paris, and Munich. There was also the imaginative, feisty group of direct marketing pioneers: Alan Booth, Wil Cahoon, Jim Hess, Manfred Heuser, Tim Horan, Jim Howard, Francine Humbert, Bill Keisler, Jean Larue, Claus Mayer, Leah Roth, Ralph Siegler, and Joel Tucciarone, who helped create an industry.

Later, there were the CEOs of Young & Rubicam: Ed Ney, Alex

Kroll, and Peter Georgescu, who helped us become part of the Y&R family.

Now there is the brilliant second generation of the renamed Wunderman Cato Johnson, led by Mitch Kurz, Mike Becker, Barbara Jack, Jean-Paul Lafaye, Helmut Matthies, Steve McKenna, Richard Stollenwerck, and Allan Winneker. They continue the tradition of innovation and client service and have built WCJ into one of the world's largest and most effective advertising agencies.

And there is my executive assistant, Elizabeth Villani, with whom I began an extraordinary collaboration in 1954. In addition to being friend, adviser, keeper of my finances and research files, and manager of my time, she personally converted this book from foolscap to manuscript.

In 1975, I met and married Suzanne Cott, who, as Sue Cott, was the beauteous, talented editorial director of WCBS-TV in New York City. When we married, all our friends asked if I knew how lucky I was. I did then and I do now. She, more than anyone, helped to bring this book to life, providing the time and encouragement to get it done and finally editing the finished manuscript under the guidance of Jason Epstein, the editor's editor. Jason, who first approached me with the suggestion that I write this book, combined mentoring, criticism, and high professional standards to help me get it done. Jason always had the last word, and it was always the right one.

Index

ABOUT THE AUTHOR

LESTER WUNDERMAN is chairman of Wunderman Cato Johnson and senior adviser to the board of directors of Young & Rubicam, Inc., with which his agency merged in 1973. He is also director of Dentsu Wunderman Direct in Japan. Mr. Wunderman has received countless awards for his many contributions to the field of direct marketing and was named to the Direct Marketing Association's Hall of Fame. He has served as a director and secretary-treasurer of the American Association of Advertising Agencies and was a director of the Advertising Council. Mr. Wunderman is an honorary member of the board of UNICEF and was a governor of UNESCO's International Fund for the Promotion of Culture. He is a trustee of the Children's Television Workshop and the International Center of Photography. His widely exhibited and televised collection of the art of the Dogon tribe of Mali is now part of the permanent collection of the Metropolitan Museum of Art. Mr. Wunderman's photographs of Africa and African art have appeared in books, magazines, and films. He has written many articles and delivered many lectures around the world on marketing. This is his first book. He lives in New York City and Mougins, France, with his wife, Suzanne, who, as Sue Cott, was editorial director of WCBS-TV.

ABOUT THE TYPE

This book was set in Galliard, a typeface designed by Matthew Carter for the Merganthaler Linotype Company in 1978. Galliard is based on the sixteenth-century typefaces of Robert Granjon.